Carol Shields
The Arts of a Writing Life

Carol Shields
The Arts of a Writing Life

Edited by Neil K. Besner

Prairie Fire Press, Inc.

Prairie Fire Press, Inc.
423-100 Arthur Street
Winnipeg, Manitoba R3B 1H3
www.prairiefire.mb.ca

Prairie Fire Press, Inc. gratefully acknowledges the assistance of the
Manitoba Arts Council.

Cover design: Doowah Design
Cover photography: Gerry Kopelow
Photograph of Neil K. Besner: Barbara Schott
Typesetting and layout: Heidi Harms

Printed in Canada by Hignell Book Printing for Prairie Fire Press, Inc.

Image, page 147: Extracted from *The Stone Diaries* by Carol Shields. Copyright
© 1993 by Carol Shields. Reprinted by permission of Random House Canada.

National Library of Canada Cataloguing in Publication Data

Main entry under title:
Carol Shields : the arts of a writing life / edited by Neil K. Besner.

Includes bibliographical references.
ISBN 0-9731608-0-2

1. Shields, Carol, 1935- — Criticism and interpretation.
I. Besner, Neil Kalman, 1949-
PS8587.H46Z62 2003   C813'.54   C2003-910166-5
PR9199.3.S514Z62 2003

To the people of Winnipeg

Contents

The Arts of Poetry, Biography, and Drama

The Arts of a Writing Life

Neil K. Besner

Introduction

It is both a grinding commonplace and a many-edged truth that a writer's life and her work are necessarily separate but inevitably related. This allegedly paradoxical proposition has been all the more contentiously debated in Canada, where writers have sometimes complained, with ample justification, that readers of fiction don't quite seem to understand that the life lived and the life written — or, at times, the writer and her protagonist — are not one and the same. Perhaps a more useful way to formulate the proposition is to pose it as a question: to ask not if, but how, a writer's life and her writing life communicate. One response that seems particularly useful when thinking about Carol Shields's writing is to begin by saying that it performs the beautifully intricate relation between art and life as if it were seamless, and perfectly natural. Hence one motive for reading the protagonist of *Unless* as Carol, her sparking anger, her family, as Carol's; as if the fiction were simply more real than the familiar. But there is much more to the story of *Unless* and all of Shields's fiction. And hence one motive for the title of this collection; another is to invoke, not only the art of Shields's unique talent for interweaving the genres of fiction, biography, and autobiography to such powerful effects over the course of her career, but also to call to mind the arts that attend her overlooked writing in other genres, in drama, poetry, and prose ("nonfiction" seems too narrowly legalistic and grudging a name for it).

The arts of a writing life: living your life in such a way as to find, steal, save the time to write; finding the time to make a past, many pasts. And then, finding the time to work words, finding the shapes and forms of stories *when* you write. Necessarily separate, and inevitably related, these lives and arts: here is Shields in her "Afterword" to *Dropped Threads*, looking back to a period when her "mother-of-small-children chapter seemed to go on forever, but, in fact, it didn't. It was a mere twelve years, over in a flash" (345). Then time bloomed for her: "I remember I spent the whole of an October afternoon working on a single sentence; I was not by nature a patient person, but for this kind of work and at this time in my life, I was able to be endlessly, foolishly, patient" (345). The arts of a writing life: recalling an era long past as a chapter in a book. The language and the plot of a writing life: moving from a twelve-year chapter suddenly closed, in a flash, to the opening out of a long afternoon in October, working with a sentence.

The memoirs, interviews, and scholarly pieces assembled here converse amongst themselves so comfortably, I hope, precisely because they take their inspiration both from the person and from the work, variously assigning themselves, like the writer and the person they evoke, no undue prejudice, rank, or pride of place. They give us Carol the person; Shields the writer; Winnipeg, Carol's home for another of those chapters, this one a mere twenty years; and, companionably jostling and nestling, a series of perspectives — critical, scholarly, and personal — on the fictions, from family, and by friends. The closing of *Swann* warmed and reprised, with less intrigue and no missing manuscripts. Shields's writing has for so long travelled an orbit at once domestic and exotic, familiar and extraordinary, that now it seems to be in the very process of forming a whole world; this collection tries to intuit this world's composite, infinitely variegated matter and spirit.

Beyond poetry and drama, beyond prose — and closely related to our contemporary fascination with film, and with visual as well as verbal art forms and techniques that promise exactitude, authenticity, and loyalty to the real, even to the super-real and the hyper-real, and all at blinding speed — ours is the new age of the novel and the short story, of a new and more demanding interest in realist fictions. We are more likely not only to tolerate, but to seek out fictional forms that set out story as if it were history (and vice versa), biography and autobiography as if they were fictions, and that do so to inquire into the timbre of the truths that attend each form. These proclivities are not, as some fear, the harbingers of fiction's blurred fall to earth; on the contrary. Each in its way — *The Stone Diaries, Swann, Various Miracles, Dressing Up for the Carnival, The Orange Fish, Unless, Larry's Party, The Republic of Love, The Box Garden, Small Ceremonies* (allow the false and incomplete chronology, and allow, too, because it is so, that Shields's short fiction is as important as her novels) — shows contemporary fiction's rich and searching weave of genres working towards important ends. The pieces here by scholars and critics from across Canada (interestingly, the two scholars from France, Vauthier and Dvorak, both focus on the short fiction), explore the protean powers of this expanding fictional universe. Among others, writers and critics — Dave Williamson on developing tactics in point of view in Shields's fiction; Perry Nodelman on Winnipeg's character in *The Republic of Love*; Deborah Schnitzer and Leona Gom on artful photographs, stone and flowers, respectively, in *The Stone Diaries*; Warren Cariou on *Larry's Party*; Clara Thomas on "Mrs. Turner Cutting the Grass"; Brian Johnson on *Swann*, authors, and Foucault; Wendy Roy on the sharpened feminism of *Unless* — all show Shields's fiction operating in inevitably related, but necessarily different domains, precincts, parishes, and neighbourhoods in one recognizable city. With winter snow *and* gardens in the sunshine, hedges *and* mazes, arching elms *and* crooked alleys. And, in all the most unlikely places, with love.

As Chris Johnson, Jacqueline Reid-Walsh, and Katharine Nicholson Ings show so ably, there is much to say and think about Shields's drama, her prose and her poetry; perhaps these pieces will serve to provoke the synthetic book on all of Shields's writing — I know of at least one in the works — which we have needed for some time. For now, it is good at least to have this substantial help in remembering that Carol's writing has never been circumscribed by her fiction.

It is not surprising, given that her work so often conjures with the intricate motions and commotions of communities, that Carol has collaborated so often in her career — with Blanche Howard to write *A*

Celibate Season, with Dave Williamson on *Anniversary*, with Marjorie Anderson to pick up many *Dropped Threads*, with daughter Catherine on the play *Fashion Power Guilt and the Charity of Families*. And so it is fitting that several of the pieces here call up a Shields in conversation, at lunch, in a back yard, at home: Maggie Dwyer, for one, brings Carol the confidante before us, while Carol's daughter Anne reveals a mother and a reader and a friend. William Neville's piece locates Carol, and Carol's writing, in a Winnipeg that finds her as she finds Winnipeg, coming home. Lorraine McMullen gives us an earlier chapter in Carol's life in Ottawa; thinking of Carol in Ottawa always reminds me of her MA thesis on Susanna Moodie — that troubling representative of British women's troubled arrival on these shores, with her prophetically conflicted imagination. It is only apt that Moodie should have provided the genesis for one of Carol's first books in 1976 and then reappeared in her first novel, *Small Ceremonies*, the same year. I mention this now because at the back of my mind there often appears an earlier Carol, not only from her Ottawa chapter, but from her Oak Park roots in Illinois; this image always carries me towards the person and her own feelings about her writing life, which is where the collection closes, like this introduction, in Carol's voice.

Discerning readers will have noticed a good while ago, perhaps with mounting disapproval, that this foreword has from its very beginning wavered unseemingly between "Carol," "Shields," and "Carol Shields" — as the essays and memoirs herein do as well. That has been intentional. The person I know, the writer I've read, the figure I have watched on television and heard in classrooms and convocations, are not only inevitably related, but intimates. I thank Carol, Don, and her family for all of her and their help, generosity, and friendship with this project, as usual, and over the years. My thanks as well to all of the contributors, and particularly to Andris Taskans, Janine Tschuncky, and the indefatigable Heidi Harms at Prairie Fire Press in Winnipeg for their unfailing support.

Meanwhile, here is Carol, singularly loved in her many voices and guises, writing in March 2000, with a few closing words for the time being:

We move through our chapters mostly with gratitude. Who isn't renewed by startling scenery or refreshed by undreamed-of freedoms? Surprise keeps us alive, liberates our senses. I thought for a while that a serious illness had interrupted my chaptered life, but no, it is a chapter on its own. Living with illness requires new balancing skills. It changes everything, and I need to listen to it, attend to it and bring to it a stern new sense of housekeeping.

But I have time for this last exercise. All the time in the world. (347)

Work Cited

Shields, Carol and Marjorie Anderson, eds. *Dropped Threads: What We Aren't Told*. Toronto: Random House/Vintage, 2001.

A N N E   G I A R D I N I

Double Happiness

Lives of Girls and Women. Surfacing. Roughing it in the Bush. As For
Me and My House. The Stone Angel. The Honeyman Festival. Fifth
Business.

When I was first beginning to take an interest in adult books, at
age twelve or thirteen, I became aware of these books. They sat
among others on a bank of shelves beside my mother's desk in her
office, a closed-in upper porch of our old brick house in Ottawa.

Children's literature had not yet exploded into a nebula of best-
sellers in the 1960s when I was a child, so I spent my time reading
many of the same books my mother had read as a girl, some of which
her mother would also have read. *The Five Little Peppers. The Five*
Children and It. Little Women. Cheaper by the Dozen. Rebecca of
Sunnybrook Farm. Swallows and Amazons. The Story of My Life. The
Water Babies. It was only logical that when I outgrew children's books
I would continue to read the books my mother was reading.

I could tell the books in my mother's office were Canadian by their
spines and dust jackets, which looked homemade and provisional.
These books lacked the solid, establishment presence of the British
paperbacks (whose uniform, banded orange jackets seemed to convey
the endorsement of some central approving body, a World War II
agency perhaps, that someone had forgotten to dismantle). Canadian
books didn't seem designed for diversion or entertainment, but for
another, more serious purpose, having more in common with an irri-
gation ditch than with a stream. And they certainly didn't emit even a

whiff of the risqué thrills promised by the American books that sat in stacks on my mother's bedside table, with their gleaming covers and come-hither titles. I worried that, in reading the short stories of the American John O'Hara for example, my casually daring mother was flirting with arrest for indecency. In one such story, into which I glanced with trepidation and hope, a suburban woman bared her breast to her (male) neighbour, a literary event that confirmed my suspicions about U.S. writers and kept me alert and anxious against the knock on the door and the removal of my mother by jackbooted authorities.

Compared to their more spirited American cousins, the Canadian books had duller jackets and denser print and a larger, unstrained measure of self-conscious seriousness. They had the wholesome, well-intentioned and earnest aspect of textbooks, which of course they were for my mother, who was working on her master's degree in Canadian literature at the University of Ottawa. I felt, when I read them, as if I were running along in the furrow my mother had made ahead of me, her passage marked by underlining and margin notes made in blue ink with 19-cent Bic ballpoint pens. And I felt how fresh-ly sprung these Canadian books were from — and not yet securely rooted in — the rocky, acid soil of my country, Canada, which I was conscious of as insecure, unformed, awkward and self-questioning. It takes one adolescent to know another. All of these books asked, in a guarded, indirect manner the same question: could a literature be cre-ated in a thinly populated country of snow and dirt and gravel roads and biting insects and uncut timber? Even if one could, would the effort be worthwhile? I was at a doubting age, and I had my doubts.

The poets whose books were strewn, slender but solid, on my mother's desk and on the floor beside her bed seemed infinitely more self-assured, doubtless because poets are a more reckless, relentless breed than novelists and story-writers. I remember among them Al Purdy, P.K. Page, F.R. Scott, Tom Wayman and others.

My mother got her master's degree a few years later, in 1975. That was a sabbatical year for my father, and we were spending it in Brittany. We lived for the first two months in an airy, broad-beamed house set on a large lot between a bend in the road that led away from the village, St–Quay Portrieux, and the sea. When the owners of this house returned, the seven of us moved into a small, ugly house close by the road, and nearer to the village. The owner, an old man who smelled of many baths foregone, lived in the basement. We were two to a bedroom, and my older brother, John, who elected to go to boarding school in a nearby town, Guingamp, stayed in a box room under the rafters when he came home on weekends.

My mother was writing a book, *The Box Garden*, and, lovely though it must have been to have us out of the house at school all day so she could work, her French was rudimentary and she was lonely, which I sensed even through the fog of my self-absorption. She had left her enormous electric typewriter at home in Ottawa and was using a clumsy manual machine. When I asked her about that year recently, she told me that she felt that *The Box Garden* suffered from having been written on that typewriter, which discouraged revisions and the process of adding layers or "thickening" that she loves to do (she compares it to making a stew) and that has become so effortless in the era of computers and word processors.

When my three sisters and I got out of school, we watched bad French TV, justified on the basis that it would improve our vocabularies (we could all croon the latest pop tunes), and read from the stock of books we had brought with us. Before long, we had exhausted our supply. My engineer father, to whom every problem has one or more logical solutions, arranged for Foyles, a bookstore in England, to ship us boxes of books. Each parcel was greeted with the joy of the shipwrecked. Books were fought over, shared, even torn in half or thirds to meet competing demands. The organizing principles behind the orders that were placed were, as far as I recall, that the books we ordered had to be paperback (to reduce price and shipping costs) and should appeal to anyone between the ages of seven and forty. It was also preferable if they were long and densely printed. I remember reading *The Black Prince* by Iris Murdoch, all the short stories of Somerset Maugham, Hardy's *Far From the Madding Crowd*, *Working* by Studs Terkel, Mary Stewart's King Arthur books *The Crystal Cave* and *The Hollow Hills*, and *Watership Down* by Richard Adams.

When we returned to Canada, I found and read, among my mother's books, John Updike, more Iris Murdoch, John Cheever,

Kingsley Amis, Mary McCarthy, Alice Munro, Marian Engel, most of Margaret Laurence, all of Jane Austen. It would have been logical to talk to my mother during that time about what we both were reading. But I was at a secretive age, and I moved away to go to university when I was seventeen. My three sisters were still at home and, during the next few years, my parents moved from Ottawa to Vancouver, and then to Winnipeg. My mother was writing steadily. I was studying. We continued to read, but I don't think we were reading the same books. In any case, we seldom talked of them. It is the regret of my life that there was a time — it lasted far longer than it needed to — when I worked diligently to distance myself from my mother. I chose to study economics, not unconscious of the fact that it overlapped not at all with my mother's studies or work. We once went more than a year without seeing each other. I had been seized with the idea that becoming an independent person meant breaking ties, reckless of whether they were necessary or could be replaced or mended.

I started a law degree when I was twenty-one. I had few bookish friends and no guide, and eventually ran out of notions from high school and university courses and boyfriends of what kinds of books I should admire. The need for something good to read may have driven me home in the end. On visits, I studied my mother's bedside table and shelves, and then looked for the same books at the library. This meant that my mother and I were again reading the same books and, in our letters and on the telephone, we were beginning to talk about what we were reading, even if it meant no more than sharing titles.

I was lying on the floor of my apartment on West 12th Avenue in Vancouver one afternoon when I was in my early twenties, when a sentence in one of these books, a novel or short story by John Updike, made me breathe in sharply and throw my head upward. That sentence sliced cleanly into my muddled brain. Because I was my mother's daughter, I had been reading good writing all my life. But I had taken it all for granted. Almost everything I read was good; the bad stuff almost never came to hand. That Updike sentence was very, very good. It could, I realized, have stood alone as a line of poetry. I scanned at random for other sentences just as good. They almost all were. Updike was a good writer! I pulled a book by Barbara Pym from my bookcase. She was good too. Like a carefully packed suitcase, each sentence that Pym and Updike wrote was precise, hard-wearing and balanced. Their sentences zipped up neatly, confidently. There was nothing bulging from the seams, nothing left out. Before that moment, bad writing had always made me feel uneasy, but I could never have said why. I am what my mother has always claimed to be herself, a slow learner, but a long apprenticeship of reading my mother's books had finally made of me a critical reader. This trick my mother had, of understanding the mechanics of excellence, I realized I could finally do too.

It can't be a coincidence that my friendship with my mother flourished when we were once again reading the same books and talking about them critically and thoroughly. Both my mother and I have a gift for happiness, for anticipating it, relishing its presence, recollecting its texture. We have called this a talent for double happiness, after the name of a Chinese restaurant on West Broadway in Vancouver. Few joys, apart from the constant astonishment of being mother to my children, and the inverting topological loop of sexual pleasure, have made me as perfectly happy as a well-made book. When my mother and I enjoy the same book, I feel that my delight is easily doubled again, magnified and refracted like light through cut glass. I have come to know many good and serious readers, but none I trust to understand my thoughts about a book as much as my mother, and none whose pleasure in a book I can anticipate so perfectly.

An important book in our discussions, when we were talking about books again, was Annie Dillard's childhood memoir, *An American Childhood*, which we read shortly after it was first published in the mid-eighties. We talked about the orderly but unbounded way in which it is strung together, the honesty and intimacy of Dillard's description of a girl's awakening at age ten or so into consciousness. This discussion broadened into a conversation about children and families that has never ended. We pick it up after months or years with an opening line such as, "Remember when Annie Dillard found a butterfly she had collected, still alive on its pins?" Novels are often praised for assisting the reader to escape the confines of her own life, but books like Dillard's also offer vigorous ideas that creep like vines through the stories, moral quandaries sufficient for any university ethics class, and different ways of living and of experiencing life.

My mother and I have read and discussed the claustrophobic plots of Joyce Carol Oates, the giddy cleverness of Nicholson Baker, the dependable Margaret Drabble, the not entirely dependable but usually interesting A.S. Byatt, and the closeness to perfection of V.S. Naipaul's *The Enigma of Arrival* (notwithstanding the almost certain odiousness of Naipaul himself). We have admired the glorious Ian McEwan, the stalwart Mavis Gallant, the cunning Muriel Spark, and Updike's relentless self-consciousness. My mother has talked me into reading such different and enormously rewarding books as Richard Fortey's *Trilobite: Eyewitness to the Evolution* and L.M. Montgomery's journals — "It groweth darker," said my mother of the third volume. I persuaded her to read Sarah Hrdy's *Mother Nature*, which both of us credit, along with Jared Diamond's *Guns, Germs, and Steel*, with reshaping the way we understand the way the world works.

Reading is usually thought of as a solitary act, although a reader in the act of reading is the opposite of self-absorbed. A reader journeys infinitely further from self than can be achieved in travelling across the globe or into space. A reader interrupted can be vague, disoriented; she has been returned abruptly, without benefit of decompression or debriefing, to one specific point in geography and time, from somewhere else altogether. To admit to having been lost inside a book is not to resort to metaphor but to admit the truth. A reader reads blindly (even books that have been read before hold new directions and dimensions) and so must have confidence in the writer. Reading is like the game of trust in which one person falls straight back into the arms of a stranger whose job it is to catch the faller and hold her fast.

When I was a girl of nine or ten, I liked to ride my bike a dozen or more blocks away from my home, to the margins of my knowledge of the neighbourhood, to where the streets and intersections became unfamiliar. I would ride on unknown roads for as long as my nerve held. Then I would turn and try to trace my way back home. I didn't describe these expeditions to anyone else. Although I could have drawn a rough map of my route and of the landmarks that had caught my interest along the way, I felt that it was impossible to describe the texture of these short trips. The thrill of growing less and less sure of where I was on the outward journey. The enchantment of discerning the partly known, the one-eighth familiar becoming over a few blocks one-quarter familiar, one half, three-quarters, then finally home. Books take you on this same journey and there is no adequate way to describe what you have read to someone who has not read the same pages, no shorthand for the full experience as the writer caught it. The members of a book group who have read the assigned book have had an experience that excludes in every important sense the one or two who come unprepared. To know the journey the reader takes, you have to follow the same path at or close to the same time.

The books my mother and I read open new questions, or new ways of exploring old questions, and there is no one else with whom I am as comfortable confessing how little I know, or how much a book has surprised or taught me. Discussing a book with another good, close reader is part of what the essayist Judith Shulevitz has referred to as "the lifelong struggle with good books" (51). Shulevitz points out that talking about books should not be limited to striving to agree. "This process . . . has nothing to do with coming together and everything to do with breaking apart, with figuring out how to live as an independent intellect and a soul loyal to its own needs. Literature takes root in a rich and stubborn particularity, not in some powdery notion of communal uplift" (51).

In recent months my mother's cancer has kept her increasingly close to home. Her illness has made her if anything even more in need of the information and ideas and promise of books. She has lived somewhat longer than her doctors predicted, no doubt assisted by the "bibliotherapy" administered by her dearly loved friend Eleanor Wachtel, who has provided her with a stream of judiciously selected books that are more nourishing than chicken soup, and as sustaining as love. My mother's life will not be as long as we wish, but the books she has read and written have expanded her life incalculably and have provided her with the surest route to double happiness.

Work Cited

Shulevitz, Judith. "You Read Your Book and I'll Read Mine." *New York Times*, 19 May 2002.

MAGGIE DWYER

My Friend Carol

Carol has a gift for friendship. Everyone who knows her agrees on that. Ours began in the summer of 1980 when she and Don moved into the house next door to mine on Harvard Avenue in Winnipeg. When I knocked on their door, my welcoming gift of freshly baked muffins in hand, I was greeted warmly, as if the appearance of a friendly neighbour was the next small turn in the plot of the novel she was writing. The Shields had arrived before their furniture, and Carol and Don and their children were ensconced in their lawn chairs. I do not recall our conversation. Only our laughter.

This was at a time in her life when the world was not as interested in her as it is now. She had published three novels, *Small Ceremonies, The Box Garden,* and *Happenstance,* but was far from being the literary superstar she is today. When she came across the lawn to ask me to witness her publishing contract for *A Fairly Conventional Woman* in 1982, I asked her about the writing life. I thought being a writer seemed an impossibly remote goal. Carol replied that she did not always identify herself publicly as a writer. She added that then people want to know if you are published, and where they may find your books, and you can almost see a hint of doubt cross the face of your new acquaintance. Often, she said, I say I teach. It is this characteristic modesty — and her genuine interest in people and their lives — that draws them to her.

She was a more experienced mother than I and I know we discussed mothering and what it makes of women's lives from the beginning. Her two younger daughters, Meg and Sara, babysat for mine. We began with the domestic, the family, with ourselves as women and mothers, and with the impositions that those roles imply. But no topic has ever been out of range: food, sex, death; clothing, writing, popular culture; men, husbands (what do they want?); politics, modern manners, or young women (what do they think?). We talk about what we are reading, what is being read, and why. All of this discussion gives us a shared history of good talk and more laughter. It is an ongoing conversation, full of stories featuring all the unnecessary details that we enjoy.

Friends often ask favours of each other, and Carol is generous to her friends. When I found myself in the early, bedazzled stage of my whirlwind romance with my husband John, I asked a group of friends including Carol and Don to meet him. I was in starry-eyed love, floating high over the full moon; I needed to see the reactions of good friends to give me some sense of perspective. Is he as wonderful as I think he is, I asked, the veritable man of my dreams? Or am I infatuated? Am I merely in a swoon? Delusional? Strictly gone? So eager to dwell in The Republic of Love that I could not say?

With Carol, there is an urge to confide, to confess. That's how safe you feel in her friendship. I felt at ease knowing that I was having my choice vetted by a friend whose insights into the workings of the human heart are fine. A woman who knows how a good marriage works. Who understands the alchemy of love and who takes love seriously in this cynical modern age. Who knows how to sweeten the nature of the certain tasks that threaten to coarsen the quality of everyday life, and how to accomplish that great high wire act: the good, the successful marriage.

She took my dear unsuspecting John aside at the party and said, "Now tell me about yourself." Although he continues to refer to this episode as "the night she grilled me," I know that Carol meant her words to be taken as an invitation rather than an interrogation. He tells me that for close to an hour she questioned him closely about childhood and family, his education and previous marital history and his children. His intentions, his character and his prospects were deemed satisfactory, and so, with my friend's blessing, though obviously not entirely on the strength of her approval, I married him.

Though I have five dear sisters, I have lived away from them for more than thirty years. In every community I have settled in, I have recognized that eventually I find an equivalent number of friends as surrogates for them. Carol is one of my sisters. Our friendship has continued over our various moves and crises, carrying us forward to where we live now, on the same island, within shouting distance of each other. We visit and talk as always. We take a sisterly concern in each other's joys and sorrows.

We puzzle over things Victorian, laugh out loud at the personal ads in the local paper by elderly seniors who clearly seek romance, try to imagine beginning a love affair at age seventy-eight. We talk about our writing. We talk about forgiveness; is it necessary? Are some acts unforgivable? If we do not forgive, will the echo of that vow follow us, mirroring our heartbeat?

The four years since her breast cancer diagnosis have been difficult for her friends. There is the harsh and undeniable knowledge that this good life will end much sooner than any would prefer. We are face to face with the very human, very humbling experience that Carol describes as a change in the script that we did not expect to encounter. We give little time to grieving now. We would rather discuss the political scene, gossip, or reminisce. Or consider why there is no feminine equivalent for the adjective cocksure. There are, we know, overconfident, presumptuous women, those whose assurance rests on inadequate grounds. But what word could describe them with the nice accuracy of the strident cocksure?

Carol is, if possible, more brilliantly alive. She continues to write. It is her shimmering intelligence, her goodness, her kindness and humour that mean so much to me. I hold her responsible for my interest in Jane Austen, things French, my happy marriage and more than she'll ever know.

WILLIAM NEVILLE

Carol Shields and Winnipeg: Finding Home

In 1960, the American writer and critic Edmund Wilson published a review essay on the work of the Canadian novelist, Morley Callaghan. At the essay's conclusion, Wilson wondered

> ... whether the primary reason for the current underestimation of Morley Callaghan may not simply be a general incapacity — apparently shared by his compatriots — for believing that a writer whose work may be mentioned without absurdity in association with Chekhov's and Turgenev's can possibly be functioning in Toronto. (20)

The world has changed a good deal since 1960. Since then, there are and have been many internationally recognized writers living in Toronto. But, in Winnipeg?

This last — with Carol Shields the source of the puzzlement — is a question that might well have been asked. It was not, to be sure, that her work has been underappreciated in Winnipeg or elsewhere. Indeed the "incapacity" would rest on a presumption of the improbability that a writer of her stature would come to Winnipeg, choose to stay — and actually stay.

To understand how that possibility could arise requires an understanding of Winnipeg. Like many cities, it is a community of contradictions. There is, for example, a long and strong tradition of excellence and leadership in the performing and visual arts — music, theatre, ballet, sculpture, painting — and of substantial interest in and support for these enterprises. It has nurtured or been associated with writers as diverse as Ralph Connor, Nellie McClung, Paul Hiebert, Gabrielle Roy and Margaret Laurence. It has been a crucible for a remarkable range of greatly significant social, intellectual and political ferment which, historically, had far-reaching implications for Canada as a whole. Winnipeg was, moreover, truly multicultural long before the term had been coined to describe it.

The social and political traditions of Manitoba, and of Winnipeg more especially, have encompassed a large part of the political spectrum, ranging from establishment conservatism, toryism, and classic liberalism to socialism and communism. This is a community where diverse political and social doctrines have competed for so long as to have acquired a kind of legitimacy even with those of other persuasions. And showing civility and granting legitimacy to unorthodox opinions has, indeed, been one of the things that keeps Canada functioning. Certainly those who live in Winnipeg have long since been forced — by harsh reality — to come to terms with political as well as cultural and ethnic pluralism. The truth is that they have endured the tensions and learned the penalties of not doing so. One striking result is that it is possible to characterize Winnipeg as a rather pragmatic community, which is to say, a conservative city with a strong radical tradition.

These phenomena were noted by Governor General Adrienne Clarkson in a speech to the Canadian Club of Winnipeg in December 2001. Speaking of the enduring impact that settlement patterns had on the character of the Prairie West, the Governor General observed that

> Manitoba was — and remains — the microcosm of multicultural life . . . Here we see the triumph of a different vision of society — one that is egalitarian, diverse, multicultural . . . [which] has produced a remarkably rich vein of artists and writers, business leaders and political visionaries. It is not too much to say that Manitoba, with Winnipeg its capital, is the cradle of the

great Canadian experiment in people of all backgrounds living together in relative harmony and toleration. We have had very rough bumps along the way, and you in Manitoba are aware of them. But we get over them and, when we do, we've created something much stronger.

The "rough bumps" were real, and if Winnipeg possesses many of the attributes that tourism bureaus promote and chambers of commerce celebrate, pride (or boosterism in its more crass manifestations) has always competed with an element of fragility and self-deprecation in the way Winnipeg perceives itself. Weather and mosquitoes are the least of it. Religion and language, more than once — most notably in the 1890s and the 1980s — were seen as driving and defining sharp political cleavages. The assimilation of non-British immigration to the dominant culture, in the first half of the twentieth century, was not achieved painlessly. The social and economic cleavages in the society, most dramatically reflected in the Winnipeg General Strike of 1919, corresponded to a significant degree with ethnic and cultural divisions. Over time, these tensions were ameliorated by the experiences of accommodation, changing public opinion and processes of political evolution. Madame Clarkson was correct in saying that, as the community got over these bumps, something much stronger did indeed emerge.

This evolution produced a community with interesting social dynamics that might appeal to the creative imagination, but for much of its history, it was also a city possessed of a strong sense of its own isolation. Until the 1960s Winnipeg was the largest city between Toronto and Vancouver, but it seemed a long way from everywhere, with no other large urban centres within easy reach. This perceived isolation was not calculated, perhaps, to lure creative and imaginative outsiders seeking the stimulation of their peers, nor would it console fainthearted local talents who longed for the bright lights to the east and the south. This was not, however, an altogether bad thing: it imbued many of the community's early visionaries with an understanding that if they wanted the cultural and intellectual amenities of a large city they would have to create rather than import them.

In many respects this approach worked well, but it made for a bad case of what was then a well-known Canadian syndrome: the belief that local achievements were of uncertain value until validated in Toronto or, better still, in the U.S. In the case of accomplished local artists or writers, this often meant full appreciation at home only after recognition had been accorded elsewhere and, more regrettably, only after they themselves had moved on. To all this must be added the significant phenomenon, in the last half of the twentieth century, of sluggish growth which, over many decades, contributed to the departure of many very bright and creative people. These developments had corrosive effects on morale and self-confidence.

The reality, of course, is that neither achievement nor underachievement accurately reflects the normal daily life of Winnipeggers. They do live in the oldest city of the Prairie West and one with historical claims to having been the gateway to the West, but such thoughts do not usually fill the day or give meaning to one's life. Most people in Winnipeg — as most people everywhere who expect never to have Andy Warhol's fifteen minutes of fame — would see their city as essentially ordinary and conventional, as, indeed, they tend to see their own lives. There are many indicators to suggest Winnipeggers see themselves as members of the same community and celebrate that fact on numerous suitable occasions. They do not, however, except during occasional outbreaks of boosterism, much reflect on their status as a city or wonder whether — by whatever standard is currently in vogue — it is "world-class." Nor do they spend much time considering whether — as they are periodically told — it is one of "the best kept secrets" in Canada. Indeed, those who do believe it often feel that such a secret is best kept secret. Generally, these are people whose lives are lived largely in circles defined by their workplaces and by their families, friends and neighbours, and who tend to live ordinary lives even in extraordinary cities. Outside the realm of politicians' rhetoric, Winnipeg has not usually laid claim to being one of those.

Enter Carol Shields.

She arrived in 1980 with her husband Don Shields, who had accepted an appointment in the Faculty of Engineering at the

University of Manitoba. Though he had family in Manitoba, it was professional opportunity that initially brought him to Winnipeg. What was opportunity for him was largely happenstance for her. She would later recount how their reasons for staying altered rather quickly: "Don had a job there, but we soon realized that everything was there that we needed or wanted . . . we had our daily rituals and a huge network of friends . . . it provided the most complete sense of community that I had known since growing up in the American Midwest. . . ." In due course she too was offered an academic appointment at the University of Manitoba. Much later, she was also given an office of her own at the University. It was she, observed, "One of the happiest moments of my life . . . it provided its very own perspective on all the other honours."

Though she had been writing and publishing for some time before her arrival in Winnipeg, the 1980s proved to be the most productive years of her writing career: an important, but by no means the sole, measure of this was the fact that nine books were written during her Winnipeg years, beginning with *Various Miracles* (1985) and concluding with a biography, *Jane Austen* (2001). The years from 1980 to 2000 (the year in which the Shields moved to Victoria) proved to be the longest period she had ever lived in any one place. Eventually — almost inevitably, some would say — as her work proceeded, and her writing was more widely read and acclaimed in Winnipeg and elsewhere in Canada and abroad, the Callaghan-in-Toronto syndrome would occasionally surface. How could such a perceptive writer flourish in so unlikely a place? How could such a gifted novelist thrive so far from the country's cultural capital in Toronto, to say nothing of the imperial centres of culture, such as New York and London? She herself never felt isolated or cut off from Toronto or anywhere else, come to that, but she remembered with wry amusement a CBC Toronto producer, wanting her to come to Toronto for some event, saying somewhat in the spirit of *noblesse oblige*, that "we would be willing to fly you *out*," her first realization, she said later, that she "lived in the hinterland — in their view." Carol also recalled with equally wicked pleasure, "a reporter from Eastern Canada writing 'Carol Shields works out of Winnipeg,' as though I didn't actually live there."

Looking back, in the spring of 2002, she observed, "It had become my home in the truest sense. I felt like a Winnipegger and a Manitoban . . . I discovered lots of very interesting people, made great women friends there and realized that I was rediscovering the social networks I grew up with." "It was," she said, "a perfectly wonderful place to write and all of my best writing was done there." At least two considerations thus seemed to be at work: Winnipeg proved to be the kind of community in which she wanted to live and it provided an environment conducive to better understanding the things about which she was inclined to write. The two were intimately connected.

Carol acknowledges some slight sense of isolation at the beginning, but even then the Shields were not idle: "We were very interested in theatre and the arts and there was plenty for us to see." And they found they were meeting people and settling in very quickly. At the outset she "wanted to live in a real neighbourhood." This proved to be Crescentwood, a pleasant area of large older homes on tree-lined streets, scarcely ten minutes' drive from the downtown. Later they moved into the immediately adjacent district of Fort Rouge and lived in a bright, spacious apartment whose balcony provided a panoramic view of the gently meandering Assiniboine River. In both cases, they were literally as well as metaphorically close to the heart of the city rather than in its far-flung suburbs. They met a great many people very quickly, including their neighbours in these two communities. She concluded early on that Winnipeg was a very open society and one that offered a range of social and cultural amenities more usually associated with a much larger place, even while retaining much of the sense and community values of a smaller one.

An example of the latter came during their first winter in Winnipeg. Returning from the university late on a very cold night, the Shields's car ran out of gas and they found themselves stranded on Pembina Highway, the main thoroughfare running from the southern perimeter of the city. As the two of them struggled to push the car in the direction of what they hoped would be a service station, a Winnipeg Transit bus pulled alongside them, and stopped. The bus driver ordered all the able-bodied men off the bus to push the car to the nearest gas station, which was enthusiastically accomplished.

Recounting this story many years after the event, she still conveyed her sense of surprise, delight and gratitude for an act of kindness of a sort not conventionally expected in a big city.

Gradually it became clear — to her and to others — that Carol Shields was not simply a writer who happened to live in Winnipeg, nor one whose location and community had little relevance to her work. It was not that she became a "Winnipeg writer" but that she was a writer who became a Winnipegger. Her keen observation of the way Winnipeg was, the way Winnipeg worked, and the way people connected one to another provided a crucial insight into a world in which her own characters might observe, feel and reflect their own communities; and how people in such situations interact, relate and deal with the problems and events of daily life. This understanding was related directly to the way in which her own life had become intimately connected to the community of which she was now a part. "There were days," Carol said, "when I thought I knew *everyone* in Winnipeg." It was reciprocal: untold numbers of her fellow citizens felt they knew her as well. One key to this, beyond the obvious impact of her writing, lay in her own personality: modest, soft-spoken, observant and curious about people and events and, what was frequently remarked upon, an extraordinary listener. There was never, either with her or for her countless friends, acquaintances and admirers, any sense of a great writer having "come amongst us." As her celebrity increased exponentially during the 1990s, this did not change: she was utterly unaffected by her own celebrity.

The need to live in a community to which one feels connected and for whose rhythms one has feeling was articulated quite clearly by Carol herself. In an interview relating to her book *Dressing Up for the Carnival* (2000), she explained that she had spent some time in the United States while the book was taking shape in her mind, but knew instinctively that she would be quite unable to situate the book there. She had to come back to what was now home — Canada and Winnipeg — to write it. "I couldn't imagine writing a novel set in the States: I don't understand how it works now or how American society thinks."

These observations about living in the United States are by no means unrelated to her own political and public concerns. As her children were growing up, she found politics and the nature of public discourse of growing interest and fascination — in both its serious implications and its comic dimensions — but her first significant awareness of politics came in the U.S., during the "investigations" of Senator Joe McCarthy in the 1950s. She was offended by him and what he stood for. More deeply, she was troubled by the long-term implications of McCarthyism for an American polity that, to her, seemed increasingly conservative. In time she concluded that the values preached within the Methodist tradition in which she was raised, pointed, at the level of political identification and action, to the political left. In Canada from the late 1950s, she joined and worked for the NDP, an affiliation which, apart from an early six-month flirtation with the Trudeau Liberals, proved enduring.

She came to believe strongly in the maxim "live like a bourgeois but think like a radical" (and believed that writing itself was a subversive activity), an attitude that would have placed her well outside the mainstream of American political life, even as it simultaneously placed her squarely within Winnipeg's eclectic political culture. That culture embraced bourgeois values and radical politics, just as it expressed both individual and collective values — and often, as in her case, in the same people. She was thus distanced from what she saw as the prevailing social and political values in the United States: she was not an enthusiast of George II of the Bush dynasty and had numerous American friends who shared her view. But their opinions, she observed, seemed never to be reflected in the polls or in American public debate, reinforcing her conviction that she could not set a novel in the United States with any feeling of authority or confidence.

In due course Carol became a Canadian citizen. She was, in a very particular way, the epitome of the "good citizen" in Winnipeg where she accepted enthusiastically the opportunities and responsibilities that were the marks of citizenship. Along with her professional duties at the university, and a steady stream of increasingly fine writing in many genres, she was engaged fully by a wide range of community enterprises, particularly those relating to the arts, and especially to literature and education: she served on the Public Library Board, which she regarded as a rare and valuable opportunity to seek books from the *other* end of the process; she worked individually and with numerous local organizations, including the Manitoba Writers' Guild, in assisting aspiring local writers and artists; she served on the Canada Council and on the Manitoba Rhodes Scholarship Selection Committee; she was elected Chancellor of the University of Winnipeg. In turn, the community's awareness and appreciation of the depth and breadth of these contributions were reflected in various ways: in her promotion to full professor at the University of Manitoba, in the establishment by the city of an annual Carol Shields Winnipeg Book Award and in her election to the Winnipeg Citizens' Hall of Fame.

If it is thus clear, in so many ways, that Winnipeg proved a highly congenial place in which to write, there is still the consideration of the possible relevance of Winnipeg to the things that mattered in her writing. Here, one must draw inferences, though they are compelling. Three of her books — *The Republic of Love* (1992), *The Stone Diaries* (1993) and *Larry's Party* (1997) — are actually set, wholly or in part, in Winnipeg or in Manitoba. In these books Winnipeg provides the locale: it is not, as might be argued in the work of some other writers, that the city is in some sense a character in and of itself. Given, however, her need to understand the society in which her characters live — if they were, indeed, to live — it would seem to follow that the characters of these novels do indeed "live" in Winnipeg. Add to this her comment that "I love . . . and am most at home in a society that values its writers, and where a society of writers feels embraced." (And in these years that society valued, along with Carol Shields, such other nationally known writers as Robert Kroetsch and Sandra Birdsell and a host of other excellent local writers with voices increasingly recognized.) The assurance with which the Winnipeg novels were written, and the acclaim they subsequently received, leave little doubt that writer, characters and place were at one.

There is, implicit in her comment about societies that value writers, a political observation about a community's broader priorities and values. And in fact, she thinks of her novels as being about politics. By that she means that they are about what governs relations between people. In that sense they are about the often implicit terms and conditions by which relationships work and, indeed, by which people manage to stay alive in this world. These issues bear on how communities work, how individuals struggle with and within their communities, and how they come to fit — or not — into those communities. And they are, she says, ultimately concerned with coming or discovering or finding home, the place one needs to be. Carol realized early that in Winnipeg she had found home.

What is characteristic of the Winnipeg novels and of so much of her work, is her ability to see in the ordinary what is — when recognized — extraordinary and meaningful. Her characters do not typically occupy exalted stations or enjoy even fleeting fame, but their experiences, as conceived and illuminated by their creator, reveal depths and feelings, intensity and humour that are real and palpable because they are immediately recognizable in the normal mortals that most of us are and know. In her novels she demonstrates insight, sympathy and the capacity to see in others what they do not often see themselves — or, just as often, things they notice but do not see until a Shields narrator or character sees it for them. Through her characters, as in her personal dealings with the community, she has the capacity to encourage us to believe, or at least to contemplate the possibility, that in our depths we are just possibly worthier than we think ourselves to be.

A private conversation with Carol can be lively, light-hearted, intense and full of laughter; yet one knows from subsequent conversations or subsequent writing that nothing goes by her, gets lost, or is forgotten, and this is because of her remarkable capacity to observe and to listen even while gently or laughingly making her own points. Her eyes and ears pick up and register things that most people notice with incomplete awareness until it appears suddenly in Carol's depiction of a moment. Some of these things, including her characters' own reflections, strike us as universal even as others seem particular to characters who are fundamentally of their environment. The discovery of both the universal and the particular or idiosyncratic in lives that are not, on their face, extraordinary, is one of the most compelling characteristics of her work. It is difficult to divorce this aspect from her own sense of connection with the places in which she has lived and, more especially, with the place where she spent the longest period of her life.

In all of this one becomes conscious of the ways in which Carol identified with her adopted city. Winnipeg somehow imprinted itself on her very soon after she arrived; and she imprinted herself indelibly on Winnipeg. If she is justified in believing that Winnipeg contributed something of value to her life, the reciprocal is also true. She had a significant impact on a wide swath of the community who enjoyed her books, and with others who admired the gentle nature of the unassuming public figure in their midst. With her induction into the Winnipeg Citizens' Hall of Fame in 2001, Winnipeg laid claim to Carol Shields till the end of time — or till the end of Winnipeg, whichever comes first. For a city whose self-esteem is sometimes easily shaken, Carol Shields provided a reassuring reminder of what the city could be: a place where artistic creativity could flourish, a city in which the uncommon depths of its common life could be discovered and articulated, and whose idiosyncrasies could be relished; a city in which, perhaps most of all, the dilemmas, trials, triumphs, and small ceremonies of daily life could be as readily understood as those anywhere in that wider world beyond Winnipeg, in whatever language her books are read. But she conveyed these things with particular clarity to the people in the community she called home.

Yes, Winnipeg.

The author is grateful to Carol Shields for her generosity in clarifying numerous factual matters and for her characteristically forthright comments on her life in Winnipeg; and to Todd Bruce for his exceptionally helpful comments on an earlier draft of this essay.

Works Cited

Clarkson, Her Excellency The Rt. Hon. Adrienne. *Address to the Canadian Club of Winnipeg*, Friday, December 7, 2001.

Wilson, Edmund. "Morley Callaghan of Toronto" in *O Canada: An American's Notes on Canadian Culture*. New York and Toronto: Farrar, Straus and Giroux, 1965.

LORRAINE MCMULLEN

Carol Shields and the University of Ottawa: Some Reminiscences

When I was invited to write something about Carol Shields as a graduate student at the University of Ottawa, I thought it seemed a good idea. Carol and I have been friends since that time, and our paths have crossed in various places from Victoria, BC, to London, England, but probably more often in Ottawa. A great fan of her novels, I have followed her career from the beginning and have been delighted with her success.

But writing about Carol's graduate student years proved more difficult than I had expected; it all happened some time ago. In 1969 Carol's husband Don accepted a position with the University of Ottawa Faculty of Engineering. Carol immediately took advantage of the opportunity for free tuition offered to professors' spouses and enrolled as a part-time graduate student with the Department of English. At that time she had five children; all but one of them, the baby Sara, were then at school.

The period of Carol's tenure as a graduate student coincided with the great surge of enthusiasm for Canadian studies in the late 1960s and early 1970s. Our Canadian literature courses were oversubscribed, we were opening new sections of the Canadian survey and adding new courses on the novel, on poetry, on earlier Canadian literature to our undergraduate syllabus. At the same time graduate students, too, were moving into Canadian studies and choosing

Canadian literature for their thesis topics for both the master's and doctoral degrees, so we were expanding our course offerings at those levels too. Carol was here when we initiated the Department of English series of annual symposia on Canadian writers. Canadian poets and novelists were travelling from campus to campus reading from their works to appreciative audiences of students. It was, then, an exciting period for Canadian studies.

Carol was an enthusiastic participant in departmental activities. She attended most of the many poetry readings and guest lectures arranged by the Department during her years here, readings by Al Purdy, Hugh Garner, F.R. Scott, and others. In fact it was at a university poetry reading rather than in a class setting that I first met Carol and Don. Peter Stevens of the University of Windsor, poet as well as scholar, was reading his poetry, and, after the reading, a group of us adjourned to the old Bytown Hotel to continue the discussion. Don and Carol were among the group. It was a pleasant evening. Carol was quite animated; I assumed at the time that she was excited at the opportunity of meeting Peter Stevens and talking with him. I was right. Later I learned that she herself was a poet and that she was especially eager to meet Stevens, who, as editor of the *Canadian Forum,* had just accepted some of her poems.

Carol was enthusiastic about the symposia on Canadian writers she attended here, which included conferences on A.M. Klein in 1974, Lampman in 1975, and Isabella Valancy Crawford in 1977. Of the Klein symposium she recalls, "I remember being thrilled by it all, especially the rather emotional final session in which Irving Layton castigated the ghost of Klein for abdicating his role as a poet and selling out to commerce." The Lampman and Crawford symposia she also found exhilarating, albeit recalling that when she heard someone's analysis of "a log jam as a metaphor for gang rape . . . a certain skepticism about literary scholarship was born in my head that day."

The graduate seminars Carol took ranged from Old English to Hemingway, and included Renaissance Poetry, Bibliography, Seventeenth-Century Literature, and two of my Canadian literature seminars, the Canadian Short Story, and New Directions in Canadian Poetry. As a mature student with time for only one course a year,

Carol did not get to know other students as well as she would have as a full-time student, but when I succeeded in contacting several former students who had been in the graduate program with Carol, I discovered that they remembered her well. They recalled her as having a quiet manner; they noted that she was perceptive and refreshing in her outlook and contributed to class discussion in a thoughtful manner. One former classmate commented that she had a "certain quality of set-apartness." Neither aggressive nor pretentious in her manner, she was inclined to be rather diffident in presenting her views. I remember that in class her comments were acute and thoughtful, they were not startling, and were expressed in a quiet, self contained, yet confident manner. She had the observant air we tend to associate with the writer: watchful, considering, and always very aware of the dynamics of the group. Several former classmates mentioned that they were impressed when they discovered inadvertently toward the end of their course with her that she was a successful poet. By this time she had published her first book of poetry, but she never spoke of her own writing.

My general impression of Carol at the time was of someone who was quiet without being shy, relaxed but quick in her movements. Wasting neither time nor energy, she clearly must have been very efficient and well organized to have accomplished as much as she did. She published one book of poetry in 1972, and a second in 1974, all while completing her course work. Later she was involved in writing a novel at the same time that she was writing her thesis, and that same year held a part-time job as editorial assistant for *Canadian Slavonic Papers*. When one considers her home responsibilities, of which I was only vaguely aware at the time, she had even more energy than I appreciated. While friendly and open, and always a lively conversationalist, Carol was not given to talking about herself or her accomplishments.

Directing Carol Shields's MA thesis was a joy. She approached me with her proposal to examine the novels of Susanna Moodie, having becoming acquainted with Moodie through studying *Roughing It in the Bush* and writing an essay on it for a seminar course. As I remember, she was particularly intrigued with Moodie's portrayal of male and female characters in *Roughing It in the Bush,* with the presence in female characters of such traditional virtues of the hero as determination, courage, and virtue, and the absence of such qualities from the males. She was curious to discover whether a similar portrayal of strong women characters and weak men carried through to the novels. She set to work immediately, located the Moodie novels, some in the university library, others at the National Library; one she had located earlier in the British Library. As well, she read widely in related works, such as the writings of Moodie's sister, Catharine Parr Traill. I remember her coming to me with a first edition of one of Traill's books which she had found in the stacks of the university library and thought should be in the Rare Book Room. I agreed and made the arrangements. Carol was very interested in the Strickland sisters' British background and early lives as well as in their Canadian experiences, and in considering the importance of that earlier background to their reactions to their lives in Canada.

She was writing the thesis during one of Ottawa's better winters, 1975. The ice on the canal was excellent. Living alongside the canal, Carol would give herself a break from her thesis for a mid-afternoon skate, then return to her writing. She worked quickly and wrote with facility, bringing a chapter for me to read and, when I returned it shortly for only minor corrections, having another ready. Carol reminded me that I corrected her spelling, which, she hastened to assure me, is much improved. She worked longer to complete the introduction, which in itself is as important and thoughtful a piece of criticism and evaluation as any single chapter. Completing her thesis in short order, no doubt given added impetus by the family's impending move to France for Don's sabbatical year, she defended it with aplomb, as articulate in speech as in writing. Titled "A Critical Study of Three Major Themes Occurring in the Novels and Nonfiction Books of Susanna Moodie," it was published under the somewhat more glamorous title *Susanna Moodie: Voice and Vision.*

The day Carol defended her thesis, Don, Carol, and I went to lunch to celebrate, and Carol gave me a copy of her second book of poetry, *Intersect,* published a few months earlier. I accepted it with pleasure, but, it must be admitted, with some apprehension, as yet unaware of Carol's skill as a poet. I was impressed and delighted with the calibre of the writing. The poems reminded me at times of Emily Dickinson and also of Philip Larkin, who I learned later was an early influence on her poetry. That was the spring of 1975.

Carol and her family went off to France that May, and there she began her second novel. The first novel and her thesis were published within a year of completion. She returned after the sabbatical with the second novel completed and enrolled in our doctoral programme.

When Carol's first novel *Small Ceremonies* was published by McGraw-Hill Ryerson, I was among its many admirers. The sparkle and wit did not surprise me at all. Nor did the fact that Susanna Moodie figures largely in the novel. (The protagonist is in the process of writing a biography of Moodie.) Having spent so much time thinking about Moodie, Carol had found in fiction a more flexible and creative form for expressing some of her views on her subject, and had written the novel, as she had the thesis, very quickly. Later Carol explained that one of the impetuses for the novel was a desire to use in an imaginative way some of the Moodie material which she could not use in her thesis. In my view, the novel, like her thesis, reveals Carol's interest — which continues — in our literary past, in women writers, in biography, and in the sense of a Canadian and a women's tradition in writing. I was impressed that a first novel could be written with such grace and unobtrusive skill. A fine novel, it deserved its excellent reception by critics and public. It received the Canadian Authors Association Award for Best Novel of 1976, was selected as a Book-of-the-Month Club first alternate, and was published the following year in paperback.

In the meantime, Carol's second novel, *The Box Garden*, written during her year in France, was published in 1977, the same year as her study of Susanna Moodie.

That year Carol began her doctoral course work with a seminar on the Canadian novel given by Professor Glenn Clever. Her choice of essay topic, Sara Jeannette Duncan, and her choice of seminar topics, Frederick Philip Grove's *Master of the Mill* and Sheila Watson's *The Double Hook* confirm, I think, her special interest in form and narrative technique. That year Carol also had her first experience teaching at the university; she gave a course on Creative Writing, and at the end of the year her class gave a public reading from their works. Joy Kogawa was writer-in-residence, writing *Obasan* that year, and the two writers became friends. Carol, too, was working on a novel, her third, which was to be named *Happenstance*.

From the time of our meetings about her master's thesis, Carol had often spoken of her interest in nineteenth-century women writers. Now, continuing to enjoy graduate work, she was considering writing her doctoral thesis on these earlier writers. But, unfortunately, since her days, like everyone else's, had only twenty-four hours, the combination of teaching, studying, family responsibilities, creative writing, and all the myriad concerns of dealing with publishers, became more than even someone as efficient and energetic as Carol could continue indefinitely. At best, she had time for only one seminar a year, and at that rate it would take a very long time to complete a doctoral program. By the end of that academic year Carol decided to withdraw from the program. While I did my best to persuade her to reconsider, at the same time I recognized that, given the necessity of choosing, her creative writing was more important in the long run than a doctorate. Nevertheless, Carol's interest in early Canadian women writers and in a tradition of women's writing continues, as both her fictional works and her conference papers demonstrate.

The next year the Shields family moved to Vancouver where Don, a civil engineer, worked as an engineering consultant, and Carol soon found a position teaching Creative Writing at the University of British Columbia, while continuing with her own writing.

This was not, however, the end of Carol's association with the University of Ottawa. In May of the following year, 1978, we organized a conference on InterAmerican Women Writers, which involved writers and critics from all the Americas. The languages of the conference were English, French, and Spanish. Carol was a participant, both as writer and critic, first reading a critical paper and then joining in a writers' panel discussion about women's writing. A selection of the conference papers was published in a special issue of *Atlantis* 4, no. 1 (Fall 1978), including both of Carol's papers. Her "Three Canadian

Women: Fiction or Autobiography" explored the question of genre, and the attempt by some critics to categorize writing, objecting to the incorporation of personal experience into a fictional work or of fictional elements into an autobiography. In opposition to that attitude, Carol maintained that each writer has the freedom to choose her own means to express her truth, and that no writer should be proscribed from expressing that truth in any way she finds appropriate. She cited examples from works by three nineteenth-century women: Susanna Moodie, Jane Ellice, and Susan Moir Allison, and concluded: "It may be that there is no such thing as pure autobiography or pure fiction, but only varying degrees of assimilated and transformed experience" (54).

On the writers' panel, which included Margaret Atwood, Elizabeth Brewster, Elisabeth Harvor, Gwen Pharis Ringwood, Dorothy Livesay, Audrey Thomas, and Miriam Waddington, Carol addressed differences she saw in the subject matter chosen by male and female writers, suggesting that women are more likely to choose relationships, especially relationships between women and men, as their topic, and she also expressed the view that women tend more often to use the present tense and the first person in their fiction than do men, citing examples from earlier writers Frances Brooke, Susanna Moodie, and Sara Jeannette Duncan, and contemporary writer Alice Munro. Both of these papers evidence Carol's continuing interest in early Canadian women's writing and in questions of genre. It was in discussions at this conference, Carol tells me, that she first became aware of the growing realization by women writers and critics that the traditional use of the masculine must be replaced with inclusive language.

Carol Shields's connection with the University of Ottawa continues. In April 1988 she participated in a panel discussion at the symposium on Nineteenth-Century Canadian Women Writers. On this panel, published in *Re(Dis)covering Our Foremothers: Nineteenth-Century Canadian Women Writers* under the title "'Thinking Back Through Our Mothers': Tradition in Canadian Women's Writing," Carol spoke of the random reading of childhood, recalling that the first books she read were popular children's books she found on her mother's bookshelves, books from her mother's own childhood. Such early reading from family libraries of the books read by mothers and grandmothers forms an important part of the shared experience of women, including women who, like Carol, become writers themselves as well as readers.

In the 1989 fall term Carol accepted an invitation to be writer-in-residence with the University of Ottawa Department of English. During that term she met with students, gave a reading from her most recent novel, *Swann,* and worked on her novel-in-progress, tentatively titled "Bodies of Water." When the time came for publication of the novel, she discovered that someone had just published a book with that title, so she had to find another. She chose *The Republic of Love.*

It is not surprising that so many of the concerns evident in Carol's novels had been evident in her graduate student years — in her choice of courses, essay topics, and thesis topic. Her interest in women writers continues, especially in earlier writers, as does her interest in genre, especially in the relationship of biography to fictional writing, and the influence of biography on writing. She continues to experiment with voice. She writes often of the academic world, which may be central as in *Swann,* or more peripheral, as in *The Stone Diaries* and the early *Small Ceremonies.* In retrospect, it seems to me that those busy years in which she juggled domestic responsibilities, academic studies, and creative writing, were formative years for Carol Shields as a writer. Reading widely and thinking about what she was reading, exploring her ideas in seminars, writing scholarly papers, taking the opportunities offered by poetry readings, guest lectures, and symposia to learn from the wide range of poets, novelists, and critics one meets in the academic world, she took full advantage of her milieu. Her academic experience, the combination of studying, listening, writing, and considering, gave Carol the opportunity to determine her own essential convictions about literature and writing. She was in the right place to explore and discover her own distinctive voice, the voice which best expresses her original creative spirit. And now she continues juggling multiple lives with skill, obvious enjoyment, undiminished energy, and ever increasing success.

B L A N C H E   H O W A R D

Collaborating with Carol

Our family has a cautionary tale, part of the family folklore. It seems that two sets of aunts and uncles on opposite sides of the family became fast friends and decided to travel together for three months in Europe. (European travel was considered more exotic then than it is now.) After the travellers returned and my mother phoned to hear all about it, she found that neither couple was speaking to the other. Furthermore, they were never known to speak again. Explanations were not forthcoming. The aunt on my mother's side confined herself to a disparaging sniff and made remarks about some people not knowing the limits of civilized discourse nor the need to accommodate anybody but themselves. Nothing, as far as I know, ever emerged that was so beyond the pale as to account for the disruption of what had seemed a solidly entrenched friendship.

How much more dangerous, then, is it for two artists to collaborate on a work! Gilbert and Sullivan, for instance, were renowned nearly as much for the depth and ferocity of their animosity as for their witty lyrics, and, indeed, at a forum at the annual Sechelt Writers' Festival, one of the participants asked Carol Shields if she and her collaborator in *A Celibate Season* were still on speaking terms.

We were, and we are. Carol's reputation, when we started the novel, was burgeoning, whereas mine had languished after my three novels were published. I jumped at her suggestion that we do a novel together, recognizing her generosity in wishing to spend time on a work that might very well not further her career, and indeed might use up valuable time more beneficially spent elsewhere.

Carol is generous, and she is loyal. I emphasize this because generosity and loyalty have not been givens among the writerly-talented, a goodly number of whom have used and abused their gifts in the disservice of others. In his final years Truman Capote alienated lifelong friends and benefactors not so much by his drunken and obnoxious behaviour as by the cruelty with which he lampooned them. The Bloomsbury crowd, too, thought nothing of accepting hospitality and favours from the likes of Lady Ottoline Morrell and then, with amusing (in retrospect) bitchiness, or downright malice, cutting her to ribbons. Virginia Woolf comments in one of her letters to her sister on the appalling behaviour of those gathered at Garsington, including Lady Ottoline herself.

Carol and I first met in Ottawa in the early 1970s, when a mutual friend took me along to the Shields's large brick house on the Driveway where Carol was hosting the University Women's Club book discussion group. My first novel, *The Manipulator*, had been accepted, and Carol's first small book of poems, *Others*, was being published. We each soon recognized the other as a "book person" — by that I mean that the reference points we used for living our lives had come to a large extent from the voracious reading habits we had developed in childhood.

In 1973 the exigencies of politics booted my husband and me back to Vancouver, and I suppose Carol's and my tentative friendship would have stayed at that level had it not been for the contract she was offered in 1975 for her first novel, *Small Ceremonies*. At the time she was in France where her husband, Don, was attached to a university during a sabbatical. My next two novels had been accepted, and so I must have seemed like an expert to whom Carol could write and ask for advice.

I don't remember what nuggets of wisdom I offered other than "Grab it," but I do remember well the astonishment I felt when I read *Small Ceremonies*. I had not read Carol's prose before, and I was, perhaps, unprepared for its magic: mature, elegant writing with the nicely turned and unexpected phrase. By the time I got to the very funny party scene where a woman is saying, "remember this, Barney, there's more to sex than cold semen running down your leg" (78), I knew, with bolt-from-the-blue revelation, that I was dispensing advice to a quite extraordinary talent.

Somehow we fell into regular correspondence. Carol loves to get letters — once, visiting them in Paris, my husband and I were amused at the enthusiasm with which she watched for the daily mail, or twice-daily, as it is in France. She swoops down on the mailbox as if it might contain the meaning of life — and perhaps it does. Still, I suppose our regular letters back and forth over the years, even in the '70s before e-mail and faxes had begun whittling away at formal communication, was and is a somewhat Victorian diversion.

I stuck Carol's letters in a file, and eventually I began to put in copies of my answers as well. The file of letters is three inches thick now, and as I riffle through them trying to determine when it was that we decided to collaborate, I settle on April of 1983 when she came to Vancouver for Book Week.

By then the Shields were living in Winnipeg while we were still in Vancouver. They *had* spent two years in Vancouver between 1978 and 1980, a time that gave Carol and me a chance to know that we enjoyed one another's company and not just one another's letters. And that our husbands liked one another. As everyone in a relationship of any sort knows, it frequently happens that the significant other is bored by or can't stand the sight of his/her counterpart. Carol's and mine is a lucky friendship; our husbands hit it off from the first. We had dinner parties; they sailed with us; we went dining and dancing with them.

Only two years and they were off to Winnipeg, where Don had accepted a job at the University of Manitoba. Now, besides writing letters about books, families, work, the state of the weather, and so on, we were beginning to read one another's manuscripts (a practice we still continue) and in 1981 I was commenting on *A Fairly Conventional Woman*, wondering if Brenda should have slept with Barry in her old flannel nightgown. (Carol was sensible enough to keep the scene.)

I suppose an epistolary novel was a natural for us, although at that time it was a form that was being shunned. Carol was the one who noticed that the feminist revolution had so liberated women that there were bound to be career conflicts, and so we decided to have our husband and wife faced with separation. Beyond that we didn't plan, which is the way I operate but is unusual for Carol. Usually she knows where she is going with her novels and is able to write three polished pages a day.

Separation has never happened to either of us in real life. Unlike our protagonists, Chas (for Charles) and Jock (for Jocelyn), Carol and I have settled quite happily wherever our husbands have taken us. This may be due in part to the social strictures of the times that shaped us; I was a young wife and mother in the '50s while Carol was still an adolescent, but in that decade when housework and husband-support was raised to what Galbraith dubbed a "convenient social virtue," it seemed a natural thing to do and be. Indeed, to yearn otherwise carried social disapprobation. When entering the hospital in labour, Erma Bombeck attempted to have "writer" entered under vocation, but a no-nonsense nurse scratched it out and put in "housewife." And, as Carol has pointed out, writing is a portable vocation that can be done satisfactorily whenever the children (five for Carol, three for me) are tucked into bed or off to school.

In *A Celibate Season* Jock says she's not prepared to abandon the middle class, since "the good old middle class has, after all, been good to us" (33). The middle class is where most of us hang our hats, although, following the century-defining '60s, many were bent on denying it. Jeans and headbands were in and skirts and pearls were out, and Carol and I joked at Writers' Union meetings in Vancouver about the need to shed our middle-class images, since writers above all were not supposed to be co-opted by the middle class.

In the end it is Carol who has done the co-opting. With her Jane-Austen-like gibes that prod our foibles and pretensions, she has carved out her territory from the milieu in which she lives. In the theatre programme for the Winnipeg production of "The Heidi Chronicles," Carol wrote, "Feminism sailed into the sixties like a dazzling ocean liner, powered by injustice and steaming with indignation." Carol's own feminism is reflected in the equal billing she gives her fictional women, although in an article in *The Canadian Forum* after the publication of *Swann* she was characterized as *not* a feminist, or not sufficiently a feminist. The family unit as portrayed by Carol is too nice, the reviewer says, too lacking in the sicknesses ferreted out by Freud. Of her protagonists the reviewer states, "Class renders these people completely homogeneous." One publisher characterized *Happenstance* as being "too housewifely" — ("Who does he think reads novels?" Carol asked) — meant in a pejorative sense, and thereby underscoring the lack of importance that, until recently, was attached to women's roles.

Fiction is not the handmaiden of politics, any more than the bleaker side of sexual politics is the honest experience of every writer. We don't lack for novels that crawl into the many hearts of our darkness, and bookstores are lined with thought-provoking essays by articulate feminists like Gloria Steinem. What we have lacked, and what Carol has brought us, is an intelligent and articulate witness to the ordinary and often happy lives of women and families.

Carol and I met — or rather, didn't meet — Gloria Steinem once. At breakfast the day after *A Celibate Season* was launched in Regina, we sputtered over an unpleasant *Globe and Mail* review whose main preoccupation was with the names we had given our protagonists. By way of a restorative we hurled ourselves against an icy gale in minus twenty degree temperatures for several blocks to a bookstore. Almost nobody was there, except for a lone woman who was sitting in a chair waiting to sign books. "Who is it?" Carol whispered to me. "I think it's Gloria Steinem," I whispered back. It was. We didn't introduce ourselves. Carol thought it might be intrusive — and I agreed — since we hadn't read Steinem's new book. I regret it now.

But I'm getting ahead of myself. When we began *A Celibate Season*, Carol wanted to write the male part, and so I kicked off the process with Jock writing from Ottawa, where she has accepted a position as legal counsel for a Commission looking into "The Feminization of Poverty." I sent the chapter off to Carol on October 26, 1983: "Well here's chapter one, and I can't tell you how much more fun it is to write something for someone else's eyes than just to write for the faceless mass who may or may not read it."

Carol responded with her usual modesty: "I'm not sure I can live up to chapter one. I think humour is your thing . . . Jessica's fart was delicious." When the chapter was done she wrote: "It was harder than I thought it would be. I think I thought it would be as simple as rattling off a letter. In fact, it was as hard as a, well, a novel."

It was enormous fun for us, lobbing curves at the other. "Killing off Gil was a stroke of genius." "Please feel free to revive Gil." I wrote that I laughed out loud at Chas's irritated postscript, "Fuck the purple boots."

When both Jock and Chas do something they can't risk telling the other, we had, somehow, to transcend the limitations of the epistolary novel. The only solution in a two-way correspondence is the unsent letter, although Carol was bothered, initially, by what she feared might be "the narrative dishonesty of it."

Since I was coming through Winnipeg in November of 1984, we vowed to complete the first draft by then. I stayed in the Shields's lovely Victorian-style home, the kind with oak panelling and big halls and a wide, sweeping staircase. On a bitterly cold and slippery night (me smug in the superiority of Vancouver rain), we went to the university to see Carol's delightful little play, *Departures and Arrivals,* and the next day we worked diligently all day at the dining room table, each reading aloud our own letters and interrupting one another with corrections, cutting, adding, changing, arguing over commas. At five o'clock Carol announced that eight people were coming to dinner so we had to clear the table.

I remember that the evening was merry and that we involved the guests in a vigorous discussion of whether or not "A Celibate Season" was a good title. Some said yes, some said no, but nobody (including the authors) knew of a possible derivation that was pointed out later by an astute reviewer: St. Paul, in a letter to the Corinthians, asserted that celibacy is desirable within a marriage, but only for a "season." As far as we knew the title was entirely original, but we may have been deceived; the brain has its hidden ways: it can explore forgotten recesses and toss used tidbits up like newly mined gems.

Carol sent along two reworked chapters in short order, and in December came the "big" chapter, the one where Chas admits to his somewhat bizarre episode of infidelity. She worried that I might think it "unacceptably kinky"; instead I found the letter wonderful, pathetic and touching.

The end was in sight. Letters flew back and forth. We started sending the manuscript to publishers in January of 1985.

I thought it would be fun to try adapting the novel to the stage, and by September, while publishers were (very slowly) considering the novel, I was sending drafts of the play to Carol in France. "Davina is better in the play than in our book, funnier and fuller, also more likeable," she wrote back. As for the novel, when Carol came to Vancouver in the spring of 1986 we still hadn't sold it, and again we went over the manuscript. The first third, Carol wrote to me after spending a July weekend on it, was perhaps too slow, the second third really crackles, and the final third was perhaps too amiable. Reworked once again, and once again I started mailing it out until we had racked up nine rejections. In the meantime, the play was faring well; it was being workshopped by the New Play Centre in Vancouver and when I sent it to the Canadian National Theatre Playwriting competition, it was a finalist and came back with soul-restoring comments.

The Shields invited us to spend a week with them in Paris in the spring of 1987, and while there I read the galleys of *Swann* and was quite sure it would win the Governor General's Award. It didn't, although it *was* shortlisted.

That was a wonderful week. Carol had been working hard all winter, without the society of the fellow writers and teachers she had been used to in Winnipeg, and I sometimes wonder if it was occasionally lonely when Don was off at the university. I remember that we talked and talked, as though floodgates of ideas had been held back waiting for the spring thaw, until sometimes Bruce and Don would be shutting our respective bedroom doors on us in mid-sentence.

By now the manuscript had been temporarily abandoned. Then at a conference in Edmonton I bumped into fellow writer and mutual friend Merna Summers. How did we expect to sell the novel, she asked, from a desk drawer? Get it out there, she urged, and she suggested Coteau Books. I sent it in September, and in May of 1990 Coteau agreed to publish it. In June we got word that the play would be produced by a small North Vancouver drama company in the fall.

That summer my husband and I rented a *gite* near the stone house the Shields had bought in France, and once more, in the sunny days of June, this time looking out over the lovely Jura mountains, serenaded by cows in the neighbouring fields, we went through the manuscript and began editing for publication.

It wasn't all work and no play, by any means. Carol and Don knew the wonderful little out-of-the-way restaurant in Bresse, the tiny church where the bones of the twelfth-century St. Lucipine rest under glass, and when to go to the market in Louhans. One formidable day, when the temperature reached forty degrees, we took our tiny rented Renault and drove to IKEA in Lyon and came back with an entire chesterfield tied securely to the roof, along with innumerable lamps, two chairs, rugs and cushions tucked into every available space. Two large cardboard cartons separated Carol and me in the back seat so that we had difficulty talking, and our husbands threatened to make this a permanent condition.

One day we toured the wine *caves* of Burgundy and purchased a bottle of local champagne. We drank it at a sparkling picnic on a high hill with a deserted stone tower that overlooks a vista of fields and small villages. There was a mysterious square of concrete beside the tower, and when we got out of the car Don danced Carol around it to the hum of a Strauss waltz.

My mother used to say that nobody knows anything about the true state of a marriage except for two people, but on that magic day in the glistening heights above the painterly background, with the ragged hum of "The Blue Danube" and Carol's black sundress splashed with orange flowers and the two of them twirling on the cracked and weedy concrete, it seemed possible, probable, that sometimes we get it right the first time, and that these two incredibly lucky people do love one another romantically and passionately, even after thirty-some years together.

Coming events, they say, cast their shadows before, but no passing cloud, as far as I know, formed itself into the shape of the hospital bed where Don would lie for the rest of the summer and on into the autumn. In the dreadful weeks that followed their car accident in mid-July, when Carol was thrown through the air but not seriously hurt and Don was badly battered with internal injuries and a broken shoulder and hip, I hope that sometimes the memory of that sparkling day slipped in and eased the long, hot nights. Carol spent them with Don in the hospital room, sleeping curled up on a chair, until he could be flown back to Winnipeg.

I suppose it is never entirely true that all's well that ends well. Bones mend, but a ghostly intruder lingers to haunt us: the reinforced and nagging knowledge of transience, of vulnerability. Don was well enough for Carol to come to Vancouver for the production of "A Celibate Season" (the play) in October of 1990, and the following spring we did the final editing of *A Celibate Season* (the novel). Margaret Allen, our excellent editor, immediately spotted the lingering and haunting problem (for me) of Jock and her lack of empathy, and under her wise and careful guidance I rewrote until I was able to say in April, "The final (?) draft went back to Margaret yesterday, and thanks to your good ideas it wasn't nearly as horrendous to come to terms with Jock's shortcomings as I had expected it to be."

After that we had to rush because Carol was getting ready for their summer in France and Coteau wanted to clear up galleys, covers, and so on. I sent a snapshot of my grandchildren that found its way onto the cover, and on the back is a picture my husband took of Carol and me in the house in the Jura, the manuscript between us on the kitchen table and coffee at hand. I came up with the dedication (Carol was by then back in France): "To Carol from Blanche and to Blanche from Carol, and to the letters woven into the fabric of friendship." At the end of October I went first to Winnipeg and then we both went to Regina for the book launch.

Carol once told me that if she didn't write she would become neurotic. I think this is true of most writers; Freud may have merely put a new spin on an old truth. Certainly writing is a search that may, like psychoanalysis, lead us into secret labyrinths where thoughts we had never suspected are discovered, where ancient and forgotten fears thrust themselves, like stalagmites, into consciousness, where we catch glimpses of desires so evanescent that they scatter like cockroaches before the light. And always, the compulsion, the need, to know more.

The following summer we were returning on the ferry after Carol's appearance at the Sechelt Writers' Festival and Carol was gently probing me about my thoughts on aging. (I am twelve years older than she is.) "Carol, are you asking me for the meaning of life?" I asked, and we both laughed, and then I said, "I'll tell you what, if I find it I'll phone you," and, after a pause, I added, "and if you aren't in, I'll leave it on your answering machine."

Works Cited

Groening, Laura. "Still in the Kitchen: The Art of Carol Shields." *Canadian Forum* Vol. LXIX, No. 796 (Jan./Feb. 1991): 14-17.

Shields, Carol. *Small Ceremonies*. Toronto: McGraw-Hill Ryerson, 1976.

Shields, Carol and Blanche Howard. *A Celibate Season*. Regina, SK: Coteau Books, 1991.

MARJORIE ANDERSON

Interview with Carol Shields

MARJORIE ANDERSON: *If I had to name one central assertion of your text* The Republic of Love *I would cite the need of the intimate other as fundamental to life. Would this be a fair definition of a central thesis of your text?*

CAROL SHIELDS: Yes I think it is. That isn't to say I don't feel uncomfortable with this assumption because there is something rather smug about it. Certainly I think that people who live alone, who are not part of a couple, are not necessarily living a life that is pathetic in any way, or even lonely; but there is a part of human need that involves a search for the other, that ultimate intimacy, and I suppose in our society and our culture we arrive at that traditionally through marriage. For all the things that are wrong with marriage, it seems to give us that one chance to know an other.

Is this knowledge of the other truly a knowledge of someone who is alien or other, or is the "other" a type of self projection? In other words, is love essentially narcissistic?
No, I don't think so. There is a certain amount of the wish to be adored that accompanies the so-called "in love" stage. But I think love, the reaching out for another human being, is truly the Martin Buber "I-thou" relationship; one feels one's self is that person. You touch the other so intimately and your care for him/her is so great that you can actually feel what it is like to be that person. I think that is one of our great longings in life—to be that close to another.

Is this longing also one of the causes of the emptiness of modern life? There seem to be a lot of people who do not have that "I-thou" relationship.

I don't know. Most of the people I know are involved in a friendship, in a relationship with a child or a relative, not just a marital partner. There are ongoing, continuing relationships in their lives that they value, and what are those relationships composed of? They are obviously composed of very sensitive intimacy. I used to hear people talking about how we search for the one who completes us. I am not sure I would think of that. We search for the one who answers us in some way and touches us at that intimate place where we touch that other person. I don't know many people who are not involved in intimate relationships, but I do know that loneliness is the disease of our times, so I suppose that there are people who don't have a perfect assurance about their relationship, who feel that they are always having to have it affirmed. I am talking in this book about the kind of relationship that doesn't need constant affirmation, that, for want of a better phrase, we can take for granted; we can relax into it and just let it become part of us.

You seem to be talking about some of the dangers of loneliness, of not having the other. Are there some dangers in having the intimate other? Is there a certain amount of distance and difference necessary in a relationship so that we don't become subsumed or, in the terms of Fay's father, "smothered"?

Yes. I think that getting this love relationship just right must be the trickiest thing in the world — too much love, or not quite enough, or always having it just the way you want it — and yet it does happen. I think people are able to find that balance, maybe not at first, maybe it takes a long time for it to happen, but I think it can happen. I always think it is such an extraordinary miracle, the sperm just hitting that egg and conception happening, but it does, doesn't it? Most of the time there is a healthy baby. I think that conception is no more miraculous than finding a happy balance in a love relationship.

So conception is an analogue for what happens with the meeting of two souls?

Yes. It is possible.

Can we use the relationship between author and reader as analogous to the relationship between self and other, and are there some boundaries to this relationship, some areas of shared reality that can't be inscribed?

Well, when I am writing I don't usually think about the reader because that would paralyse me; and it is not that I am talking to myself either. The sensation I have when writing is that of talking to the typewriter, or to the paper, or to this thing that I am making. So the reader, at that point, is outside. But then, of course, I do think about the reader, particularly in an area as delicate as this because the last thing you want to do is to shut the reader out of your story in any way by smugness or by making declarations about the only way that things can be done or achieved.

So you accept that there are boundaries to this relationship that the artist shares with the reader?

Yes, and I also think that I can't expect to connect with every reader. I can only talk to a certain kind of reader, and I don't expect everyone who opens my books to connect with me. I don't connect with half the books that I open. It is very much like the network of one's friends. I always think that the people who read my books and respond to them are people who would be my friends; in fact, I met a woman who said she feels that she is me when she reads my books. It was the nicest thing anyone ever said to me.

You mention friends as important kinds of readers whom you would like to reach. Are there any other terms that you could use to describe a reader whom it's important for you to reach? Can you describe this reader in gender terms?

Well, sometimes when I am in the middle of writing a book, when confidence fails, I think, who would be interested in this and then I have to think, well, maybe there are one or two others. Sometimes I can imagine them, and often they are my daughters. Then I think, if there are two or three others, then maybe there are two or three hundred others. So there is this sort of mythical readership that I can call on and feel friendly toward and talk to.

Is a readership often, always, sometimes female gendered?
I hope not. No I don't think of that reader as being a particular sex. My earlier books were very much considered women's books, but that was in a very curious time in our history when the kind of books I wrote were described as domestic. We all now agree that everyone has a domestic life. We used to just pretend we didn't. I never thought for a minute that the domestic life wasn't important to write about. I never doubted its validity but, I must say, other people did. Of course now that men are writing so-called domestic novels they are not called that at all; they are called sensitive, contemporary reflections of modern life.

Carol, you spoke of having your novels labelled as fiction for women, and from what I read of your reviews they certainly aren't considered that now. Did going to the dual perspective, having both male and female characters sharing the narrative, grow out of a concern that your novels would be considered for women alone?
I will give you the old answer — yes and no. The first two books that were from a woman's perspective, from the first person perspective, had men in them, so although it wasn't a shared perspective I felt that the weight of those men's lives in the book was fairly heavy. So in a sense men were included, and I like writing about men. It was at a time when I was thinking a great deal about gender (and I seem to be doing that still), but I was curious about the way in which we understand each other and fail to understand each other. So, yes, the idea of writing *Happenstance* from a male point of view did come out of being tired of being called a women's writer. Although to tell you the truth not that many people did call me that, maybe one or two, but I took it very much to heart. Men review books in this country, and a lot of men were reviewing my books. For example, my books were reviewed by William French who always damned me with faint praise, thinking I would be a fine writer if I ever found a subject worthy of my abilities. That was how he put it, meaning he thought I should stop writing about women in domestic situations, I suppose. So I did think that I would try to write from a male perspective; I did not have the courage to write from the first person point of view though and I

wanted, in any case, to try to write a third-person book and see what happened. So I wrote those two books, first *Happenstance* and then *A Fairly Conventional Woman,* one about a husband, one about a wife. But the person I feel closer to is Jack Bowman, the husband, in terms of his sensibility. Although Brenda is an artist, and I feel that part of her is part of me too. But Jack's basic life posture is one of watching rather than doing; he is someone who always stands slightly outside of events. This is how I have always felt. I had to write that book to know that. There are rewards in that stance and also losses. Nevertheless, I do feel that is where I am located and where, probably, most writers I would read are located.

You are the watcher in your own life? You are the watcher in others' lives?
Well, not in my personal life, I suppose in my relationship to the world. I've never hurled myself into positions of organization, of doing, or of real activism. I have tagged along now and then, but basically I have watched it happen. The '60s were very interesting years for me, but only because I was watching them happen, not because I was involved.

Do you think then that to become a writer one must have a strong component of the watcher?
I do.

You can sense that the author has that? Was the male perspective in the first person as easy for you to do as the third person?
Swann was a very interesting book to do because of finding different ways, different narrative lines. I found it far easier to make the gender hop in that novel than I did the age hop. It was easier for me to write about Morton Jimroy, who was a man about my own age. Even though he happened to be a man and his sensibility was very different from mine, he was easier to create than Sarah Maloney because I found it harder to imagine what someone twenty-eight years old was thinking.

That's interesting.

I have a romantic belief that men experience life very much as we do emotionally. There is the question of language, but that just requires paying attention to how language operates and what is really behind it. But men are as damaged as women are by power, by powerlessness, by loss, by loneliness, by their need for the other.

In The Republic of Love, *you write that Fay and Tom inhabit different vocabularies. Is that what you meant, that they share emotional needs but they speak of them differently?*
Yes.

Are you conscious of trying to resist male and female stereotypes when you are writing?
No, I guess I am not. I try to resist other kinds of stereotypes. I was very anxious to usurp the stereotype of Winnipeg, for example. I wanted to show Winnipeg as a civilized society, a gentle society, an integrated society, and a society in which there was a summer, not just a winter. I didn't write all this down, but I made a mental list of the ways in which Winnipeg and Manitoba are thought of and tried to turn this upside down.

I have talked to you about your desire to play with genre and you have mentioned subverting genre. What were you subverting in Republic? *You mentioned subverting the idea of Winnipeg as a winter city. What else were you subverting?*
The whole stereotype idea. I don't very often see decent people in novels, and why not? Some don't believe in them perhaps; but I do. I think there is an awful lot that doesn't get into fiction. I wrote about this idea in the essay in *Anthology*. Love is the same thing in trying to find a love poem. One would think that love would be the subject of a huge bulk of our poetry writing. In fact, it's not. It's difficult to write about, and people have avoided it and have written about loss and longing instead. So I wasn't trying to usurp the love story; I felt more that I wanted to rescue it, hold it up against other major themes, like war for example. Do I think love is a lesser subject than war? I do not. I think it is far more important than talking about war, or race relations, or these other things. Love is the basis of our lives. I don't think

of it as a minor theme and yet we all know it's been relegated to Harlequin romance novels. Serious, reflective people do not fall in love; it's embarrassing even to say so. I don't believe that for a minute, so I want to write about love.

You want to write about love. What do you not ever want to write about? What stories would you not be interested in telling?
I would never write a war story, I mean the war story, as it were, is entirely a male-modelled genre, and I have no interest in it at all. I think it doesn't involve much reflection.

You are not interested in war in its pure form. What about the other types of war that go on and are really microcosms of macrocosms — the wars between people that lead to all sorts of human pain and agony right up to murder and death?
In *The Box Garden* I wrote about a kidnapping and I was very sorry I did that. It is one book I would recall if I could. What do I know about kidnappings and police? I felt I did it very flimsily, and I don't know why I did it. I don't think I'll make these kinds of mistakes again. I am interested in people's perversions and dishonesties to a certain extent and how they work those out, but violence has not been a part of my experience and I am far too fond of my characters to want to do them violence.

Ah, a wonderful authorial perspective. The other day I heard you make a statement about conflict, and you have to tell me if I have quoted you correctly here. You said that conflict isn't about two people fighting, it's about the human heart fighting with itself. Is that accurate?
Something like that.

Explain that to me.
Well, I think most of the dialogue that occurs in the world is what goes on in our own heads — us talking to ourselves — and this is where we are conflicted, I suppose, about right and wrong or attachment and detachment — all the things that humble us and trouble us. This type of conflict is a more realistic one in my life than actually battling it out with my colleagues or my family.

What type of conflict are you concerned with in Republic*? Another time you said that you were not interested in depicting the traditional type of conflict in your works, that there was another type. What is that other type of conflict?*

I am interested in "what is important?" It seems to me that a lot of people think that one particular kind of thing is important. I want to jiggle that scale a little bit, and say, "Look, this isn't important. This is important." Some writers, especially playwrights, will often say, "the purpose of my play is to disturb you," and I sometimes say, "how dare you disturb me; you haven't earned that right yet. Why not bring me some wisdom, tell me what you've discovered, bring me some harmony, give me something else, you don't have to disturb me. We go into the theatre disturbed already." I need someone to throw out an intellectual puzzle (I do love that) but I resent (here we are getting into ageism), I resent a twenty-five-year-old playwright poking at me and saying "I want to disturb you."

What do you want to do for your audience? Not disturb them, but what?

In a way, writing is like a conversation you might have with someone. You want to talk about these things. In *Thirteen Hands,* I want to present this notion I have of what goes on in small groups of people, how groups feed us and sustain us and in a way become an alternative to the family which has failed us to a certain extent in our society. I wanted to show how those stereotypical, "blue-rinsed" women are thinking individuals, worthy individuals, and how they often feel brilliantly alive in those moments when they come together with other people.

Do you feel an affinity with nineteenth-century women writers because of the artistic desire of yours that you just expressed?

Yes, I think I do, and I feel a particular affinity with early nineteenth-century writers such as Jane Austen. She understands, I think, that fiction writing is making scenes. She knows how to create a scene, and this is one of the things that I am interested in doing, not just presenting the scene but furnishing it and lingering in it as long as I can, at least as long as it is paying for itself.

Are there other nineteenth-century writers with whom you have a strong affinity?
Yes, George Eliot and Charlotte Brontë, not Emily Brontë.

Tell me about George Eliot and Charlotte Brontë and then also tell me about Emily. Why not the affinity with Emily? But tell me about the affinity with George Eliot and Charlotte first.
I read George Eliot before I read Jane Austen, which is not very sensible, I suppose, but theirs were the first novels I ever read about intelligent women, and I wanted to read about intelligent women, thinking, reflecting women. I was not finding these kinds of women characters in my reading of contemporary novels in the '60s and '70s. I was reading about distraught, troubled women who didn't seem to have much power of reflection, much of a sense of loyalty, for example. George Eliot's women understand what loyalty is, and integrity. I think contemporary women do too. I don't see why they have so much trouble finding a place in fiction, why we are not writing about those women.

So with George Eliot, it is intelligent women; what is it with Charlotte Brontë?
Oh well, Charlotte Brontë has so much wonderful narrative energy. I suppose I love that novel because of the narrative energy in it.

Which novel in particular?
Oh, *Jane Eyre.*

And Villette?
It was so long ago when I read *Villette* that I can't really talk about it except that I know it was a kind of novel that I just crawled into and happily stayed in as long as I could. What Charlotte has is the power to enthrall. With Emily it is exaggeration, a poetic exaggeration that I don't feel happy with.

What are some other affinities you have with nineteenth-century writers?
Oh, the other thing is that they did understand the love story. They understood the importance of finding the other and weren't ashamed of it.

Did they have to write their love stories in a covert as well as an overt way? Do we have to do a lot of subtext reading in nineteenth-century fiction?

I think they did. I can talk for a minute about Susanna Moodie's stories. She wrote terrible novels and there are people who think that her Canadian books aren't that much better, but there is a subtext in them. A lot of people think that she was conscious of the subtext and felt that she had to hide things. I think that she was unconscious; she was very much a feminist who didn't know she was a feminist and perhaps hadn't articulated these things even to herself. Nevertheless, if you read *Roughing it in the Bush* carefully you find the same motifs coming back and back, that of the strong female figure nursing and nurturing the weak, prone male. So that has to tell us quite a bit, I think.

You see that as subtext?

Yes, when Susanna Moodie talks about her better half you can almost see her winking.

Ah yes, I understand that. What about the differences? How are you as a twentieth-century woman novelist different from your nineteenth-century role models?

Ah, that's an interesting question. Well, I suppose just the furniture that I am dealing with.

Is there a difference in artistic licence?

Well yes, I suppose, although there is this wonderful thing about nineteenth-century novels — I'm thinking about Trollope. He was very free with his narrative technique and did interesting narrative things that we think we have just discovered now and we call them postmodern, but ninteenth-century novelists were doing this. They were using different points of view and interruption of the text all the time. I think we can still feel an affinity with nineteenth-century novelists that we are working in the same tradition. Of course we can go further in terms of the social context. We can be a lot more immediate in terms of our physical lives, for example, but I'm not sure that that has made such a tremendous difference.

Has the women's movement had some effect on changing the kinds of perceptions that we all have of the world? I am thinking now of the use of the image of the sphere in the nineteenth century to represent the domains of the sexes — the domestic sphere and the public sphere. I don't detect those separate worlds in your novels. I see that what had been represented as a sphere has elongated and flowed into parallel lines. So, if I were talking about how you represent the world of the two sexes I would talk of parallel lines rather than spheres.
Yes, probably.

Would this perception, which is possible now, not have been possible in the nineteenth century?
I think George Eliot did that too. She brought male consciousness into focus as well as the consciousness of women. The interesting thing is that the novel is the only literary form in which women have participated from its very beginning. They have had a strong foothold in it, and I think it is the most important literary form that we have, partly for that very reason, that it has had two eyes to it instead of just one. Certain kinds of novels — the novel of action, the political novel, and some of the adventure novels — were out of the females' sphere, so women concentrated on the novel of relationships. Just by accident they arrived at the most fertile territory for novel writing. They were, in fact, handed this very small corner to cultivate, and it proved to be the most interesting corner, at least for me.

Where should women's writing go now?
I would like to see more novels about intelligent women, instead of novels about women as victims. We were talking about Jane Smiley's *A Thousand Acres.* I think the book would have been better if the women characters had been stronger. Everything revolved around victimization: the quarrel between the sisters was over a man, the quarrel over land was the result of the father's perversity, their own destruction was the result of their being victims of sexual abuse. Everything seemed hinged to victimization and to male authority. It would be interesting to see what would happen if women could be stronger in their novels and fully human.

What do you do with the topics of male authority and hierarchy?
Laugh at them a little bit. I wish we had more comic novels. Women's novels have not been very comical, and men haven't written many comic novels either.

So not take these issues too seriously?
No, I think we can look at male authority ironically, for example, or comically, for these are ways we can arouse a kind of distrust in it.

Are you aware of having done a reversal in Republic? *I think of Tom as anything but an authority figure, and I think of Fay's father as the more nurturing of the two parents. He is the one who listens and he is the one who gives her licence; her mother is the one who makes authoritative statements. Were you aware of inscribing particular traits on a male and particular ones on a female?*
No, I don't think so. I didn't start to divide the screen between the male and female and balance them. I am never that deliberate about how things work out. Someone once said to me — this was after I had just published two or three novels — "Carol, do you know how feminist your novels really are?" And I said yes I did. I knew right from the beginning, but I thought there might be another way to do it.

Other than confronting?
Other than novels of polemic.

Were you also conscious of showing a type of male that isn't often depicted in fiction?
No, I wasn't very conscious of that. In fact, maybe my characters are just the kinds of males I know.

Have you had people comment on that before?
Yes, only once about *Happenstance*; a CBC reporter said he thought that Jack Bowman wasn't very masculine because he didn't do any sports.

I have another question on the male/female theme in Republic *that is of interest to me. Do you think that there is such a thing as "maternal instinct," and if there is, is this instinct an exclusive territory of females?*

I certainly think there is maternal instinct. It is enormously strong biologically and inscribed in our culture. This is an extraordinary feeling, the desire to protect the creature who comes from us and is bound to us, and it's astonishing how it does work out. Often, young mothers talk obsessively about their children. This has to be biological. The focus of women is necessarily divergent in those early months. Mothering is all-consuming because that infant is so helpless and needs complete protection, supervision, and total nurturing. It's frightening but also exhilarating to find that you are totally responsible for another human being. That is the bond of love I think. Most people who have children are astonished; they have never thought of themselves as having a maternal instinct and then they feel it. The biological attachment may make it more pronounced in women, but probably it is culture that has divided the father from the child.

In The Realms of Gold, *Margaret Drabble writes about Stephen Ollerenshaw, who is looking after his infant daughter and is very much involved in the parental obsessiveness of care and protection. In fact, this obsessive concern causes him, in a fit of compassion, protectiveness, and insanity, to kill both himself and the child. In that text, there is a parallel character who is also very concerned about her baby, but the woman character survives and the male character doesn't. Drabble seems to be saying that a strong, parental instinct is there for all of us but maybe women have been socialized into knowing how to handle it.* Well, maybe it is socialization, but women are able, for whatever reason, to care deeply outside themselves for another, whether it's their children or not. I do think that women have this capability to a greater degree than men. Why would that be, I wonder?

Is it nature or nurture — the old debate. I am also interested in the types of female imagery that you have in Republic. *I have noticed that your text opens with a powerful representation of the maternal, twenty-seven mothers, and it ends with the iconography of the mermaid. What are we to make of the movement from maternal to mermaid?* I wandered into each of these stories simply out of curiosity, and I never intended to set up anything, but I suppose unconsciously it may have been there. The story of the twenty-seven mothers, this shared motherhood, is thought by some to have been very damaging to Tom, but by me to have had exactly the opposite effect. I would think the more nurturing one would get, the better off one would be, and I think Tom felt that. He was getting mixed messages from so-called therapists who felt his early experience either damaged his love or developed it, I don't know which. The mermaid interested me for other reasons. The mermaid is one of the most interesting parts of our iconography because the mermaid doesn't reproduce; she has no reproductive organs, and is always alone. She is a sort of double figure and conveys an irony that I love. The figure of consolation for the drowned seaman is also the one who lures sailors to their deaths. All the fears of women could be located in this sea creature. I was astonished to find that no one has looked at mermaids from a feminist perspective, and I wanted to do that. At first I thought I would write a book about mermaids and then I thought I would write a book about a woman who was writing a book about mermaids. What I did in the novel was to present Fay's different theories; she goes from one to the other, and, true, she ends up with a kind of Jungian theory, but I don't expect for a minute that she will stay there. One thing that I think women have learned to do is to say "I've changed my mind" and not have a closed system of belief. I wanted Fay to keep testing her theories, but always underneath she would be doubting what she was doing.

What would you like your readers to take away with them after reading your fiction?
I never think in these terms when I'm writing, although, unconsciously, I must be imagining another eye sweeping over the print. I don't pretend, ever, to impart even a small ray of wisdom; writers, in fact, seem almost singularly unequipped to do so. I suppose I imagine the reader-writer relationship as a joint venture in the world. I remember Jean-Paul Sartre saying that "to read a book is to write it." This seems a profound statement to me, suggesting as it does a partnership of creativity, a decision to travel the same hills and valleys of language, not in search of enlightenment but of the experience that language can return to us.

What is the purpose of fiction in our lives?
I've been thinking about this for years. It comes straight out of the puritan guilt of my childhood — fiction is lies. But it's not. Judith Gill in *Small Ceremonies* talks about narrative hunger: why do we need stories? Her conclusion — and mine — is that our own lives are never quite enough for us. They're too brief, too dark, too narrow, too circumscribed, too bound by geography, by gender, by cultural history. It is through fiction that I've learned about the lives of women. And about how people think; biography and history have a narrative structure, but they don't tell us much about the interior lives of people. This seems to me to be fiction's magic, that it attempts to be an account of all that cannot be documented but is, nevertheless, true.

May, 1993

JOAN THOMAS

"... writing must come out of what passionately interests us. Nothing else will do": An Epistolary Interview with Carol Shields

I've interviewed Carol Shields once in the traditional fashion, tape recorder running. This was shortly after her nomination for the Booker Prize. She had just come back from Europe, from several weeks of being constantly interviewed, and she told me that she was struggling not to repeat herself, not to develop the routines that writers fall back on in self-defence. Her responses to my questions were unfailingly thoughtful, precise, often surprising and challenging.

Nevertheless, when the opportunity came to interview Carol again for the special issue of Prairie Fire *in 1995 (Vol. 16, No. 1), Carol talked about her reluctance to be interviewed in the usual way — and so, we settled on an exchange of letters.*

Winnipeg
7 September 1994

Dear Carol,

You've been interviewed probably more times than you care to remember in the last year, and I wonder if this has made you wary of the conversation as a form of communication?

In your contribution to *Writing Away,* the PEN Canada Travel Anthology, you talk about the benefits of reading while travelling — the way a book can throw a new landscape into relief, and vice versa. This summer I spent a week on a houseboat on a Saskatchewan lake rereading *The Orange Fish* and *Various Miracles,* and in this strange, minimalist landscape (some days there seemed to be nothing but a quarter inch of land between water and sky), I was sensitive to a social context in your writing that is not *prairie,* a world of decorum, thank-you notes, and real art on the dining room walls. Was this your world as a child?

Can you give me a sense of what you expected of your life when you were an adolescent?

You have what we now consider a large family, and I'm astonished to read that you began your first novel when your children were small. Aside from the fact that it's very hard for a parent to find time to write, I find that it's tricky to sustain the often tenuous world of the imagination, and simultaneously be emotionally present in that intense childhood world where peanut butter and dead AA batteries predominate. How did you sustain these two realities at once — or are they two realities?

Was it hard for you to give yourself permission to write?

Looking forward very much to your reply,
Joan

15 September 1994

Dear Joan,

I'm glad you suggested a written interview, though I am aware, and I'm sure you are too, that a considered and shaped response sacrifices the fizz and spontaneity of a conversation. But since I'm given to conversational blurts, and can't resist jumping in with "my theory for the day," a written exchange seems a more prudent way to go.

What an odd word, prudent. I doubt if I've used it more than a half dozen times in my life, and I can't say that I admire genuine button-down prudence as a quality. And yet it is the word I would have to use to describe my childhood, which is something you've asked specifically about. Prudent parents, careful, conventional. A prudent school system, too.

There was a period in my life when I went around, rather ostentatiously, saying I'd grown up in a plastic bag. I've got over that, or perhaps I've reassessed what Oak Park, Illinois, meant. Oak Park in the forties and fifties was a place where behaviour patterns were fairly rigid. Everyone went to church — well, there was one family who admitted to being atheists, but I never quite believed this could be; it seemed too preposterous. There were Catholic and Jewish minorities, and it was the great fear of our families that we might acquire boyfriends from these sectors, and heaven only knows where that would lead. The city of Chicago, which bordered Oak Park, might have been a hundred miles away. Once a year we visited the Art Institute, generally with the Girl Scouts, and occasionally we would be taken by our teachers to the Museum of Science and Industry or the Field Museum.

Oak Park society was in those days completely white. Before I went away to college I had never spoken to a black or Asian person, never tasted garlic, and had never heard the word "shit" uttered aloud. On the other hand, I knew how to write a thank-you note, which occasions demanded hat and gloves, and how to conduct polite introductions. The three transfer points (as I think of them) in Oak Park were school, church and library, and the library was where I felt most at home. Church was the domain of men; this seemed reasonable to me in those days. A male God, a male heir, and the board of elders at the Methodist Church where I attended Sunday School. Libraries and schools, on the other hand, were overseen by unmarried middle-aged women, remarkable women for the most part, and even one or two who were devoted to their vocations in a way that made me suspect work could be a joyful undertaking.

This society, when I describe it, appears seamless and banal; in fact, I've come to see that there were hundreds of disruptions in its surface, signs that I seem almost deliberately to have suppressed, persuaded as I was that Oak Parkishness represented a desirable reality, perhaps the only reality. The father of one of my friends was America's leading Lincoln scholar, but I didn't know it then. Another friend lived with her mother on welfare, but this was, somehow, never acknowledged or made clear. A neighbour fell into depression and jumped in front of a train, but I — ten years old — was told he had a heart attack on his way to work and "fell" off the platform. A local clergyman made inappropriate gestures towards teenage girls in his congregation. All these anomalies, and many more, failed, somehow to enter the record I was assembling. The one exception was the Walsh family across the street who were described as bohemians; they painted their living room ceiling chartreuse, they hung abstract art on the walls, they listened to jazz, and the children of the family called their parents by their first names. (I am in close touch with this family today, and grateful to them for offering another vision of what life might be.) Taking the El downtown I glimpsed vast and puzzling slum areas which in no way accorded with the vision of America I was given in school. Sitting in Sunday School I came to suspect — but not articulate — that the Christian story was more metaphor than historical fact. I was, as you can see, a rather fuzzy-headed dreamy kid, ready to accept other people's assessments and to distrust my own.

I very early formed the notion of being a writer, all the while knowing that this was impossible. Writers were like movie stars. Writers were men. Hemingway grew up in Oak Park, but aside from him I suspected that suburbia did not produce writers. My real life, as I saw it, was entirely predictable: I would get married, have children and live in a house much like the one I grew up in. Along the way I would acquire a university education so that I would have "something to fall back on," should any part of the plan fail. I have,to say I was quite happy with this future; in fact, I was enchanted by it. (Many of my girlfriends were starting their silver patterns while in grade nine or ten.)

I met Don Shields when I was twenty-one, and we were married the following year. Our meeting took place in the UK where I was a third-year student at the University of Exeter and Don an Athlone Fellow (from Saskatchewan) at Imperial College in London. Our marriage is now in its thirty-eighth year. We held similar ideas of the life we wanted to lead — children, our own house, but I can't say we thought any of this through very clearly.

It was Don, though, who encouraged me to start writing again. He knew I had won a couple of writing prizes in university and had worked on school literary magazines, and I suppose he wondered what had happened to this strand in my life. I picked it up in a small way by taking an evening course in magazine writing at the University of Toronto. This would have been in 1959. I don't remember much about it except that the instructor — a woman who never took off her hat — told us never to write about old people. "The world belongs to the young," she said. She also advised using a paper clip instead of a staple on manuscripts. I remember writing this down carefully in my notebook. I wrote a short story for this class, and to my astonishment she sent it off to the CBC, who bought it for their series *Stories* with John Drainie.

This early sale, while extremely modest, gave me the kind of permission I needed in order to write. It made me feel less foolish, less self-indulgent, about the whole business of writing and telling people that I "did a little writing." Nevertheless, it wasn't until the late seventies that I could look the census people in the eye and say, shuffling my feet all the while, "I am a writer."

I'm frequently asked how I could write with small children in the house. I'm a little baffled myself, looking back. I wrote while they were in school, mostly, grabbing an hour in the morning, and perhaps another in the afternoon. I seemed able at that time in my life to write through a great deal of noise and distraction and to produce a couple of pages on even the busiest of days. I did come to realize that one needed "time around the time" in order to enter that other reality and then to resurface to real life. The older children knew more or less what I was up to in my second-floor room, but I suppose the younger ones thought only that I was a mother who typed a lot.

Like many writers I've written in kitchens, in the corners of bedrooms, in cafés, on trains, at a quiet library table, but for many years, starting in 1970, I had a room of my own to work in. In our household it was always referred to as my office. And luckily I had my children one at a time so that the noise and confusion was incremental. For some reason I never minded interruptions; the telephone was left on the hook (you never know when there might be an emergency) and the children were free to come in and out. There was a sewing machine in one corner of the room which was used less and less by me and more and more by one or the other of my daughters. I'm not sure how I managed to type to the accompaniment of the sewing machine, but it didn't seem a problem in those days.

Nowadays the house is empty in the daytime, too empty and too quiet, and I prefer to work in my office at the university. Writing habits have shifted as I've grown older. I can sometimes manage three pages instead of two. I do far more revisions, and enjoy them more. The work I'm doing now demands a little modest research, oddly pleasurable trips to the reference room, telephone calls or letters to verify points of information. And I love to talk over my writing projects with friends, soliciting ideas and impressions, getting their experiences.

Carol

3 October 1994

Dear Carol,

It is interesting to me to see the way we continue to modify the constructs of our childhood. I'm finding that this isn't something that just happens when we first leave home and do our first big revision; it seems to keep happening. This must be a tremendous source of interest and material to a fiction writer.

In response to your reflections on the "prudence" of childhood in Oak Park: There is, of course, the belief that people are made into artists by a difficult childhood, that they create to exorcise the past, or that they were moved out of the mainstream somehow by their childhood, turned into observers. I thought after I sent my first questions away that you are often asked about your childhood in the way that I asked it. I wonder if you sometimes get the sense that you have to account for having had an ordinary childhood, as the North

American middle class defines ordinary, that there are a lot of people out there who do not believe that happy homes in suburbia produce writers?

You talk of yourself as a dreamy and fuzzy-headed kid, who didn't integrate any of the anomalies into the sanctioned view of Oak Park. I wonder if children ever can do this without someone to open the door a crack for them?

Has it been a conscious decision for you not to write about what shows through the fault lines — the racism and sexual abuse, for example — but to take on the more delicate job of excavating the "ordinariness"?

Margaret Laurence talked about having "a fiction writer's memory." Do you think that such a gift exists?

You've written some of the most beautiful images of love and family. Jack walking into his parents' living room in *Happenstance*, for example, and seeing his father unself-consciously painting the fingernails of his wife, a woman who has been crippled for many years with arthritis. The fireplace in "The Orange Fish" where everything is fuel for the family fire. But against this I think of Daisy Flett in *The Stone Diaries*, who is married to a decent enough husband, has kids that are as nice as one could reasonably hope for — and who has become invisible in her own life. I wonder whether the meaning of Daisy's tragedy is (for you) principally existential, about the hazards of life that all of us face, or whether it's social, having to do with the meaning of marriage for women.

Joan

14 October 1994

Dear Joan,

I'm not sure we "modify" the constructs of our childhood; that word seems a little too active to fit my own experience. I like to think we see further and deeper with time (does this mean wise — I hope not). "Adjustments" come about because we have a longer perspective, because we talk about these things as we get older, weighing and comparing, and I suppose, because we see our own children grow up. I was never interested in childhood when I was a child, but only when I had children.

There are so many myths about writing, and writing away a miserable childhood must be the most romantic and the most firmly rooted. I'm not convinced that we write to complete something in us that is incomplete or to amend the unbearable; writing seems to me much more an act of "making." There are so many things for which I have no patience, but for some reason I am willing to bring enormous patience to this one task: of "making" something out of words. Sometimes a ridiculous amount of patience. An afternoon will go by with only a few sentences down on paper, and I will have experienced that happy distortion of time that makes four hours seem like fifteen minutes. (I've talked to other writers about this, and it seems it's a fairly common experience.)

You ask if we require something to help us break out of the reality we're born into. We're lucky, I suppose, if we have books to read, a few decent teachers, and enough family security to let our imaginations wander. In a story I wrote called "Scenes" I talked a little about what it was like learning to read; it was, in fact, as close to a spiritual experience as I've ever felt. I was about ten or eleven when I had another experience (which I also put into "Scenes"). I was walking home one summer evening, probably from a friend's or from the library, when I passed a house in my immediate neighbourhood. I couldn't see the people sitting in the darkened screen porch, but I could hear them, and they were speaking in a foreign language. Their voices were excited. I couldn't tell if they were angry or just impassioned. I'd heard snatches of other languages on the radio or on the El going downtown, but it was a shock, a wonderful and liberating shock, to know that my utterly familiar neighbourhood could reveal such a surprise, such a mystery. To hear strange voices from a dark front porch — this seems to me now a most unremarkable event, but at the time it offered an almost transcendent form of promise. The promise was that there was *more*. The sense of *more* came out of the radio too, from Chicago's gospel churches that broadcast their services on Sunday afternoons, and from the solid, stately sound of applause that followed musical performances. I was drawn to these things.

I don't think I ever made any conscious decision about what I would write about, and certainly I had no idea who my audience would be. I found myself writing about certain recurring ideas, mainly about the unknowability of other people, and about those odd, chancy, redeeming moments of connection. Racism? Abuse? Neither of these were realities for me, though certainly I lived in a racist environment; it was just that I didn't know it.

I'm not sure what Margaret Laurence means when she speaks of a "fiction writer's memory." I wonder if she is speaking about the recognition of what a story is. So much slips through the net unrecognized, unarticulated. Perhaps she is speaking about how to hold on to material by an act of recognition. I've always believed that everyone experiences a few instances of transcendence in their lives, and that many such happenings are discarded because they don't fit very well into ordinary experience. Moments of craziness, we say, shrugging them off. It's almost as though we don't feel we deserve these random illuminations.

Someone, a stranger, wrote to me after *The Stone Diaries* was published to say that she wished Daisy had tried harder. (I do too.) But like the huge majority of women she felt the full force of social stricture. Her real sadness, as I see it, is that she never knew what she was allowed, what she was owed. She settled for exactly what she was offered, without ever forming the sentence parts for "I want . . ." She believed what the women's magazines said about women's work. She absorbed, unquestioningly, the notion of what a woman's life might consist of, its rewards, its bargains. If only one person had said to her: Your life is your own and there is work you can do. (A lot of women never heard this articulated before *The Feminine Mystique* was published.)

On the other hand, Daisy knew economic security, she was able to have children, she was at least partially educated, she had women friends, and she stumbled, for a time, into meaningful work. Her garden offered her a form of creative expression. Her health was reasonable. What do people need and what do they want? — surely this is what fiction writers write about, regardless of genre.

I don't think I would have become a writer if I hadn't had children. Children changed my life completely, changed me completely, the way I thought, the way I functioned. Having children woke me up, in a sense. I knew I had to pay attention. I *wanted* to pay attention. All my senses seemed sharpened, and I seemed capable of more. Like many a parent, I was astonished to discover how much love I was capable of feeling. Blown away, people say. In some way, this revelation spilled over into writing. I didn't know if I'd ever get published or not, but I never doubted for a minute that I could do it!

Carol

4 November 1994

Dear Carol,

I'm interested in your swift repudiation of the thought that the widening of perspective that comes with age is *wisdom*!

It's striking that those almost transcendent moments in childhood, when you were struck by the possibility of *more*, all have to do with language, written, spoken or sung.

I loved what you said about the effect of having children — how in a sense it made you a writer. I found that having a child was a final blow to the narcissistic sense that I was the centre of the universe; it was the first time I really deeply understood that I would grow old and die, that my parents' lives had the same poignancy and meaning to them that I ascribed to mine — a recognition which does open up things for writing. Since I read your letter, I have been thinking so much about the link you make between a deepening of the experience of love, a recognition of the value of the lives of others, and the readiness to write.

Sorry, I should have put Margaret Laurence's comment into a context; by a "fiction writer's memory," I understand her to have meant an unusual ability to recall details . . . the flowers in the borders of one's childhood home, a grandparent's idiom, the details that allow a writer to create the texture of a time and place. I think of "Chemistry" in *The Orange Fish*, currently my favourite of your stories. I am "blown away" by this story, astonished by your selection of details and the way these evoke what it was like to be the age that these earnest, shy, smug recorder players in Montreal in 1972 are. Could you tell me a little about the process of making this story, whether you were able to hold onto some of this material through "an act of recognition" as you lived through certain experiences — or does the act of recognition come later?

You talk about the way writers recognize and articulate moments of transcendence, and you put your finger on, I think, why literature is so important to us. Is a big part of being a writer the courage to see?

If the first generation of women's writing in Canada enlarged the subject matter of our literature to include childbirth, aging, housework, rape, harassment, abuse, what is the second generation doing?

Recently, at a reading, you talked about writing stories that "soar off into mystery and disruptiveness" instead of ending in epiphany. You said that the traditional structure of rising action and resolution doesn't seem to fit women's lives. Does it fit men's? Did it ever fit anybody's?

Would you say that you ask different things of your readers than you did at the beginning?

And finally — what is your theory of the day for today??

Joan

15 November 1994

Dear Joan,

About wisdom — if only it were true that we grow wiser. Perhaps there is some wisdom (understanding's probably a better word) that attaches to the midpoint perspective and our ability to see further, both backward to our children and forward to our parents. A privileged viewpoint, you might almost say. Everyone I know who's my age marvels at growing more tolerant. On the other hand, there's the danger of turning into a walking bundle of opinion. If I prayed, that would be my prayer: deliver me from opinions.

I'm delighted you asked about "Chemistry," since it's one story that I can track right to its inception. It came from my first teaching job, a creative writing class at the University of Ottawa, 1977-8. It was a night course, and you know what that means in our climate: that we come through the cold and the dark to be together. In that class of about sixteen students there was an extraordinary degree of bonding. We loved and protected each other almost from the beginning. After just three weeks another student wanted to late-register, and the class — I did consult them — said no, they couldn't bear an intrusion. (In "Chemistry" the late student *is* admitted.) I remember that one of the students had a play produced. We all went to see it. It was awful, got terrible reviews in the local press, but we refused to see its flaws. Another student was close to being illiterate, but we praised his poems extravagantly, and they did have a rough complexity. I think everyone got an A. I pondered for years the reasons for the human "chemistry" of that class. Was it because it was my first year teaching? — I don't think so. I wonder if there weren't three or four generously minded people in the class, and whether this perhaps set off a chain of contagion. We did give a reading at the end of the term, inviting families and friends — and, unlike the story, we had a roomful of visitors. Rapport would not begin to describe the quality of love in that classroom, and I knew I wanted to write about it someday. For the story I turned the class into a recorder group and moved them to Montreal. A couple of years later I read an Updike story about a recorder class. He had clearly done his research, as I had not, on the technical aspects of the recorder. His story revolved around erotic connections in the class, as I remember, and in that respect was very different than mine.

You ask about the courage to see, whether this is part of being a writer. It seems to me it's very close to that: the power to say what you see. I felt like a writer for the first time when I was twenty-nine years old and writing a series of poems. I was very strict with myself for some reason, and each time I finished a poem, I put the question to myself: is this what I really mean? It's so easy to be charming. Anyone can be charming. It's a lot harder to say what you really mean, especially women who've grown up hearing an echo of "Woman, hold your tongue." Women were told to hold their tongues for the very good reason that they might scatter the seeds of unorthodoxy, thereby turning the established order upside down. Even women who don't consciously want to give the world a good shaking up should bear in mind that they have the power to do so.

What will the next generation of women write about? I can't imagine that there will ever be a shortage of material. I've just finished Alice Munro's new book, *Open Secrets*, which is about the stories we tell each other, the strategies we devise in order to survive the lives we're born into. These stories use traditional materials radically reshaped. She has neatly jettisoned that old line of ascending action, finding a structure, or lack of structure, more suited to women's lives. Our stories are fragmentary; they neither ascend nor descend; they go along. Some intersect, some get plowed under, but their separate strands sustain us. I hope we can trust readers to live inside these new kinds of stories. When *Thirteen Hands* was produced at the Prairie Theatre Exchange, I had to defend, endlessly, it seemed, the play's seeming lack of "conflict." Couldn't I have two of the women have a misunderstanding, it was suggested. The conflict, in fact, was centred in the question: how do we value a human life? It is a question that has always interested me; my life theme, you might say, and my most passionate concern.

Perhaps you can call that "my theory of the day." That writing must come out of what passionately interests us. Nothing else will do.

Carol

WARREN CARIOU

Larry's Party: Man in the Maze

Whenever I was sick as a kid (tonsilitis, strep throat, flu, sniffles), I got to stay home and do mazes. Mom had several books of supermarket pen-mazes stashed away for every occasion of illness, and if she brought them out in the morning before school started, it meant I was sick enough to stay home. I spent hours in bed with these maze books propped against my knees, squinting through the addled haze of my illness, tracing my pen back and forth along the incomprehensible route, as if to wend my way back to health. When I reached a dead end, I went back to the previous fork in the road and tried again. Eventually the goal would be attained, and I would look back at the sorry record of my mistakes, trying to understand how there could possibly be so many.

I imagine Mom thought these games would simply take my mind off my symptoms — and they did. But they were also a depressing lesson in the pragmatics of free will and determinism. As my pen wandered those circuitous hallways, I came to see how bloody arbitrary choices are, and how uncertain are rewards and punishments. I also learned that while an action can be undone, it can never be fully erased: it leaves a path there for all to see.

However, one day as I doodled around the exit to an uncompleted puzzle, I stumbled upon the most crucial and empowering of my maze lessons: how to cheat. I discovered it was far easier to solve a maze if I began at the ending. I could zip right back through the various choices with nary a mistake. And to anyone viewing the pristine finished product, it was impossible to tell what direction I had taken.

"Hey Mom, take a look! Perfecto!"

All hail to the powers of hindsight.

Who would have believed that such a lesson would ever be useful again, but now I have been asked to write about Carol Shields's novel *Larry's Party*, which is all about mazes. And in approaching the maze that is *Larry's Party*, I've known from the start that I will follow my cheating instincts and begin with the finale. It's my only way to avoid getting lost, so forgive me. I could invoke the Kierkegaardian maxim that life is lived forward yet understood backwards — but it would only be an excuse, and why would I need that? Who said critics were ever interested in playing by the rules?

So, beginning at the ending. Larry's party, the chapter: the culmination, the *goal* of the novel. What is it, this perilous dinner party that Larry throws? Who in his right mind would invite two ex-wives and a current girlfriend to a party? It is of course a recipe for all manner of disasters, especially when we consider what happened so many years earlier when Larry's poor mother, Dot, invited her in-laws over for dinner. The sudden demise of Mum Weller provides ample evidence in the novel that a dinner party can be a fatal mistake, can be murder. Even so, Larry tempts fate at his party by serving beans, the same "treasonous vegetable" (53) that killed his grandmother and made his mother's life a purgatory. It's as if he is purposely loading the dice against himself, as if he knows at an unconscious level that he must dance through the minefields of his past relationships if he is to reach his goal (more about that goal anon). This party is his most crucial test as a maze-man. If he can get through it unscathed, he might after all be a hero.

Yes: the party is itself a kind of interpersonal maze, a psychomachia maze, the barest grid of which is outlined in Larry's sketch of a seating plan (304). *This is where they begin*, we tell ourselves, tracing the sight lines across the table, *but where will they end up?* The situation throbs with treacherous potential. Mistakes will certainly be made. And the only way to know exactly what these mistakes will be is to follow the game through to the end.

In a sense every narrative is a journey through a maze. There is the branching of paths, the illusion of freedom, the irrevocability of actions once they have occurred. John Gardner in *The Art of Fiction* suggests that the plot of a novel should be both entirely surprising and entirely preordained. When we are reading through, it should seem that anything could happen, but when we look back from the end, every event should seem inevitable. That's all time is, I suppose: the transforming of the possible into the inevitable. And we try to capture this mystery of time whenever we recount a story, or whenever we receive one. Gardner's characterization of fiction seemed right to me when I first read it, and I remember feeling a tremor of recognition a few years later when I reached the ending of David Adams Richards's *Nights Below Station Street*, where one of the main characters, Joe, thinks back on the events of the novel, "not knowing how this all had happened, only understanding that it was now irrevocable because it had" (225).

This prompts me to return to Kierkegaard's dictum that life is lived forward but understood backward. Living, by such a definition, is confusion. But confusion is not always a cousin of dementia and delirium, not always an occasion of crisis. As Shields illustrates in Larry's recollection of his first wanderings in the Hampton Court Maze, confusion can also be a balm, a revelation, or even an occasion of *ekstasis*:

> He has never been able to identify what happened to him during the hour he wandered lost and dazed and separated from the others, but he remembers he felt a joyous rising of spirit that was related in some way to the self's dimpled plasticity. He could move beyond what he was, the puzzling hedges seemed to announce (217).

What an elated confusion this is for lost Larry, who says much later to Dorrie when recounting the incident, "I wanted to be lost" (335). For me such language perfectly describes what it's like to get lost in a story, a novel, a memoir. In them or through them we are able to slip beyond ourselves, to explore the wilds of otherness, the shaggy hedgerows of unreason. They are a pleasant madness, a holiday from selfhood, and as such they are indispensable.

Indeed, books and treed mazes are similar in many respects. Larry's onetime neighbour Lucy Warkentin explains to him, "A paged book was called a codex. . . . the word comes from the Latin, meaning wood" (86) — which reminds one of Dante's dark wood, the entrance to the maze of the Christian universe. Similarly, the bizarre reversals and transformations of *A Midsummer Night's Dream* occur entirely in the labyrinth of a darkened wood. And it is not quite too much of a coincidence that the word "wood" also once referred to the state of insanity, so that characters in medieval plays and poems could remark cleverly, "I was wood in that wood."

That might well be Larry's refrain throughout the novel. His expertise as a maze-maker does not exempt him from the confusion that is felt by those who simply muddle through the mazes of existence. He is just like the rest of us. That is indeed one of Shields's primary points about Larry. He is normal, average, typical. And yet his work and his luck are extraordinary. By this analogy a writer is not, say, a diviner or a leader of men or some other variety of paragon, but rather a humble maze maker, a creator of structures that confuse and delight, structures that have only a tenuous relationship to the rest of the world. A maker of systems, not a seer into the life of things. I suspect this is how Carol Shields would characterize her own role as an author, mingling a postmodern view of the human subject with a refreshing aesthetic of humility.

OK. Larry's party is a maze, and narratives are mazes, and writers are maze-makers, and this novel is a series of interconnected maze-chapters. Even Larry's body is "an upright walking labyrinth" (269). I'm getting somewhere now, tracing my way back from the inevitable, covering my pen-tracks.

But I'm left with another possibility, a road not taken that I wish I'd at least had a peek down. It's about this party. I'm thinking the word itself is a forking path, a place where two roads diverge in a wood. Larry's party is his celebration, yes, his attempt at domestic entertainment. But it is also his partiality, his side, his affiliation. Larry is not a joiner, but still he has inherited some affiliations, the most important one in this novel being his membership in "the company of men" (331). His party is his gender. And I suppose it is also his race and his class and sexual orientation, though these aspects of Larry are given less attention in the novel. He is a white middle-class heterosexual male — stereotypically the most boring, yet most culpable, demographic on the planet. He is "a walking, head-scratching cliché" (165), as he himself is aware. He and his party have been blamed for much of the degradation, violence, abuse and mendacity in the history of Western Civilization. And what does he have to say for himself, for this great luck of having been born a privileged, powerful, imperialistic man?

Uh, not too much. When one of his guests asks point blank, "What's it like being a man these days?" (315), Larry is conspicuously silent. He reflects, suddenly, that this is the first party he has ever hosted in his life, and this realization bespeaks a sea change in him, though it's one he hasn't begun to analyze. Midway along the path of his life, he has stepped into a darkened wood and has become Mrs. Dalloway. But he doesn't know this, of course, and he doesn't have more than the slightest inkling of how significant this transformation might be. Because if Larry's dinner party is a maze for him to negotiate, then so is his other party. He really has little idea what it's like being a man. He is forever wandering the mirrored hallways of gender, understanding precious little about the roles of son and husband and brother and father which he mimes.

In this too, he is average, typical. Men, the current daytime TV stereotype goes, are the ones who don't ask for directions, who don't read the manual, who try to bully or bluster or fake their way through. And this is why they always get lost. But I wonder if the order of this progression might need to be reversed: perhaps the lostness is what comes first, and the bluffing and the acting out derive from it. When someone moves the shrubbery halfway through the maze (as Larry's wife Dorrie does with his Lipton Street effort), the result might well be a particularly overwhelming disorientation.

But Larry, with his dinner party, does something other than wander aimlessly in the ruined avenues of identity. While this dinner party is certainly a disaster waiting to happen, it is also in another sense a triumph, because it announces a change in his approach to gender roles, and specifically because it reveals Larry to be for the first time an active participant in those roles. Larry is not the uncommunicative couch potato that his own father was, nor is he the freewheeling tomcat of the masculine postmodern novel, nor the reactive backlasher of concern to feminists, nor the predator, nor the buffoon. He has become instead a man for whom there is as yet no available template, a man who is not effeminate but who also understands and deeply appreciates what the women in his life have meant to him: "Oh, these women, these beautiful women. He regards them with wonder. These women are separate selves, but also part of Larry's self" (330).

By placing himself in the social role of a Mrs. Dalloway figure, Larry unknowingly creates the maze of gender anew for himself. Or, in the metaphoric timbre of the novel's first chapter (steering now toward the entrance of the maze), this change in Larry is like the removal of an accidentally acquired garment. Late in the party he recognizes this, or almost does, remembering a gesture from twenty years earlier that suddenly acquires new significance:

> Walking alone on a Winnipeg street, twenty-six years old, he'd seen, perhaps for the first time, the kind of man he could be. He'd felt the force of the wind, and impulsively he'd whipped off his tweed jacket, offering himself up to the moment he'd just discovered, letting it sweep him forward on its beguiling currents (331).

Without understanding it, Larry here is casting off the mantle of his forefathers, shucking received notions of maleness, opening himself to a new kind of masculinity that will evolve haphazardly and unconsciously in the coming years. And this new male self will only become clear to him in the moments before he solves his dinner party maze and reaches his heretofore unknown goal: a reunification with Dorrie, who has herself travelled a path of change in the intervening years.

I can't help feeling disappointed when Larry arrives at this goal, partly because finding the goal means that the confused pleasure of maze-wandering is at an end, but also because it seems to me that in the mazes of gender and other accoutrements of the self, there is no real place of arrival, of finality. It is rather a process, a continuing one. For me, Larry's joyous return into the arms of his first wife feels contrived. But then, I wonder, what is a maze but a contrivance? What is luck but the occurrence of the unlikely, the unbelievable? Larry has always been a lucky man. He makes all the right mistakes. That he should be blessed with a happy ending worthy of a Greek hero is perhaps perfectly appropriate. Dorrie and Larry: Penelope and Ulysses: Hera and Zeus: Titania and Oberon. All is well again in the world.

I am left contemplating one of Carol Shields's enduring preoccupations: the blind happenstance that is the mother of superstition and that has so much weight in our lives, whether we want it to or not. One manifestation of this chimera for me was the unusual fact that the day I moved to Winnipeg was the day Carol Shields moved away. I was coming from Vancouver; she was going to Victoria. I learned about this changing of places about a week after it had occurred, when she and her husband were already gone to the land of prairie retirements. I didn't know she was planning to move. She didn't know I existed. So what meaning could there possibly be in our transcontinental crisscrossing? For most people it would mean nothing at all. But for me it had at least a pleasing symmetry. It was something that might have happened in a novel — especially a Carol Shields novel — and might have had significance there. And I suppose I wanted it to have some larger purport, to be some token of luck for me as a writer moving to a new place. I will admit I even hoped for some kind of transmigration of talent and determination and grace. Why not hope? Happenstance inspires it.

I've never met Carol Shields, but often these days I feel that I inhabit her mazes. I write this in the Wolseley house that my partner Alison and I bought last year, only a few blocks away from Larry and Dorrie's fictional Lipton Street house, just down from the friendly bakery where everyone knows Larry's name (and mine). This spring I drove out to the Tyndall stone quarry at Garson, Manitoba, and witnessed what must have been the inspiration of *The Stone Diaries*. This city has become for me an extension of her novels.

And two weeks after being asked to write this essay, I found (or lost?) myself in London with Alison, on what was a kind of honeymoon three months before our wedding. There, near the end of a mad week of galleries and theatres and charging through the clamouring, dustblown streets of the city, we took a brief detour out of town to visit Hampton Court Palace. After a tour of the royal gardens, resplendent with rhododendrons and lilacs and withering daffodils, we found our way to the goal. There, we paid our three pounds each, pushed through the turnstile, and entered the shrubby realm where so much of everything started for Larry Weller.

But our experience of the Hampton Court Maze was somewhat different from Larry's. For us, the greatest challenge of the maze was not the arrangement of the hedgerows but rather the crush of our fellow humans. Larry in this same maze, on *his* honeymoon, had "will[ed] himself to be lost, to be alone" (35), but for us the latter was impossible. We had chosen a Sunday afternoon, not the best time for maze exploration. Hundreds of people were jammed in there with us, filing up and down the pathways, talking and laughing and catcalling as they went. It was a thrumming, cacophonous hive. One young couple wheeled a huge and ungainly pram down the narrow avenues, barely negotiating the hairpins, while their red-haired baby entertained us with his one-toothed grins. "Help me!" someone cried out, and there was a general outburst of hilarity.

People called to each other through the foliage, and even reached through to clasp hands with their compatriots. Yes, the maze was full of gaping holes, through which we could see the neighbouring alleyways and sometimes even the ones beyond them. Strangely, this made it more difficult to find our way, since being able to see your goal — as we did several times through the fringes of ragged plant stock — can be more misleading than helpful. There was a wrought-iron grate running down the middle of each hedgerow to prevent us from breaking through to the goal prematurely.

Despite our best efforts to seek the contemplative mentality of aloneness, the quest became a collective effort. "Dead end!" someone would say, and we would all turn on our heels and follow each other back out. It was like an absurd dance routine, something from

Charlie Chaplin, and I thought of Larry's characterization of mazes in one of his conversations with Beth: "A maze . . . is a kind of machine with people as its moving parts" (218). Often we didn't even see the dead ends ourselves; we just had to take someone's word for it. Certain leaders or would-be leaders distinguished themselves (mostly by their height) and they would charge ahead of a group, at which point the question became: to follow, or not? We wanted to maintain our own autonomy, to make our own mistakes, to have ownership over our confusion, so we tried not to follow. But then resolutely choosing the alternate path from the self-appointed leaders was in its way a relinquishment of choice too, so sometimes we did follow after all.

We tried to read the maze on the faces of the people going back the other way. Was that the disappointment of the blind-alley visitor, or the subtle elation of someone who had already found the prize and was on their way back out? It was hard to tell because almost everyone had a pleasant puzzlement in their features, as they bumped and jostled through the narrow tunnels of ragged shrubbery. The throng was almost indistinguishable from the crowded streets of London, or Toronto, or even the busy avenues of Winnipeg on crazy pre-Christmas days — except everyone was clearly *loving* this. I had never seen such happy lineups.

In the tiny courtyard at the centre of the maze was another tumult. Children, mothers, octogenarians, wheelchair users, and many other maze-walkers were gathered under the two big elms that marked the spot. At the base of one tree, three boys of about fourteen were sitting, slouch caps pulled down over their foreheads, oblivious to the traffic around them as they passed a bottle of cheap champagne back and forth. At the base of the other tree, various tourists jockeyed for position, posing for the panoply of cameras that aimed at the scarred trunk. Its bark was torn away and the bare wood was riddled with initials.

The spectacle didn't feel like much of a goal to us, so we turned back quickly into the mazeway itself, wanting not to savour this feeling of dubious accomplishment but rather to share again the sense of common movement, of linked mistakes. And as we threaded our way back through a flow of human faces both new and already familiar, I arrived at what seemed like a labyrinthine epiphany. We are each other's mazes, I thought. The structure itself is hardly necessary. And I stood for a long minute at the entrance to a little cul-de-sac while my fellow denizens of the maze surged past me in both directions. Here we were, all of us, a community of convolution, a single seething organism of recreation. I wondered at us all. And as I did, I thought of how Larry also wonders at almost everything in his life: his boy Ryan, "his two magnificent wives" (330), his amazing luck. I had believed this was a byproduct of his innocence, his prodigious confusion, but now for the first time I saw that it might instead be a genuine talent. Yes, I thought. Maybe Larry Weller's greatest gift is his capacity for amazement.

Works Cited

Adams Richards, David. *Nights Below Station Street*. Toronto: McClelland & Stewart, 1988.

Shields, Carol. *Larry's Party*. Toronto: Vintage, 1997.

CLARA THOMAS

Stories Like Sonnets: "Mrs. Turner Cutting the Grass"

In one of her journals, May Sarton says, "If novels are the epics of prose, Journals are its sonatas." And, I thought, short stories are its sonnets. I had been thinking for days about Carol Shields's "Mrs. Turner Cutting the Grass," admiring the economy of its form and the elegant "rightness" of its language. It is certainly no more than five thousand words long, every word weighted with its maximum — and optimum — meaning. Analysing it is like dissecting a butterfly with a hoe. But the sonnet analogy gave me cheer; it can be applied; it does work. Long ago I noticed the likeness of certain passages of Thoreau's prose to the sonnet. I was charmed to find such a likeness again. This prose "sonnet's" octave is the story of Mrs. Turner's life, the remarkable total of experiences behind her introductory appearance; the sestet is the counter-story of the Professor. At the end, the final distillation of ironic meaning swings us back to Mrs. Turner as she first appeared, but with a vastly increased depth of referral and respect.

The story's theme encapsulates the three elements that have become Carol Shields's trademarks: her celebration of the astonishingly extraordinary behind the most "ordinary" of façades; the sturdy reliability and actual beauty of the daily, the "quotidian" that all her works celebrate; and the amazing entanglement of dailiness with fate, coincidence, the "Various Miracles" of this collection's title. The story of Mrs. Turner begins: "Oh, Mrs. Turner is a sight cutting the grass on a hot afternoon in June!" It ends with: "Oh, what a sight is Mrs. Turner cutting her grass and how, like an ornament, she shines" (27). It moves between these two polar points, the meaning of "sight" finally having changed from its first colloquial connotation of "outlandish spectacle" to its final connotation of "remarkable spectacle," conferring privilege on those who see her, and given a boost of glory in the final added clause, "and how, like an ornament, she shines."

At the start, Mrs. Turner is all visual, a two-dimensional figure: "Oh, Mrs. Turner is a sight cutting the grass on a hot afternoon in June! She climbs into an ancient pair of shorts and ties on her halter top and wedges her feet into crepe-soled sandals and covers her red-gray frizz with Gord's old golf cap. . . ." The space for development of a third dimension is signalled by that word, Gord, and opened out by the sentence's final clause, "Gord is dead now, ten years ago, a seizure on a Saturday night while winding the mantel clock" (19). Mrs. Turner's initial image is as clear as a photograph in an album, a still-life representation of a figure in motion, all surface. As seen from the outside, by passing high school students, by her next-door neighbours, the Saschers, this could be expected to be a trite formula-story, irony on its simplest level. But the omniscient narrator is looking on as well, and her affectionate, understanding voice has something quite other in store. At the end of the story, Mrs. Turner has been both revealed and vindicated to us as a lifelong truster of surfaces; furthermore, that very quality is her glory. Her enjoyment of the trips she now can afford to take with her sisters has nothing to do with depth of experience or an awareness of history:

> . . . she never did learn, for instance, the difference between a Buddhist temple and a Shinto shrine. . . . What does it matter? She's having a grand time. And she's reassured, always, by the sameness of the world. She's never heard the word commonality, but is nevertheless fused with its sense. . . . Everywhere she's been she's seen people eating and sleeping and working and making things with their hands and urging things to grow. . . . it is amazing, she thinks, that she can understand so much of the world and that it comes to her as easily as bars of music floating out of a radio. (26)

"Commonality" is the climaxing and summarizing pointer to the narrator's intention in that paragraph, occurring close to the end of the story. For the rest, the vocabulary could be Mrs. Turner's. With grace and great good humour and in the most matter-of-fact language, the narrator has entrusted to her readers the highs, the lows and some breathtaking surprises in Mrs. Turner's life, and finally, has interwoven her story with the "sestet," the advent of the Professor and the impinging of Mrs. Turner's life on his.

Word by word, and sentence by sentence, the narrator reveals herself as a friend and partisan of Mrs. Turner: "The grass flies up around Mrs. Turner's knees. Why doesn't she use a catcher, the Saschers next door wonder. Everyone knows that leaving the clippings like that is bad for the lawn. Each fallen blade of grass throws a minute shadow which impedes growth and repair" (18). They don't say anything to Mrs. Turner, because to them she is an old woman who will soon be going into a Retirement Home and then they won't be annoyed by her ignorance. How little the Saschers know about her though! In fact, each tiny event in her life, like each flying blade of grass, is an airborne celebration of her own resilient pleasure in living. The Saschers, with their earnest concern for the ecosystem, are meagre and stunted by comparison, and the young girls passing, repelled by her pudgy thighs, and enclosed in their dreams of Neil Young, their folk-rock hero, are denizens of another element, artificial by comparison.

The first vivid frame picture of Mrs. Turner and her surroundings introduces us to the astoundingly adventurous and adaptive being living inside the ungainly, unknowing, carelessly dressed old lady. She was Girlie Ferguson from Boissevain, Manitoba, "who got herself in hot water" by being caught in a hotel room one night with a local — and married — farmer, Gus MacGregor. She was nineteen. In the face of her father's "soppy-stern voice — 'Girlie, Girlie, what have you done to me?'" she left town and went by bus, in wretched, uncomfortable stages, to New York. It was 1930. She worked for eight and a half months, until the baby came, as an usherette at the Lamar Movie Palace in Brooklyn, writing to her sisters, Em and Muriel, that she had a job in the theatre business.

New York was immense and wonderful, dirty, perilous and puzzling. . . . Every last person in the world seemed to be outside, walking around, filling the streets, and every corner breezed with noise and sunlight. She had to pinch herself to believe this was the same sunlight that filtered its way into the rooms of the house back in Boissevain, fading the curtains but nourishing her mother's ferns. (20-21)

She met a man named Kiki, "*black as ebony*. . . . the phrase she uses, infrequently, when she wants to call up his memory, though she's a little doubtful what *ebony* is" (21). Kiki was kind, and he stayed with her for some months, even after the baby was born, but he couldn't stand the baby crying, or so she thought, so one day he left $50 on the table and left her. She didn't know how to find him, and she didn't know how she was to keep looking after the baby, so one "murderously" hot night, she took him to Brooklyn Heights and left him in a beautiful wicker baby carriage she spotted sitting on a verandah. That night she was free and happy: when she remembers that time "all she thinks is that she did the best she could under the circumstances" (22).

After a year she had saved enough money to take the train home to Boissevain, carrying gifts for her family. But she didn't stay long, because her father's greeting, "Girlie, my Girlie . . . . Don't ever leave us again" (22) frightened her. Instead she married Gord Turner and they settled down in Winnipeg, finally in the little house in River Heights, beside the Saschers, around the corner from the high school. The narrator doesn't even tell us what Gord worked at — all we need to know is that "he was a man who loved every inch of his house. . . . And he loved every inch of his wife, Girlie" (23). He earned Girlie's love and loyalty by his tolerance — "as far as he was concerned the slate had been wiped clean," and by two far from humdrum pledges of his love: "Once he came home with a little package in his pocket; inside was a diamond ring, delicate and glittering. Once he took Girlie on a picnic all the way up to Steep Rock and in the woods he took off her dress and underthings and kissed every part of her body" (23).

After Gord died, Girlie and her sisters, Em and Muriel, began to travel. "She was far from rich, as she liked to say, but with care she could manage one trip every spring" (23). They thoroughly enjoyed the most touted of tourist attractions, Disneyland, Disneyworld and the rest, but "three years ago they did what they swore they'd never have nerve to do: they got on an airplane and went to Japan" (23). Here enters the Professor and his counter-story, the sestet of the sonnet. Here enters the element of chance as well, that random and far-reaching collision of circumstances that Shields manipulates to such effect both here and throughout all her subsequent work. The Professor is a misfit among the package tour members; he really is a Professor at a small Massachusetts College, a would-be poet, but one who had so far published only two small chapbooks "based mainly on the breakdown of his marriage" (24). Set beside Girlie, Em and Muriel, so thoroughly and thoughtlessly loving the novelty of the tour, he is a sadly comic figure, "as he scribbled and scribbled, like a man with a fever, in the back seat of a tour bus traveling in Japan" (24). But in himself, he was undergoing a totally unexpected epiphany: "Here in this crowded, confused country he discovered simplicity and order and something spiritual, too, which he recognized as being authentic" (24).

When the narrator is "inside" Mrs. Turner's experience, she uses a discourse that is convincingly hers: "Once they stayed the night in a Japanese hotel where she and Em and Muriel bedded down on floor mats and little pillows stuffed with cracked wheat, and woke up, laughing, with backaches and shooting pains in their legs" (23-4). When she turns to the "inside" of the unnamed Professor, her discourse changes to his: "He felt as though a flower, something like a lily, only smaller and tougher, had unfurled in his hand and was nudging along his fountain pen. He wrote and wrote, shaken by catharsis, but lulled into a new sense of his powers" (24). Benign culture shock brought him success, for his poems on Japan were published by a prestigious Boston publisher who even deemed them worthy of sending him on a cross-country reading tour.

Now comes the unforgettable, deliciously anticipated and nonetheless eminently satisfying climax: in the midst of his readings, someone would always ask for his "Golden Pavilion poem":

> The poem was not really about the Golden Pavilion at all,
> but about three midwestern lady tourists. . . . They were the
> three furies, the three witches, who for vulgarity and tasteless-
> ness formed a shattering counterpoint to the Professor's own
> state of transcendence. (25)

And the chief offender was Mrs. Turner, "a little pug of a woman,"
with painted toenails, pink pantsuit and photos of her dead husband.
"This defilement she had spread before the ancient and exquisitely
proportioned Golden Pavilion of Kyoto, proving — and here the
Professor's tone became grave — proving that sublime beauty can be
brought to the very doorway of human eyes, ears and lips and remain
unperceived" (25-6).

Mrs. Turner and the Professor collide here with wonderful irony.
Students and colleagues, we are told, listening to the reading, all
know someone like Mrs. Turner: "They know — despite their youth
they know — the irreconcilable distance between taste and banality.
Or perhaps that's too harsh; perhaps it's only the difference between
those who know about the world and those who don't" (26). Never has
the blind condescension of the appearance-trapped, word-trapped
onlooker been skewered more neatly or the Mrs. Turners among us
vindicated more delicately and decisively. It only remains to give us a
final couplet-like, sonnet-like conclusion, encapsulating both Mrs.
Turner and the Professor. Mrs. Turner is living without a "catcher" as
she is cutting grass without a "catcher," for living, to her, means par-
taking of experience on the wing. She and her sisters enjoy remembering their lives and families, sitting on tour buses reminiscing, but
Em and Muriel have long forgotten Girlie's wild days and they never
did know about the details of her New York escapade. Em has given
several items to the Boissevain Museum, including "a white cotton
garment labeled 'Girlie Fergus' Underdrawers, handmade, trimmed
with lace, circa 1918.' If Mrs. Turner knew the word *irony* she would
relish this. Even without knowing the word irony she relishes it" (27).

The Professor's encounter with Mrs. Turner has a happy ending
too: his book of poems won an important international award, translation rights have been sold, and his picture, together with a lengthy

quotation from "The Golden Pavilion," has appeared in the *New York Times*. He is as oblivious to the reality of Mrs. Turner as she is to him, but the chance of their proximity has meant good fortune for him in the only way he understands it. Meanwhile, finally, economically, and elegantly, Shields offers us the wonderfully imprinted sparkle of the last line: "Oh, what a sight is Mrs. Turner cutting her grass and how, like an ornament, she shines."

Note

All quotations from "Mrs. Turner Cutting the Grass" in *Various Miracles* (Don Mills, Ontario: Stoddart, 1985).

PERRY NODELMAN

Living in the Republic of Love: Carol Shields's Winnipeg

For most readers in most places, fiction is about somewhere else. It occurs most often in a place made safely fiction-worthy by the thousands of stories already set there: the old West, the deep South, Paris, Shanghai, Los Angeles, New York. Or else it happens in some generic, nowhere, middle America, too perfectly generic to seem much like the place we call home. And the places like Dublin or Toronto that have produced a James Joyce or Margaret Atwood capable of persuading readers that fiction might reasonably occur there are few.

For readers in Minneapolis, Minnesota or Manchester, England or London, Ontario, therefore — and for readers like me in Winnipeg, Manitoba — the world of fiction is almost never quite the world we live in. We tend to end up believing that fiction does not — indeed, cannot and should not — describe real people like us, people living ordinary lives like ours in ordinary places like ours.

Take Winnipeg — I feel tempted to add, in this context, "please." It's cold here. There are mosquitoes. There are cankerworms. The land is flat and bleak. The rivers are brown. In Winnipeg, we're too distracted by the insects to concentrate on suffering truly fiction-worthy angst; and our lovemaking never has the intensity fictional characters achieve, simply because it takes us too long to shed our parkas and long johns. Winnipeg is too real to be fictional.

Fictional places, on the other hand, are exotic: i.e., enough unlike this one we're stuck with to seem desirably alien to us. Even when

Joyce's Leopold Bloom is doing nothing more unusual than moving his bowels, he's doing it in a scenic Irish outhouse, and it's adorable. Even when Atwood's Torontonians are suffering deep depression, they're doing it in relatively balmy weather, without cankerworms, and in close proximity to the Skydome; it's all just too damn wonderful to seem very real to us. If fiction has any relationship to our own lives, then that relationship must be indirect: allegorical or metaphorical. For us, all fiction is fantasy.

So what happens when we *do* read a book about a place we know? If the book evokes our place well, does that make the book seem less like fiction, less fantastic, less enjoyable? Or does something different happen? Might the book even teach us how to see the wonderful exoticism of the place we thought to be so dull?

For me as a Winnipegger, reading Carol Shields's *The Republic of Love* was all about asking these questions. It's one of a surprisingly small number of novels set in Winnipeg — much smaller than the number of writers in Winnipeg might suggest. I suspect a lot of Winnipeg writers suffer from a peculiar Western Canadian variation of the no-fictional-place-like-home syndrome I've just described above: they think of this unfortunately urban place we live in as an intrusive barrier between ourselves and the true essence of the prairie psyche, and therefore tend to write about bored farmers and bleak prairie towns rather than bored accountants and bleak Osborne village. But there are hardly any farmers at all in *The Republic of Love*. The Winnipeg it describes contains both accountants and Osborne village — and is anything but bleak, even though Shields doesn't forget to mention the cold, the wind, the mosquitoes, the cankerworms, or the brownness of the rivers. All are there, and all are an integral part of what the novel's about. In fact, Winnipeg is more than just background in this novel: it's very much a presence, a character, maybe even the central character.[1]

Throughout *The Republic of Love*[2] there's a relentless litany of names of real streets, actual churches, genuine landmarks — places Winnipeg readers are likely to have actually been to or can actually go to: Harvard Avenue (21), Assiniboine Avenue (23), McDermot Avenue (85); neighbourhoods such as Linden Woods (99), Tuxedo Park (99), and South Drive in Fort Garry (99);[3] the Norwood Bridge "in the center of town"(81),[4] the Osborne St. Bridge (45), and the Redwood Bridge (87); Westminster Church (90), St. Ignatius Church on Corydon (92), St. Luke's and Holy Rosary (152), and All Saints (277); The Winnipeg Inn (82) and the Northstar Hotel (281);[5] St. Vital Mall (99), Portage Place Mall (166), and Polo Park Shopping Centre (210).

The main characters, Fay and Tom, both live on Grosvenor Avenue near Stafford, and Grosvenor is accurately described as being "lined with trees and with Victorian houses, now mostly converted to rental apartments, or to condominiums" (7). In the real Winnipeg as in the novel, there is a bookstore around the corner on Stafford named Murray's (194). There is also a Dubrovniks restaurant, it does overlook the river, and it is exactly the kind of place where you might take a guest from out of town to eat something as pretentious as smoked trout salad (59). There's also a Vietnamese restaurant on Sargent (127), and there was once, a few years ago when I assume the events of the novel took place, an Act II restaurant downtown (27). There's also a movie theatre downtown on Notre Dame (291) and a Belgian bakery on Corydon (298). There's even a "radio station down on Pembina Highway" (24) like the one Tom works at. And the route Tom jogs, down Wellington Crescent past the Richardson mansion and the bridge at Academy Road to Assiniboine Park (19-20), is often frequented by joggers.

But why am I listing all of these things? Why does it matter? I'm listing them because, as a Winnipegger, I find all this fascinating; and it matters, I think, because I *do* find it fascinating, and because someone unfamiliar with Winnipeg probably wouldn't. The presence of all these real names and places makes reading the novel a different experience for me than it would be for someone who's never been here, just as reading Joyce would be a different experience for a Dubliner than it is for someone like me who has never set foot in the place and is therefore thrilled by the exotic outhouses.

The most obvious effect of these Winnipeg references is the economy with which they convey information about the characters' locations, activities, financial status and cultural background, and even their moods and attitudes — information that's often unspoken and therefore unavailable to non-Winnipeggers. This is a textbook case of what reader-response literary theorists call "blanks" or "gaps": moments when a fictional text provides a small amount of information that evokes much larger meanings for readers with the knowledge to fill them in: what theorists call a "repertoire."[6]

For instance, and most obviously: at various points in the novel, Shields tells us of characters who live in specific locations: a duplex on Lanark Avenue (63), a house on Oxford Street (92), a condominium twelve floors up on Wellington Crescent and overlooking the river (71), an apartment over a store on Selkirk Avenue in Winnipeg's North End (115). A non-Winnipegger might guess that the owner of the Wellington Crescent condo is better off financially than the dweller in the Lanark duplex. But the non-Winnipegger wouldn't catch the just-barely-hanging-on-to-middle-class-respectability status of a far west River Heights address like Lanark in relation to the world of poverty, immigrants, and Aboriginals evoked by the reference to Selkirk Avenue. Both addresses are intriguing additions to what Shields actually does tell us about the characters who live there.

Sometimes, the sociological information Shields implies by specific addresses is very exact indeed. Non-Winnipeggers aren't likely to catch the subtle clue signifying not just very substantial wealth, but the conventional and sedate atmosphere of old money as opposed to the exuberance and crassness of new which is implied by the fact that someone lives in a house "on the older end of Park Boulevard" rather than the newer one (106).

Winnipeggers will also realize that someone like Fay's mother who had a wedding reception at the Manitoba Club (132) some decades ago was not only likely to be quite well off financially, but also, decidedly not Jewish or Ukrainian. Nor is it surprising for such a person to have been married at All Saints, which conveys not just that she is an Anglican, but that she has ties to a specific church especially favoured by the old WASP establishment. And for Winnipeggers, the fact that one of Tom's former wives had the maiden name of Friesen strongly suggests that she comes from a Mennonite background, and therefore explains the exact nature of her parents' "narrowly religious" values (126) — and the distance of both Tom and his former wife from old establishment WASP families like Fay's. Similarly, the fact that someone works at the Grain Exchange, or eats at Dubrovniks, or shops in Osborne Village, or performs in musicals at Rainbow Stage (113), or attends the Folk Festival at Birds Hill (162) or Shakespeare in the Park (135) evokes far more specific information about character for those of us who are familiar with these institutions and the nature of their usual clientele than for those who aren't.

But these addresses and institutions also — and in some ways I find this much more interesting — evoke mental images of particular physical places, and the particular way they look and feel.[7] By that I mean, inevitably, the way they look and feel to *me* in addition to what Shields tells us they mean to her characters. For instance: at various points in the novel, either Fay or Tom go to a Safeway on a corner near where they live (21), a donut shop on Osborne Street (29, 83), a flower shop in Osborne village (75). Just about any Western Canadian reader will know what a Safeway is — and maybe, understand what it means about Tom and Fay's habits that he buys his flowers at the Safeway, she hers at the flower shop. But only a Winnipegger who's seen it will be able to imagine that actual Safeway on Osborne, its geographical relationship to the donut shop across the street from it, the architectural qualities of the building that houses the flower shop not just in the village but half a block down the same street, the stores on either side of that shop that Shields doesn't even mention. Similarly, only a Winnipegger will know, when Shields mentions the condo on the riverbank on Wellington and then, a few pages later, refers to St. Boniface hospital as being "across the river" (73), that she's talking about two different rivers.

Or, like me, remember my own visits to that hospital, in which, as it happens, all my children were born. Or respond to Shields's passing mentions of Harvard Avenue and Peanut Park with a complex stew of memories of the time they lived on that street, as I did once, just across from that park.[8] Those memories are far richer for me in their evocation of that place than the novel is — and, for any other reader but me, totally beside the point. But I can hardly ignore them, and they get in the way: my repertoire of private knowledge wars with the connotations Shields seems to intend.

As a Winnipeg reader, so unused to reading fictions about my own place, I don't know quite what to do about that. But I do know I'm not alone in having this difficulty. I taught *The Republic of Love* last year, in a first year literature course — in Winnipeg, at a university even named Winnipeg. It was the first time most of my students had read a novel set in the city they happened to be in at the time, a novel that actually mentions the building we sat in as we talked about it. The students told me they found it a disconcerting experience.[9]

In our first class discussion of the book, many of the students described how they'd be reading along, getting caught up in the characters and the story, and then suddenly come upon a reference to Corydon Avenue or Portage Place or even the U of W — and suddenly finding themselves pulled out of the fictional world their mind was creating. At first, they found this confusing, disorienting — I suspect because of the no-fictional-place-like-home syndrome. One student, Phil Peters, told the rest of us that he always read fiction as an escape, a way of getting away from the world, and specifically, from the life and place he knew. As he read novels he put together a different world in his head, a world satisfyingly alien enough to be worth escaping to. Corydon Avenue had no business being in that world. The vision of the real Corydon that popped into Phil's head when Shields mentioned it ripped his fictional world apart.

In a sense, I suppose, what happened to Phil is just one particular version of the main problem fiction always creates for all its readers. Because fiction requires our knowledge to make sense of it, it inevitably evokes aspects of that knowledge — matters personal to us — that seem to interfere with what it might be trying to say to us. The blanks unavoidably present in fictional texts can and always will be filled with different repertoire by different readers — including repertoire too personal to be what might seem to be required. We are doomed by the individuality of our past experiences always to misread all fiction.

But as I think about that, I realize that I could put it another, more positive way: the knowledge fiction forces us to bring to it allows us to *invent* what it says to us. Reading fiction is always the experience of making up what is being communicated to us, of manufacturing for ourselves the Harvard Avenues or the existential agonies the novelist names for us. That's what makes reading fiction such an involving process, and so much fun.

Furthermore — and this is strange and magical — the Harvard avenues of novels are not ever exactly the ones we walk on, the existential agonies not exactly the ones we experience ourselves. Even though it's mostly made up of our past knowledge, what we invent when we read is not what we knew already, but a mysterious amalgam of that and something new, something intriguingly different — something that didn't exist either in our own minds or in the text of the fiction before we got around to our acts of reading.

I suspect many of us share Phil Peters's assumption that fiction is always escape — and not just because, for Winnipeggers and other inhabitants of unlikely settings for fiction, it is so often about somewhere other than here. In the way I've just described, it *is* always about somewhere else, even when it's made up of stuff we brought to it ourselves. It's always an evocation of someone else's vision of what is: and so reading it is always and significantly an escape from the world we imagine for ourselves and call real. We would have no reason to read fiction if it showed us only what we know already.

But no matter where it takes place, fiction is also in an important sense always about *here*, where we are, and no escape at all. It's hard to imagine a novel, even a fantasy, that didn't want to convince us that the world it describes is in some important way the world we really live in — that it's actually about us. While some of us don't live in Toronto, Atwood's vision of her Torontonians' lives is clearly intended as being to some extent a fair representation of the way we all live now — even in Winnipeg.

The same could be said of Shields's Winnipeg. I suspect the events she describes in *The Republic of Love* bothered Phil because they didn't match his own expectations for what sorts of things might take place in the Winnipeg he knew. I also suspect she wanted to persuade him and other readers that such things *might* take place here: that the Winnipeg of the novel is actually the one Phil lives in.

Fiction is inherently paradoxical: an escape from the world we know as we begin our reading of it and an attempt to represent the world we know to us in new and different ways. Phil's experience of *The Republic of Love* as an unsettled back and forth movement between escape from what he knew and documentary description of it is, then, merely an extreme version of what fiction almost always tries to do to all of its readers: it tries to persuade us that what we know already can be understood in terms of what it shows us, so that what it shows us is actually the way things are.

In order for a fiction to convince us that its reality is the only reality there is, it has to persuade us that events like those it tells of might actually take place in real places we know. Doing just that is central to Shields's agenda in *The Republic of Love*. It's a story of love — deep love, bone-rattling love, love at first sight. It is, in fact, a romance, not really all that much different from the kind Harlequin publishes; and if there was ever a kind of experience that many of us believe takes place only in the exotic other worlds of fiction, then romance is it: surely the whole point of Harlequins is that they are unreal enough to be suitably wish-fulfilling fantasies. As Shields's protagonist Fay tells herself, "It's possible to speak ironically about romance, but no adult with any sense talks about love's richness and transcendence, that it actually happens, that it's happening right now, in the last years of our long, hard, lean, bitter and promiscuous century" (248). Fay then goes on to express a faith that explains much about the novel and the key role of Winnipeg within it: "Even *here* it's happening, in this flat, midcontinental city with its half million people and its traffic and weather and asphalt parking lots and languishing flower borders and yellow-leafed trees — right here, the miracle of it" (248). Romance can happen here, even here. The alien, exotic place in which fiction takes place might be Grosvenor Avenue, in Winnipeg.

Phil Peters helped the rest of us to understand that possibility by working on a class presentation with two of his classmates. Phil, Brandi Dearlove and Cory Dmytrow visited some of the locations mentioned in the novel. They came back with maps and photographs, and told the rest of us what it felt like for them as readers to be in the same places as the fictional characters, and how the reality they saw for themselves did and did not match Shields's fictional descriptions of it.

My students' response to this exercise was, I suspect, exactly the one Shields intended. Travelling the streets Shields says her characters travelled, seeing photographs of houses like the ones Shields tells us her characters inhabit, removed the fiction from the realm of fantasy. Confronted with an actual condo on Grosvenor, a building you can take a photograph of, it's not possible to escape into a fantasy world — but it is surprisingly easy to imagine Fay and Tom inside the condo, living and thinking and feeling exactly as Shields describes them. For someone standing in front of the condo with a camera, Fay and Tom's story seems as much like documentary as it does like fiction: and that means that romance is possible, even, maybe especially, here.

I say "especially" because the *here* Shields describes is already romantic. In *The Republic of Love*, Winnipeg becomes exactly as glamorous and as fiction-worthy as Joyce's Dublin or Atwood's Toronto — exactly the kind of place in which people might fall passionately in love. As the fiction becomes real, the reality becomes fictionalized.

Shields makes this fictionalizing happen, in part, by being very selective about how she describes her setting. Her characters tend to confine their activities to just a few neighbourhoods — River Heights, Osborne Village, the Exchange district — and only these parts of the city are described in any detail. It just so happens that these are the oldest, most tree-filled, most conventionally "romantic" parts of the city. Only when love seems dead do we hear much about boringly square modern apartment buildings in bland commercial districts near the airport.

Furthermore, Shields focuses her descriptions of her neighbourhoods of choice on qualities that make them sound attractive enough to be a target for touristy bus tours. She pays particular attention to the ways in which the large old trees form canopies over the streets of River Heights and Crescentwood. She speaks, for instance, of Yale Avenue, where "overhead a double row of elms met" (190), or of Wellington Crescent, where "the tall trees seemed knitted together, tobacco colored, squashed gold, swinging their branches in long easy arcs" (232) — or of River Heights in general, where "overhead the branches of the separate trees gathered together, oak, elm, ash, poplar — city trees with black tarry rings painted around their trunks, put there to discourage the cankerworm larva. The uniformity of these dark markings turned them into a tree army, marching straight up to a point of perspective" (193).

Shields also provides a frontispiece illustration depicting just such a canopy of trees, albeit without their unromantic cankerworm rings. When I first opened the book, I took only a cursory glance at this picture and assumed it represented some sort of medieval or Renaissance garden, the sort of place where courtly lovers in fancy costumes might discover their republic of love. It was only after I read the book and then came back to the picture again that I actually noticed the River Heights sidewalks and houses under the trees. In their class presentation, furthermore, Phil and Brandi reported turning their car onto Grosvenor from Stafford and experiencing a moment of déjà vu: the actual street looked to them exactly like this frontispiece. Our various experiences of this picture nicely signal how the novel manages both to move the escape of romance into a real place and to make that real place seem a romantic place to escape into.

From the point of view of tourism, even the eccentric peculiarities and uglinesses of a place can seem attractive: evidence of uniqueness, of the endearingly visit-worthy idiosyncrasy of a locale and its perversely but charmingly abnormal inhabitants. In Shields's Winnipeg, as we've seen, even tarry rings on trees become charming — unique and artistic contributors to a painterly perspective. Indeed, even the cankerworms themselves are worthy of a lengthy, scientifically exact description:

> Just when the trees have finally filled out their crowns with great glossy leaves, the cankerworms go on the march. The larvae make their way up the tree trunks and then the munching begins. It takes no more than two days to transform an avenue of foliage into ragged lace, and ten days to strip the trees bare. At night there's a steady drizzling rain which is not rain at all but the continuously falling excrement of billions of cankerworms, chewing and digesting. The

streets and sidewalks are covered with slippery syrup. The air turns putrid; the worms, grown fat, spin themselves long sticky threads, and on these they descend, like acrobats, to the ground . . . 10

Like acrobats, indeed: bring on the tour buses. Then there's the "flat blue light" (59), which makes accurate landscape paintings of Winnipeg hard to sell: "It seemed people wanted a few fluffy clouds in their skies" (342). Nevertheless, Shields finds a phrase to make the "hard flat blue" (342) beautiful as she tells how us how Tom "loves this light-filled city" (101).

Similarly, the bleakness of the city's downtown becomes a source of exotic uniqueness: "Downtown Winnipeg has its city-share of graffiti-spattered back alleys but is mostly made up of wide formal boulevards lined with handsome stone buildings, piteously exposed despite repeated attempts at landscaping" (100). Indeed, "From the bus window the streets have the gray-and-amber freshness of a foreign city, stretching purposefully toward the doors of serious institutions and office blocks where the intricacies of commerce and learning unfold" (57).

I find these descriptions interesting because I recognize them, and yet I don't recognize them. They claim Winnipeg locations I'm familiar with in the name of a vision, an attitude unlike the one I've thus far had toward them. The Winnipeg of the novel is not quite the Winnipeg I know.

In fact, that's quite literally true. For all the exactness of many of its details, there are a surprising number of inaccuracies — what appear to be silly mistakes. I've discovered in conversations with other Winnipeggers that these errors really bother a lot of readers.11 How could Shields be so accurate about so much, evoke such a convincing picture of our city — and then screw it up by getting other things so wrong? I'd like to propose an answer to that question: she did it on purpose. She wanted us to be bothered. She had a trick up her sleeve.

The inaccuracies are particularly bothersome, I suspect, because they are so close to the truth. It's not as if she moved Lindenwoods to

St. James or let her characters meet in a charming but actually non-existent park at Portage and Main. There's nothing as jarringly wrong as that; instead, Shields invents perfectly possible variations on Winnipeg realities — things much like what does exist, things which could quite easily exist without greatly disturbing the fabric or feeling of the real Winnipeg we Winnipeggers know.

For instance: while there is a radio station on Pembina Highway like the one Tom works at, it's not called CHOL. The National Folklore Center Fay works at doesn't exist at all; but if it did and if it were on Market Avenue as reported, its windows would indeed "overlook a sliver of the old warehouse district and a section of disused railroad track and, beyond that, clear to the sky, the curved crust of the Red River, which is really brown, sliding its way northward" (32).

Some specific geographical details are equally variant, and just a little more bothersome. In my Winnipeg, there is no "Knox Church over on Broadway" (20), but there is a Knox Church, and there is a Broadway. There is no Poster Plus store on Stradbrook (83), but there is one on River, one block north. There is no "Ballentyne Street" (112); there is however a Bannatyne Avenue, and there is indeed a warehouse there converted into condos. There is no Roblyn Road (124); but there are both a Roblin Road and a Roslyn Road with a large old-fashioned apartment on it. There is no Ash Avenue, no Waterloo Avenue (121), no Vaughan Avenue (297), no Smith Avenue just off Wolsley (147): but there are Ash, Waterloo, Vaughan and Smith Streets, and there is a Wolseley (note the different spelling again), albeit nowhere near Smith Street. On a stroll through her neighbourhood, Fay could indeed walk down a street named Gertrude, "and then up a parallel street called Jessie" (38), but she would be walking east and west, not north and south as Shield reports; and it isn't true that "many of the streets in this part of the city were similarly named: Minnie, Agnes, Flora, Bella and Lizzie," although there are streets with some of these names and similar ones elsewhere in the city, and local mythology suggests that they may well be "immortalizing, [as] Fay has always supposed, the patient or demanding wives of early-twentieth-century developers" (38). Elsewhere in my Manitoba, meanwhile, there is no town called Amiota, but there is one called Hamiota

(46); and there is no town with a pulp mill called Duck River, but there is one called Swan River. These are almost the real places, but not quite — and the differences are too close to reality to be mere errors.

Some of the character's interactions with the city are not so much geographically inaccurate as they are unlikely — and therefore, for a Winnipegger, very surprising indeed. On her way home from work, Fay would indeed be "turning right on Portage, bucking the worst traffic of the day, [then] turning left onto Osborne" — but if she then turned "right again onto Stradbrook," (35) she would be going the wrong way on a one-way street. Later, Fay catches her bus to work at River and Osborne (77) — a good many blocks from where she lives; for no clear reason, Fay avoids the Stafford bus she might catch on the corner of her street or the Corydon bus that runs just a block away from it. Similarly, when Tom goes to the corner to mail a letter he walks all the way to River (214). Perhaps most peculiarly, Tom gets stung by an insect while looking out his window (164); because of my local experience of mosquitoes, it's hard for me to imagine a window in my Winnipeg like this one, without a screen in the middle of summer.

It's possible, I suppose, to conclude that Shields either didn't care about these inaccuracies, or didn't realize they were inaccurate: as a relative newcomer to the city she writes about, she simply might not know that streets which run north and south like Ash and Vaughan could never be called Avenues in a city in which all the Avenues run east and west. But if we assume that the inaccuracies are deliberate, that they might be an intended part of what the novel is and does, then thinking about them offers some interesting insights into the world Shields has created.

Above all: the inaccuracies make it crystal clear, for Winnipeggers at least, how paradoxical Shields's vision of the city is. It is both itself and something else, both real and not quite what it really is — and as such it is Shields's best representation of her main topic: love itself.

As Shields describes it, love is problematic for a variety of reasons. Most obviously, and as I've already suggested, the surprise and the wonder of romance are at odds with the familiarity of normal life. The thrust of the book is to bring the two together, which requires that the strange enter the familiar. What better way to signal that connection than by setting events in a city almost but not quite like Winnipeg — a city just different enough to be unsettling, strange — romantic?

Love, Tom comes to believe, is "the only enchantment we know" (70). Romance, Fay thinks, keeps people "on edge, taunts them, then slitheringly changes shape and withdraws" (37). The Winnipeg of the novel is equally enchanted, equally slithering — both itself and something else, a meeting place of the real and the imaginary, of the self and the world. It represents Shields's success at duplicating what she herself calls "the curious and brave efforts of children to charge their immediate world with brilliance, making it glow with color as they move among common objects, bringing those objects alive with incantatory music, alive with texture and outline, alive with life" (194).

But it is more specific than that, and a more specific representation of the nature of love. Love is specifically problematic for Shields's characters because, as she insists on pointing out, they — and, presumably, all the rest of us — have to wrestle with two equal but opposite facets of the human condition:

1. We human beings, enmeshed in our own thoughts, are all, to our cost and our glory, completely and utterly isolated from each other. Connection to others is a delusion.
2. We human beings, enmeshed in our dealings with others, are all, to our cost and our glory, completely and utterly connected with each other. Isolation is a delusion.

Each of these truths individually suggests why romance might be problematic; together, they suggest why it might appear to be impossible.

If we are truly as isolated as the logic of the first truth suggests, then we cannot actually have the contact with another that romance requires. We might imagine that we do, but it's all in our minds, all something we invent ourselves, as Tom invented the three women he believed he loved and married, and then had to leave when they turned out not to be who he imagined.

Before meeting Fay, Tom ironically tells himself that he is "part of a Camus fable, a lost soul, loveless" (19). For all the irony, he is indeed depicted as "a man attached to no one" (172), despite heroic efforts to connect: he has had his three marriages, and "friends have entered and left his life. But he has no children, no relatives, no property, none of the blown aftermath other people attach to their arrangements" (100). He concludes, "All I have is this self. Not another thing. Just this irreducible droning self" (44). Unless love does actually exist, self is all there ever is.

Fay seems to represent the opposite problem: she even wonders if there is such a thing as a self. "Fay, a reasonable, intelligent woman, has long recognized that reverence for individualism is one of the prime perversions of contemporary society. It is illogical and foolish. Oh, yes. We are bound to each other biologically and socially, intellectually and spiritually, and to abrogate our supporting network is to destroy ourselves" (267). She asks, "Are human beings really so locked into their own cherished anxieties that the only vibrations they feel are solitary and private? Aren't people capable of more than this?" (183). Fay believes they are; in fact, she sees herself as so completely and utterly connected to a web of family and friends that she has no room left to be a solitary or private self. She believes she is "too dependent on the response of others and incapable of sustaining any kind of interior life for more than a few seconds at a time" (9).

But that creates another problem: it means that Fay's sense of self is totally dependent on others. When Fay claims that "she's sick of her identity; in fact, she's afraid of it" (154), it's telling that she defines herself in terms of how others see her: "she has all the identity she wants, all she can absorb. Daughter, sister, girlfriend, all her Fay-ness. . . . She's learned, too, how unstable identity can be, how it can quickly drain away when brought face to face with someone else's identity" (154). Fay feels that being connected to others deprives her of a sense of her separate being.

In terms of these concerns, love is doubly — indeed, paradoxically — problematic. It's either an illusion, a merely illusory move beyond the eternally isolated self; or else it's the essential contact with others that gives us the only sense of self we have—a false sense, of course — while depriving us of any real way of being separate and individual. If it's the former of these, then it is, as Fay suggests, "a form of vanity . . . . You know, the wish to be adored. To be the absolute center for someone else" (108). If it's the latter, it's both illusory and suffocating, as Fay's mother's equation of being centred with being possessed implies: "there's something to be said for having a center, for belonging to someone, your own family, not just one person living for himself or herself" (13).

For love to actually exist, then — and for it to be real rather than illusory, and enlivening rather than suffocating — it must represent some paradoxical mid-state between total isolation and total connection. The love that Tom and Fay find for each other represents exactly that paradoxical condition. Tom moves past his isolated self into a connection with someone else, and Fay moves past the self she knew in her connections with others into her truer, barer self:

> So this was what it was like. To open her body completely and to feel another's opening in response. She felt all his loneliness coming toward her. This was how it happened.
> For once, to lay ourselves bare. (235)

Fay and Tom find a state in between isolation and societal absorption that leaves them both wholly individual and wholly connected to each other.

Nor is that all, for the novel does not end with this expression of love. It continues long enough for Fay to make the important discovery that maintaining love requires the hard work of balancing isolation and connection. Fearing "the fragility of human arrangements" (331) and seeing Tom as completely separate from her, a "dangerous stranger" (332), Fay tells herself that "she cannot open her body to such harm" (331): too much isolation, and love ceases. But on the other hand, too much connection, and the people you love might end up like Fay's father, who leaves his wife of fifty years because "I got *lost*, that's all, in all that warmth and loving" (318), because "his long peaceful marriage had somehow overnourished him. He couldn't breathe. He felt watched, insulated, incapacitated" (349). At the end, together with Tom again, Fay wisely concludes that she needs his separation from her as much as his connection: "She prizes his on-air self, his else and his other — his absence, in fact —

and wonders if other people come to depend on this currency of separation" (365).

It's interesting how often Shields uses geographical metaphors to represent a state of balance between connection and isolation. At one point, Tom says that his ideal land form is a peninsula, "because it was separate yet joined" (121). Later, he sees the "coming together" of his friends and Fay's at an engagement party as "Two rivers meeting, a symbolically charged wha'd'ya-call it? — a confluence" (321).

A confluence such as that in the centre of Winnipeg, where the Red and Assiniboine meet. In fact, Winnipeg is Shields's main metaphor for the confluence of separation and isolation. It's a city which is "a bit too small" (32), so that you don't know everybody but often run into people you didn't expect to see; a city in which Fay has never met Tom but Tom's former wife was once married to the man who later married the woman Fay's former boyfriend Peter was once married to. In a central passage, Shields describes Winnipeg as the perfect balance of isolation and connection:

> The population of Winnipeg is six hundred thousand, a fairly large city, with people who tend to stay put. Families overlap with families, neighborhoods with neighborhoods. You can't escape it. Generations interweave so that your mother's friends (Onion Boyle, Muriel Brewmaster, and dozens more) formed a sort of squadron of secondary aunts. You were always running into someone you'd gone to school with or someone whose uncle worked with someone else's father. The tentacles of connection were long, complex, and full of the bitter or amusing ironies that characterize blood families.
>
> At the same time, Fay has only a vague idea who the noisy quarreling couple on the floor above her are, and no idea at all who lives in the crumbling triplex next door, though she knows, slightly, two of the tenants in the building across the street. Her widowed Uncle Arthur lives one street over on Annette Avenue, but she knows no one else on that street. . . .
>
> Geography is Destiny, says Fay's good friend Iris Jaffe, and Fay tends to agree. (77-78)

As a balance between the isolation of not knowing others and the tentacles of connection, the geography of the recognizable but perversely strange Winnipeg of the novel does represent Fay and Tom's destiny together. As Shields describes it, Winnipeg is, exactly, the republic of love.

For those of us who live here, and who like to complain about the cold and the mosquitoes and the brownness of the rivers, thinking about our perversely unromantic city as a metaphor for what love's all about is something of a reach. I suspect that's at least part of the reason why Shields's geography is so often so perversely strange. She wants us bothered enough by the inaccuracies to make the reach. She wants us to see the possibility of this still recognizable but transformed place, this weird combination of what we previously knew and what she has invented and is forcing us to invent. If the impossible but not improbable Winnipeg of the novel can exist in the imagination of Shields and her readers, then love, also theoretically impossible but not all that improbable, might exist too, might exist here in our normal, mundane lives — does, in fact exist in the minds of Fay and Tom and those who read about them, right in the midst of the mosquitoes and the cankerworms.

And if the love described in the novel exists, then why not its Winnipeg also? There may never be an Ash Avenue on any official map of the physically real city, just as there may never be a Fay McLeod or Tom Avery listed in the real phone book. But the metaphorical Winnipeg of the novel — the city as Shields represents it — might well become for us Winnipeg readers an accurate vision of the place we live in.

For my student Brandi Dearlove, the most mysterious evidence that Shields's fiction might actually be describing her real world occurred as she and Phil Peters drove down Wellington Crescent into the park, following Tom's regular jogging route as Shields reports it. As they stopped to take a picture, a real jogger running by tapped on the car window and greeted Brandi by name. At that moment, Brandi told us, she felt that she'd somehow entered the world of the novel; for in the novel, after meeting Fay's former partner Peter, Tom keeps running into him wherever he goes, in confirmation of Shields's view of the city being not quite big enough. On one occasion, in fact, Tom actually does meet Peter while jogging in Assiniboine Park.

Brandi reminded herself that of course it couldn't possibly be Tom out there, or Peter. But she still hadn't quite escaped Shields's version of Winnipeg, for a closer look told her that the man knocking on the car window and calling her name in a part of the city she rarely frequented was someone she had worked with the previous summer and not seen since. In the real Winnipeg as in the fictional one, "the tentacles of connection were long, complex, and full of the bitter or amusing ironies that characterize blood families." On Wellington Crescent that winter morning in 1994, the real Winnipeg became, for a moment at least, an exact replica of Shields's republic of love.

Notes

1 After I wrote this sentence, I came upon a piece in *The New Yorker* by Ian Frasier, called "The Novel's Main Character." In it, Frasier quotes a variety of reviews and articles claiming that Cicely, Alaska, Troy, New York, Bridgeport, Connecticut, Dublin, Ireland, New York City, The Bob Marshall Wilderness Area in Montana, and mortality itself are actually the main characters of various novels and TV shows. Apparently, I have replicated a cliché, without even knowing it. Too bad; I don't know about Cicely or Bob Marshall, but as I certainly will have persuaded you by the time you finish reading this article, Winnipeg is the main character in *The Republic of Love.* So there.

2 Unless otherwise indicated, all references are to the Random House hard cover edition.

3 In the real Winnipeg, Linden Woods is more usually Lindenwoods, and Tuxedo Park more usually just plain Tuxedo. I say more later about Shields's intriguing variations from standard Winnipeg reality.

4 Winnipeggers and other Canadians might be interested in noting the American spelling in this book about a Canadian city published in Canada: in the real Winnipeg outside the novel, what Winnipeg has usually is a "centre." Maybe it has something to do with NAFTA?

5 The former Northstar is currently the Radisson. This places the novel a few years in the past.

6 See, for instance, Iser's *The Act of Reading.*

7 The questions of whether fictional descriptions do or do not evoke mental visual images for readers, and whether or not such images are of any importance in the act of reading, have much exercised theorists in this century. In *The Reader's Eye,* Ellen Esrock offers a careful summary of the issues.

8 Or for that matter, know that the official name of this little plot of green in the midst of substantial Edwardian dwellings is Egerton Park — that the name doesn't actually represent an uncharacteristic moment of whimsy on the part of the dour grain merchants who built this neighbourhood. Everyone just calls it Peanut Park because it's small.

9 I'd like to thank the students in English 1001-1, section 4, Popular Reading and Serious Literature, fall and winter session 1993-94, for letting me tell about their experiences. I'm particularly grateful to Phil Peters, Brandi Dearlove, and Cory Dmytrow, whose responses to *The Republic of Love,* discussed in more detail below, led me to the speculations that form the basis of this article.

10 Pages 100-101. The paperback edition amends the texts of this description, presumably for the sake of entomological accuracy; instead of "The larvae make their way up the tree trunks," it says, "The beetles make their way up the tree trunks, the larvae are hatched," and so on (87).

11 I've had conversations about these matters with, among others, Billie Nodelman, Kay Unruh Desroches, Neil Besner, and David Pate — Winnipeggers all. My thanks to them.

Works Cited

Esrock, Ellen J. *The Reader's Eye: Visual Imaging as Reader Response.* Baltimore: Johns Hopkins, 1994.

Frasier, Ian. "The Novel's Main Character." *The New Yorker* (Sept. 5, 1994): 59-60.

Iser, Wolfgang. *The Act of Reading.* Baltimore: Johns Hopkins, 1979.

Shields, Carol. *The Republic of Love.* Toronto: Random House, 1992.

—. *The Republic of Love.* Toronto: Fawcett Crest, 1993.

WENDY ROY

Unless the World Changes: Carol Shields on Women's Silencing in Contemporary Culture

At the end of the first chapter of Carol Shields's *Unless*, narrator Reta Winters says of the new novel she is planning to write, "This will be a book about lost children, about goodness, and going home and being happy and trying to keep the poison of the printed page in perspective. I'm desperate to know how the story will turn out" (16). As the reader soon discovers, Reta's comments about her book also eloquently describe both her own troubled life and *Unless* itself, a brave, strikingly feminist examination of goodness, loss, family love, and the process of putting words to paper.

Words are important in this novel, and not just big words, but also those "little chips of grammar" (313) — prepositions, adverbs, and conjunctions — that locate, modify, and connect and thus are essential for understanding. Each chapter in Shields's book carries one of these words as its title, as does the book itself. Two separate, lengthy passages are devoted to a discussion of the way in which *unless* functions in the English language as either "the worry word" or the word that provides "a tunnel into the light" (224). One problem that the book poses begins with that word: Unless one person knows the details of another person's day-to-day struggles and life-changing events, she or he cannot understand that other person's life trajectory. But the book also poses another and more fundamental problem:

Unless women are perceived of as fully human, they will continue to be forced to choose a life of what one of the characters in the novel describes as "goodness but not greatness" (115).

Shields's novel opens with Reta contemplating the sorrow inherent in such a choice. She tells readers that she is "going through a period of great unhappiness and loss just now" (1) because her oldest daughter, Norah, "a good, docile baby" and "a good, obedient little girl," has dropped out of university and now spends her days sitting on a Toronto street corner with a begging bowl in her lap and a cardboard sign reading "GOODNESS" around her neck (11). Reta's struggle to come to terms with and understand her daughter's path toward "invisibility and goodness" (12) is the primary subject of Shields's novel. Ultimately, Reta's quest for understanding leads to an exploration of her own situation as a woman and a writer at the beginning of the twenty-first century, and the position of women in earlier generations, including her mother-in-law, Lois, and Reta's eighty-five-year-old friend, writer Danielle Westerman.

Unless is Shields's most explicitly feminist novel, one in which she deliberately, self-consciously, and courageously ties together feminist threads from the novels and short stories she has written over the past twenty-five years, and in which she expresses more forcefully and openly than she has ever done before her concerns about the continued marginalizing and silencing of women in contemporary society. Her narrative does not just demonstrate feminist strategies, as have many of her earlier works; it names them. Thus while the sometimes third-person narrator of *The Stone Diaries* says of protagonist Daisy Goodwill Flett that "She wants to want something but doesn't know what she is allowed" (117), Reta as narrator identifies "the big female secret of wanting and not getting," the way in which women reach out "blindly with a grasping hand but not knowing how to ask for what we don't even know we want" (98).

Other feminist threads pulled from Shields's earlier books and skillfully rewoven into this new narrative include the value of the domestic, as well as of mother-daughter relationships, women's friendships, and healthy and egalitarian heterosexual partnerships. If Sarah Maloney of *Swann* can comment on the redemptiveness of dailiness, Reta's two younger daughters can fill the emptiness of their home with "tiny particulars of the quotidian" (172). If Daisy of *The Stone Diaries* can find her way out of her deep depression when she realizes that "She'd like to tie a crisp clean apron around her waist once again, peel a pound of potatoes in three minutes flat and put them soaking in cold water. Polish a jelly jar and set it on the top shelf with its mates" (263), Reta Winters can control her own sorrow by recognizing the rewards offered by "dusting, waxing, and polishing" (61). (And unlike the apparently unreflective Daisy, Reta can identify the metaphoric link between her house and her daughter.)

The often fraught relationship between mothers and daughters — fundamental to Shields's first two published novels, *Small Ceremonies* and *The Box Garden,* and a glaring absence that must be imaginatively reconstructed by the sometimes autobiographical narrator of *The Stone Diaries* — is rehearsed in *Unless,* as Reta both contemplates the way her younger daughters "just see this watercolour blob that means mother" (28) and at the same time takes responsibility for her oldest daughter's predicament. Echoing Judith Gill's mutual revelations with a friend in *Small Ceremonies* and the ongoing and reinvented friendships of *The Stone Diaries,* Reta's friendships help her to cope with her sorrow about her daughter. Reta even comments on her decision to include friends in the novel she herself is writing, as a way of rewriting the modernist tradition which "has set the individual, the conflicted self, up against the world" (121). Her common-law marriage, meanwhile, demonstrates both equality and goodness, as its partners try to determine what happened to their daughter without blaming one another. Goodness is part of their family dynamic: each parent spends one morning a week on the street with their daughter, while Norah's teenaged sisters give up volleyball so they can spend every Saturday sitting quietly beside her.

Although the novel represents domestic activity, family, friends, and work in part as Reta's attempts to distract herself from her grief, these activities and interactions are more fundamentally part of her process of coming to terms with her daughter's transformation. Each chapter contains elements of Reta's quest for understanding, a quest that drives her more and more as the book draws toward its conclusion, and that involves questioning as well as questing. Is Norah's situation connected to her self-effacement as a "good, obedient little girl" and later as a young woman who is "too easily satisfied" and who "too seldom considered herself deserving" (89)? Is Norah responding to her parents' decision not to marry, despite their lengthy committed relationship? Are Norah's actions connected to Reta's fears about her "own failure as a mother" (121), or to her lack of firmness on her daughter's behalf, as evidenced by the chapter in which Reta describes searching for the perfect scarf for Norah's birthday and then silently allowing a condescending and grasping friend to claim it? Are they caused by Norah's disintegrating relationship with her boyfriend, or her conflicts with a male professor about women's limited place in literature and society? Is Norah, as the psychiatrist her parents consult suggests, "either escaping something unbearable or embracing the ineffable" (214)? Are her actions the result of some unidentified trauma she has experienced, as Reta's physician husband, Tom, comes to believe? Or, as Reta's long-time literary collaborator, French writer Danielle Westerman, asserts, and as Reta increasingly agrees, is Norah's decision to drop out of her own life the result of her dawning recognition of her invisible and silenced position as a woman in her own culture?

The significance of that insight, to Reta as a character and to the novel as a whole, is evident in the narrator's repetition of Danielle's theory, in third-person and then first-person narration, in English and then in French: "She believes that Norah has simply succumbed to the traditional refuge of women without power: she has accepted in its stead complete powerlessness, total passivity, a kind of impotent piety," and "Norah s'était tout simplement laissée aller vers ce refuge traditionnel des femmes qui n'ont aucun pouvoir" (104-05). Reta eventually concludes that after "an accretion of discouragement," Norah has understood "how little she would be allowed to say" (309-10). Norah's silence is echoed by the increasing silence, passivity, and withdrawal of her grandmother, Lois. Even Danielle, whose memoirs Reta has spent years translating, has been silent about one crucial aspect of her life. In this novel, Shields makes it abundantly clear that unless our society asks questions of women — and unless it first determines the relevant questions and asserts the value of asking those questions — it will never understand the self-blame and undeserved guilt that women such as Lois, Danielle, Reta, and Norah carry with them.

Reta addresses readers directly and didactically, telling them, "I need to speak further about this problem of women, how they are dismissed and excluded from the most primary of entitlements" (99). She points out that the television programs she watches and the books she reads almost invariably imply that only men count: only men are identified as influential authors, "Great Minds of the Western Intellectual World" (135), and problem solvers; men's books alone can provide an "entire universe" to comfort a man in his dying days (273). Reta's response to this evidence that something is missing from contemporary culture — and that that something is women's experience — is to write, or to think, letters that point out the debilitating effects of such erasure on young women such as her daughter. She signs these letters with pseudonyms that indicate her understanding that most people would not accept the seriousness of her charges, would instead accuse her of bean counting or of "constructing a tottering fantasy of female exclusion" (227).

Women's exclusion becomes concretely and personally evident to Reta in the sometimes comically drawn relationship with her new editor. He interrupts every sentence, bullies her into sending him an unfinished draft of her upcoming novel, translates French expressions for her even though she is a well-respected translator, and suggests a masculinized title and pseudonym for her new book. Most damagingly, he demands that she move in her fiction toward what he calls "the universal" — a universal that of course encodes primarily male experience. Thus while he comments on the "goodness" of her main female character, Alicia, he wants Reta to focus on the character whom he perceives as capable of "greatness": her main male character, Roman. Alicia, he tells Reta, cannot be "the moral centre of this book" (285). His reasoning — "She writes fashion articles. She talks to her cat. She does yoga. She makes rice casseroles" and, more incoherently but also more explicitly, "She is unable to make a claim to— She is undisciplined in her— She can't focus the way Roman— She changes her mind about— She lacks—" (286) — can be summed up in one sentence: "Because she's a woman" (286). Reta's repetition of this summation indicates its importance to her life and to this novel. Because Alicia is a woman, she is defined by lack and by the inability to make a claim. But instead of reinscribing this limiting definition of what it means to be a woman, Reta, like Shields herself, bravely insists that her readers accept that her female protagonist is "intelligent and inventive and capable of moral resolution, the same qualities we presume, without demonstration, in a male hero" (320).

In writing a first-person narrative about a writer, Shields spotlights her own work, something she has not done to this extent since she made the sister protagonists of her first two novels writers of biography and poetry. In the first chapter of *Unless*, Reta tells readers about the book she is planning to write. The sentence she plans to begin with — "Alicia was not as happy as she deserved to be" (15) — both echoes the first sentence of *Unless* — "It happens that I am going through a period of great unhappiness and loss just now" (1) — and reflects Shields's own life. She has told several interviewers that she translated her unhappiness about her experience with breast cancer into Reta's sorrow about her daughter (which Reta in turn translates into Alicia's unhappiness regarding her relationship). Reta is "aware of being in incestuous waters, a woman writer who is writing about a woman writer who is writing" (208), and clearly Shields is also aware of this dizzying whirlpool, even as she throws herself into it with enthusiasm. Thus Reta, like Shields, writes a bad early sonnet that begins "Satin-slippered April, you glide through time" (2), wins a writing contest as a "young voice" at age twenty-nine (4), and has the unsettling experience of being called by a reviewer "a bard of the banal" (243). In the same way that Shields wrote companion books to her first and third novels, Reta writes a sequel, working carefully to retain the style of narration and details about characters that she established in the first book. Some aspects of Reta's novel are suspiciously similar to Shields's *The Republic of Love*, especially at the point at which Reta realizes that her characters' engagement will have to be broken off, "The wedding guests will have to be alerted and the gifts returned" (173). Like Shields's *Small Ceremonies*, *Unless* takes place over nine months and is about creative gestation and rebirth. Shields even self-consciously includes bits and pieces in *Unless* from her other published narratives, including an entire short story ("The Scarf," from *Dressing Up for the Carnival*) which is transformed and reworked into the chapter titled "Otherwise." (In a similar way, the first chapter of *Larry's Party* was a reworking of her earlier short story, "By Mistake.")

Unless incorporates evocative descriptions of writing and the importance of writing, including Reta's opening disquisition on "a novel's architecture, the lovely slope of predicament, the tendrils of surface detail, the calculated curving upward into inevitability" (13). Much of the latter half of the novel focuses on details of Reta's construction of characters and plot lines. As she says, "This matters, the remaking of an untenable world through the nib of a pen; it matters so much I can't stop doing it" (208).

In *Unless*, life itself is represented as narrative. As Reta tries to understand her daughter's predicament, she asks, "How did this part of the narrative happen? We know it didn't rise out of the ordinary plot lines of a life story" (13). Her assessment is partly correct, because one traumatic event has indeed pushed Norah out of the pre-scripted plot of her quiet life story. In another sense, however, the fact that Norah's life has always followed the ordinary plot lines of many women's life stories — which demand goodness, quietness, and above all sacrifice to others — has paved the way for her eventual transformation into a street person. Like many satisfying stories, *Unless* involves the solution to a mystery — in this case, the mystery behind this transformation. Reta might have uncovered Norah's causal trauma earlier had she put together the clues presented to her and to readers: around the time of Norah's transformation, a Muslim woman set herself alight on a street corner in Toronto; another unidentified woman tried to beat out the flames; and now Norah always wears gloves, even in hot weather. In the denouement to *Unless*, Norah's silent vigil on this particular street corner is revealed as honouring another woman who, through self-immolation, put her silencing and invisibility to literal, permanent, and drastic effect. Shields's book thus turns on itself in a powerful exploration of apparently voluntary silencing that is in fact enforced by cross-cultural gender codes. In completing this circle, *Unless* expands upon and brings to a particularly satisfying conclusion the concerns about women's silencing introduced by Shields in earlier books such as *Swann* and *The Stone Diaries.*

Works Cited

Shields, Carol. *The Stone Diaries.* Toronto: Random House, 1993.
———. *Unless.* Toronto: Random House, 2001.

M ARTA D VORAK

An Aesthetics of the Ordinary in *Dressing Up for the Carnival*

In an essay entitled "The Same Ticking Clock," Carol Shields denounces the way in which serious literature previously suppressed the domestic component of our lives and replaced the "texture of the quotidian," rich in meaning, with "the old problem-solution trick," that she likens to "a photo opportunity for artificial crisis and faked confrontation" (258). Her own aesthetics of the domestic have both enthused and irritated: reviews of her work alternately dub it smaller than life or else praise it for its alchemy of the everyday.[1] Her trademark role, bard of the commonplace, is so firmly established that in "Soup du Jour," one of the stories in her latest collection, *Dressing Up for the Carnival*, Shields parodies the very aesthetics in which she grounds her writing:

> "The quotidian is where it's at," Herb Rhinelander wrote last week in his nationwide syndicated column. "People are getting their highs on the level roller coaster of everydayness, dipping their daily bread in the soup of common delight and simple sensation." (162)

The extract encapsulates the writer's characteristic combinatory tropological strategy consisting in mixing irony, paradox (*highs/ level*), or oxymoron (*level roller coaster*) with the powerful transforming figure of the metaphor (here dominantly alimentary but also carnivalesque) in order to suspend the referential function of language and set up a state of contemplation. Having overturned with light irony the journalistic mixture of truisms, faddish colloquialisms, and facile alliterative metaphorical style, Shields's extradiegetic narrator then goes on to proclaim:

> The ordinary has become extraordinary. All at once — it seems to have happened in the last hour, the last ten minutes — there is no stone, shrub, chair, or door that does not offer arrows of implicit meanings or promises of epiphany. (163)

The flow of the syntagm with its enumeration implying an open-ended amplification, an infinity of possibilities to be envisaged and celebrated, is interrupted by the figure of the parenthesis, which not only self-reflexively foregrounds the process of enunciation, but also satirizes literary fashions through the device of hyperbole (in the absurdly restrictive temporal precision), aporetically cancelling out the promises of higher meaning and epiphanic disclosures behind pedestrian objects. Yet, as I shall attempt to demonstrate, this is precisely what Shields does offer: through stones and shrubs, chairs and doors, objective correlatives or figurations of nature and culture, she transforms objects into signs — symbols or emblems of an ontological stance.

I shall argue that Shields's poetic practice functions simultaneously — and aporetically — in a vertical and a horizontal fashion. The writer paradigmatically reconfigures universal aesthetic and metaphysical concerns, all the while she syntagmatically questions the ontological existence of any reality outside of representation. Coral Ann Howells's article "In the Subjunctive Mood: Carol Shields's *Dressing Up for the Carnival*," studying the collection from the angle of fantasy and masquerade, judiciously grounds the critical discussion in an essay by Shields in which the author makes an analogy between her vision and mode of writing and the subjunctive mood of grammar:

> Diurnal surfaces could be observed by a fiction writer with a kind of deliberate squint, a squint that distorts but also sharpens beyond ordinary vision, bringing forward what might be

called the subjunctive mode of one's self or others, a world of dreams and possibilities and *parallel realities*. (Shields, "Arriving Late," 246; emphasis mine)

At the core of Shields's writing, then, is a paradigm characteristic of modernism suggesting a supra-reality beyond the senses, deeply concerned with figuration and representation, or the order of the world. But this vertical mode is enmeshed with a horizontal one characteristic of postmodernism: it is concerned not with re/presentation, but with the *presentation* of a world through the "*parallel* realities" of fiction.

From the ordered world of homely things, we constantly slide into the ordered world of language and representation. Rather than "artificial crisis and faked confrontation," Shields pursues "the real mystery" of the self, of the other, of the creative process itself. In an interview with Eleanor Wachtel, her "real mystery" takes on the contours of the following interrogations: "How do you know anyone? How does art come out of common day?" ("Interview," 41). The writer confesses her fascination with numinous moments, when we sense "the order of the universe beneath that daily chaos" (43). She argues that in order to perceive the pattern of the universe, in order to lead creative lives, we need order and safety:

I think creativity flourishes in tranquil settings . . . What the writer needs is everydayness. (Wachtel, "Interview" 39)

Recognizable in her statements is a rather neoclassical mode of idealism which marks a certain verticality[2] of the quotidian, metaphor of a higher order, sign of a supra-reality: fiction represents things *as* something beyond, which is more elevated. The preoccupation with an undisclosed meaning underlies and even catalyzes *Mary Swann*, a novel in which ambitious academics unscrupulously reconstruct, even reinvent, the biography and oeuvre of an ordinary farmer's wife who has inexplicably authored extraordinary poetry:

The mythic heavings of the universe, so baffling, so incomprehensible, but when squeezed into digestible day-shaped bytes,

made swimmingly transparent. Dailiness. The diurnal unit,
cloudless and soluble. (*Mary Swann* 21-22)

Dailiness as the doorway to the mythic heavings of the universe, but
also the thingness of Being-there or Being-in-the-world, containing
its own meaning and needing no explicatory act of language — reminiscent of Heidegger's *Dasein* — are fundamentally what the stories
in *Dressing Up for the Carnival* aporetically revolve around.

The writing, rooted in everydayness, is profoundly metaphorical.
At the core of the metaphorical network are the alimentary and vestimentary dynamics that both codify and are codified by a given socio-
cultural reality. These are the leitmotifs that provide the point of
emergence where the pattern of relations constructed by the text
rises to the surface and proclaims the power of invention.

Defying the linear plot of conventional short story structure, the
title story of the collection is constructed upon the rhetorical devices
of seriation and hypotyposis.[3] The omniscient narrator chooses one
spring day in a North American city and juxtaposes a dozen scenes
made even more vivid and dynamic through the use of the nunego-
centric present tense, grounded in the here and now, focussing in
turn on characters of different ages, backgrounds, and sexes without
ever providing a narrative interconnection. The only linking thread is
the vestimentary leitmotif proclaimed in the opening sentence: "All
over town people are putting on their costumes" (*Dressing Up* 1). As
the choice of the theatrical term indicates, the accoutrements that
the characters take up are not merely vestimentary items but accessories that include a mango, a bouquet of daffodils, a football, a vio-
lin case, or an English pram. The opening sequence sets the tone, as
a young woman, Tamara, dresses for work in an apparently non-func-
tional way. Without checking the weather, she chooses a yellow skirt
and white blouse, along with a straw belt, yellow beads, earrings,
bone sandals, and bare legs. The outfit can be viewed simply as a carnivalesque disguise or concealment, or as a form of conformity to or
transgression of social codes and conventions, yet by setting it within
the framework of the multiple segments or variations that it antici-
pates, Shields nudges it towards an ontological statement.

Yes! The yellow cotton skirt with the big patch pockets and the hand detail around the hem. How fortunate to own such a skirt. And the white blouse. What a blouse! Those sleeves, that neckline with its buttoned flap, the fulness in the yoke that reminds her of the Morris dances she and her boyfriend Bruce saw at the Exhibition last year.

Next she adds her new straw belt; perfect. A string of yellow beads. Earrings of course. Her bone sandals. And bare legs, why not?

She never checks the weather before she dresses; her clothes *are* the weather, as powerful in their sunniness as the strong, muzzy early morning light pouring into the narrow street by the bus stop, warming the combed crown of her hair and fuelling her with imagination. (1-2)[4]

The accoutrement concretizes the power of invention, the power to construct and to represent the self. Tamara's enthusiastic assemblage of the outfit that will transform her is transmitted ironically, it is true, through inner focalization signalled by a hyperbolic combination of modalizers, interjections, shifters, embryonic sentences, and markers of emphasis such as exclamations, rhetorical questions, and italicization. Behind the technically unmediated free indirect discourse, the gently mocking stance of the implied author is perceptible, particularly in the escalating tone of the concluding passage describing the transformation:

She taps a sandalled foot lightly on the pavement, waiting for the number 4 bus, no longer just Tamara, clerk-receptionist for the Youth Employment Bureau, but a woman in a yellow skirt. A passionate woman dressed in yellow. A Passionate, Vibrant Woman About To Begin Her Day. Her Life. (2)

In a pastiche of the headlines of trashy tabloids, Shields capitalizes even unstressed grammatical words that serve merely to specify the relationship among the lexical words that carry meaning, and that normally remain uncapitalized, thus placing the authorial voice as well as the receptor at an ironic distance from the free indirect discourse containing the character's inflated lexicon and melodramatic statement. Yet we cannot help noticing the multiple existential resonances. The final syntagm-sentence concluding the segment contains the single noun "life." The juxtaposition of the penultimate and ultimate sentences, with the added parallelism of the possessive adjective, generates an equivalence between "day" and "life": we construct our lives just as we structure our days. The grammatical ellipsis of the verb "to be" throughout this incantatory passage is significant through the presence of its absence. We divine that the portrait of Tamara conforms to the rhetorical convention regulating description, designed to move from *effictio* (outward appearance) to *notatio* (inward moral qualities). The surface (the yellow skirt) does not cover but rather unveils the inner truth of the self (*passionate / vibrant*). Or even more radically, the skirt *is* the self, in the Humist sense that there is no definitive self, only a collection of perceptions and habits.

The vignettes that follow vary the accessories as well as the protagonists in a metonymic fashion, antonomastically multiplying individual flat characters that function synecdochically as universal, even allegorical types. Roger, of average age, height, class, and profession, has impulsively bought a mango for the first time in his life, and carries the sensuous exotic fruit in his hand, all the while that the epanalepsis "Mango, mango" of the free indirect discourse transforms the alliterative acoustical image into a mantra. The prosaic, everyday scene — a man on the street hurrying back to work after his coffee break — is a scene of revelation reminiscent of the Hegelian quest for self through encounters with the Other, but with a light touch that invites celebratory laughter:

> he freezes and *sees himself freshly;* a man carrying a mango in his left hand. Already he's accustomed to it; in fact, it's starting to feel lighter and drier, like a set of castanets which has somehow attached itself to his left arm. Any minute now he'll break out into a cha-cha-cha right here in front of the Gas Board. The shrivelled fate he sometimes sees for himself can be postponed if only he puts his mind to it. Who would have thought it of

him? Not his ex-wife Lucile, not his co-workers, not his boss, not even himself. (3; emphasis mine)

The collision of incongruous, almost antithetical terms, such as *Gas Board / cha-cha-cha*, suggests that the self is a performance, that being is a representation, a construction. From Roger breaking into a cha-cha, to Wanda delivering her employer's empty pram home and soothing the imaginary baby in a gesture she has rehearsed in dreams, or little Mandy "striking a pose" at the traffic light as she races to the field with the football helmet that her adulated older brother, star halfback, has forgotten at home, all the characters envisage life as a spectacle, and represent themselves to themselves as well as to others on the stage of the world.

The verb *to be*, elided in the initial segment, becomes omnipresent in the subsequent scenes that equate representing and being. Running along to deliver the helmet, her breath blazing in "heroic pain," Mandy is touched by an epiphanic recognition: for the first time "she comprehends *who* her brother is, that deep-voiced stranger whose bedroom is next to her own" (8), and who previously held only a spatial reality. The process of sympathy corresponding to the aesthetics of sentimentalism set up by Adam Smith is so complete that

[t]oday, for a minute, she *is* her brother. *She* is Ralph Eliot, age seventeen, six feet tall, who later this afternoon will make a dazzling, lazy touchdown, bringing reward and honour to his name, and hers. (8)

The exploration of being-in-the-world is consolidated by the shortest vignette, made up of three brief sentences grounded in three different angles of vision:

Jeanette Foster is sporting a smart chignon. Who does she think she *is!* Who *does* she think she is? (9)

The initial objective point of view — narrator as external observer — shifts through the play of italics to, first of all, inner polyfocalization, recording in essence the struggle for control of image, the disapproval of the social group confronted with a gap between image already held

(static), and image newly-generated (dynamic), and then to the sub-
jective point of view of the omniscient narrator musing over the
nature and power of the self.

The antonomasia that catalyzes the allegorical dimension of the
apparently banal episodes is reinforced by the fact that the next to
last character remains anonymous ("a young woman"), and the identity of the protagonist of the closing scene is explicitly effaced: he is
designated by the letter that conventionally represents an unknown
factor. X is an "anonymous middle-aged citizen" who represents existential uncertainty in the form of ambivalent sexual orientation:
behind closed doors, he takes pleasure in "waltz[ing] about in his
wife's lace-trimmed nightgown"(9). In this attire, the liminal character's glance out the window discloses a world suffused with aporia, a
fertile flux of inexpressible sensations dissolved in the objective correlative of the pear tree, and grounded in the cosmology suggested by
sun and evening:

> He lifts the blind an inch and sees the sun setting boldly behind
> his pear tree, its mingled coarseness and refinement giving an
> air of confusion. Everywhere he looks he observes cycles of
> consolation and enhancement, and now it seems as though the
> evening itself is about to alter its dimensions, becoming more
> (and also less) than what it really *is*. (9; emphasis mine)

To be remarked above is the final word which concludes the story on
its major key or motif, just as a musical composition ends on the
main centre of its tonal framework. Within the verb denoting existence, Shields slides from the world of substantial things, the world of
the senses, to the mental acts of perception, thought, and representation.

Nowhere is this clearer than in Shields's trademark rhetorical
device of enumeration, such as the items listed in the story "Keys,"
that, along with a bent key just found and so devoid of any usefulness,
are contained in a cracked china cup in a kitchen drawer:

> a single hairpin, a handful of thumbtacks, a stub of a candle,
> half an eraser, a blackened French coin, a book of matches from

the Informatic Centre, a rubber band or two, and a few paper
clips. (101)

The enumeration functions on several levels: one remarks the
exophoric dimension inviting the receptor to identify with the odds
and ends of dailiness, as well as the entropic implications of dysphoric words such as "stub," "half," or "blackened." Simultaneously,
even before they become more explicitly metaphorized, the items
quietly evoke desire and despair. The cracked cup with its "miserable,
broken, mismatched contents, its unsorted detritus of economy and
mystery" (102) is a synecdoche of life, and one night when the character, a thirty-four-year-old single woman named Cheryl, sits reading
a book significantly called *The Sands of Desire*, she suffocates, opens
a window, and begins to fling out the objects that come to hand: a
package of Cheese Twists that is ironically family-sized, a brown-
edged head of lettuce, and finally the contents of the cup. The series
of word sentences that accompany the objects rattling down and that
conclude the sequence — "Ping. Tut. Tsk. Tick. Gone." — shift from
the phonic symbolism of the opening onomatopoeic lexeme evoking
an objective physical act/sound to the phonic symbols of regret,
transgression, and mortality, in which the final component of the
series is an abstract odd man out. Remarkable throughout the whole
sequence revolving round this character is the ontological vehemence, to borrow a term from Paul Ricoeur, that underlies the nam-
ing process. When Shields names or enumerates, she is in effect creating the be-ing of the object, affirming that it exists. Yet by limiting
herself to the point of view of the same character, the writer aporetically questions the existence of any material reality outside the perceptions of the mind:

> The real world, of course, is in her own head, which she some-
> times thinks of as a shut room provisioned with declaration
> and clarity, everything else being a form of theatre. (100)

In this, Shields reconfigures the pre-existent aesthetic traditions that
have subtended the texts of writers from Shakespeare to Milton and
Shelley. The relationship between external and internal, mind and

matter, thought and thing have been since the Renaissance at the core of seminal works such as *The Tempest, As You Like It*, or *Macbeth*, as well as *Paradise Lost* or *Prometheus Unbound*, to take but a few of the best known examples. Shields's originality in reconfiguring what is essentially an ancient metaphysical as well as an aesthetic preoccupation may consist in the manner in which her reclaiming the familiar entails not only a cosmological assessment, but also an assessment of commodity culture.

The short fiction I have been discussing posits that life is spectacle, an artistic performance in process, while art, in a complementary fashion, is a constructional craft grounded in the daily world of things. The writer's preoccupation with representation is an attempt to make sense of what we call reality, to make sense of our past and present in order to allow us to at least begin to picture — as one of the child protagonists in "Keys" cannot yet do — the "unscrolling of a future" (106) in which a key ring represents the societal comforts and obligations of house, office, club, and cottage. Yet Shields's aesthetics of the ordinary are also grounded in postmodern aporia. On the one hand, her self-conscious writing, language-centred rather than plot-centred, calls attention to itself and to its own process. On the other hand, her stories are suffused with the ontological vehemence that seems to be the metaphysical equivalent of Austen's concept of the performative. When Shields announces "This is," she is in effect creating the be-ing of the object, making her scene operate with a centripetal force, revolving and closing in upon its own centre. In poetic texts, as Ricoeur argues, such a practice contains the ex-tatic moment of language, when language is outside of itself, expressing a desire to efface itself, to vanish within the confines of "l'être-dit"(313), the being-said — in turn the consequence of the act of speech. The Word creates: telling engenders being.

The cosmological reckoning subtending Shields's aesthetics of the commonplace does not deny the referential function of language: on the contrary, her texts seem almost to defy the Saussurean principle that a linguistic sign unites only a concept and an acoustical image, so intensely do our senses perceive the materiality of the objects conjured up. They seem to be the verbal equivalent of the still lifes of baroque painters such as Chardin, which suggest that the meaning of life is right here at hand, in the very substance of the silently luscious fruits. Yet at the same time, objects are often signs or figurations of something beyond — or *meta*. Grounded in postmodern aporia, Shields's poetic practice reconfigures universal aesthetic and metaphysical concerns, confirming Benveniste's affirmation that language literally re-presents or re-produces reality (25), the writer all the while questioning the ontological existence of any reality outside of representation. We cannot fail to recall the "diurnal unit" of dailiness in *Mary Swann*, or the writer's confessed fascination with the "diurnal surfaces" in her essay "Arriving Late, Starting Over," which etymologically suggest daily occurrences or realities, but also evoke coexisting paradigmatic and syntagmatic dimensions. They evoke invisible realities — the hidden world of the diurnal flower that closes at night, that the figurative "squint" cultivated by the writer and resulting in sharpened vision promises to disclose. Yet they also evoke a juxtaposition of the diurnal and the elided nocturnal: two worlds placed side by side. The writer's poetics, in which the texture of the quotidian is distorted but also sharpened, takes us effectively into a world of parallel realities in which the ordinary exists extraordinarily.

Notes

1 Cf. Joel Yanofsky's delight in Shields's alchemy in his review of *Dressing Up for the Carnival*, or Ajay Heble's professed boredom in his review of *Larry's Party* with respect to what he qualifies as the "non-meteoric rise of Larry Weller from one kind of ordinariness to another" (256).

2 Interestingly, the suggested verticality is inverted. In the phrase "the order of the universe beneath that daily chaos" it is expressed in the term "beneath" rather than "above," implying the possibility of stripping away the layers that veil the core of meaning.

3 The technique seems to be an elaboration of the scenic epanalepsis that Simone Vauthier remarks in her study of "Mrs. Turner Cutting the Grass" in *Various Miracles* (*Reverberations* 126).

4 Emphases in the text unless otherwise indicated.

Works Cited

Benveniste, Emile. *Problèmes de linguistique générale I*. Paris: Gallimard, nrf, 1966.

Heble, Ajay. "Letters in Canada" 1997. *University of Toronto Quarterly* 68.1 (1998): 235-254.

Howells, Coral Ann. "In the Subjunctive Mood: Carol Shields's *Dressing Up for the Carnival.*" *The Yearbook of English Studies* 31 (2001), Maney Publishing for the Modern Humanities Research Association: 144-154.

Ricoeur, Paul. *La Métaphore vive*. Paris: Seuil, 1975.

Shields, Carol. *Dressing Up for the Carnival*. London: Fourth Estate, 2000.

—. *Mary Swann*. Hammersmith, London: Flamingo/HarperCollins Publishers, 1993.

—. "Arriving Late: Starting Over," in *How Stories Mean*. Eds. John Metcalf and J.R. Struthers. Erin, Ont: Porcupine's Quill, 1993: 244-251.

—. "The Same Ticking Clock," in *Language in Her Eye: Views on Writing and Gender by Canadian Women Writing in English*. Eds. Libby Scheier, Eleanor Wachtel. Toronto: Coach House Press, 1990: 256-259.

Vauthier, Simone. "Closure in Carol Shields's *Various Miracles*," in *Reverberations: Explorations in the Canadian Short Story*. Concord, Ont: Anansi Press, 1993: 114-131.

Wachtel, Eleanor. "Interview with Carol Shields." Ed. E. Wachtel. The Carol Shields Issue, *Room of One's Own: A Feminist Journal of Literature and Criticism* 13.1-2 (1989): 5-45.

Yanofsky, Joel. Review of *Dressing Up for the Carnival. Quill & Quire* 66.2 (2000): 14-15.

D E B O R A H   S C H N I T Z E R

Tricks: Artful Photographs and Letters in Carol Shields's *The Stone Diaries* and Anita Brookner's *Hotel du Lac*

In a *Prairie Fire* interview with Joan Thomas, Carol Shields explains the risks of the biographical and autobiographical idiosyncrasies in *The Stone Diaries*: "It is tricky, and you never know if this works, and if people really connect with it. There will be plenty of people who won't. There's a sort of postmodern box-within-the-box, within-the-box. I mean, I'm writing the novel, and I'm writing her life, and writing the knowledge of her life — so that's one. But it's also her looking at her life, so I think she has to be in first person sometimes to comment from outside. But the really tricky part was to write about a woman thinking her autobiography in which she is virtually absent" (58). I'm always intrigued by the trickery that is required when an author explicitly tests the virtual realities shaped by points of view and pieces of evidence. Of course, the seemingly antique and family photographs within the novel contribute to the enigmas that develop. Shields refers to them along with point of view as techniques that she worked with to create illusions of presence and absence, virtuality and provisionality: "Someone said — a reviewer in Edinburgh — that when she read it [*The Stone Diaries*], the pictures shocked her, she hadn't known they were coming. I can see it would be a shock, because suddenly you are asked this question, 'What is fiction, what's real and what isn't?' and I suppose that is useful to what I want to have happen in this book — the contradiction and correspondence" (59).

As a reader, that's the tension I love best: texts that argue intense loyalties to seemingly contradictory illusions. On the one hand, mimesis operates as description where the concept of representation is understood as the reproduction of external objects, an assurance of stable and reliable correspondences between sign and thing signified. On the other, mimesis develops as construction, where the concept of the nonrepresentational is understood as the replication of perceptual processes rather than surface appearances, an insistence on the volatile and assailable nature of possible correspondences and competing frames of reference. There are so many delicious terms that establish this dialectic, and one of the best is *trompe l'oeil* — that trick that artists in visual media, for example, often use to enchant the eye, to seduce by encouraging the flat plane of the canvas to run off with a third dimension. Objects appear to recede. Picture frames open windows to the actual. The correlative in a verbal medium might be the *trompes l'oreille* — tricks of the ear that nibble at the reader's sensibilities so that the silent word on the printed page speaks. The suggestion of depth and volume, of things on tables and voices in texts, is conjured by the tricks of the trade, creating what Anita Brookner describes in a *Spectator* review as an "impeccable performance" in Shields's novel (28).

Shields's photographs masquerade as fact in the fiction, a masquerade we repeatedly confer with during our experience of the story. In fiction, we're more predisposed to detect the masquerade than we are in biography, for the latter produces illustrations that chaperone our desire to presume they reproduce the genuine article. In *The Stone Diaries*, Shields's photographs provide a tempting fraud. In the interview with Thomas, she reveals, in part, the status of the photographs which encourage an illusion of biography in the novel: "I wanted them to be random photographs, and not very good photographs, like the kind you find in the bottom of your drawer. Everyone wants to know where they came from . . . The editors found some of them in antique shops, and I found some in a postcard market in

Paris. Some of them are from our family album, everyone thinks they're me, but I'm not in any of them" (59).[1]

The first photograph in the novel is identified as "Cuyler and Mercy, 1902." I take this figure to refer to the courtship Daisy recreates in the novel's "Birth, 1905" chapter, though for a while I thought it might be the wedding portrait that Daisy mentions as "the one

Cuyler and Mercy, 1902

photograph" she has in her possession. I recover from this potential error by remembering that the wedding took place in 1903; Cuyler and Mercy meet in 1902. Mercy and Cuyler are fictions, while the novel's photographs appear to correspond to extra-literary persons once living, now dead. The issue of correspondence is academic in the best sense. There's something about the photograph, of course, that embodies the awkwardness between Mercy and Cuyler that has fascinated their daughter. The speculative energy of the space between them seems to corroborate this impression. They are sure not to touch one another — her hand is pulled back behind her hip, his folded on the crease of his pant leg. I'm struck by the boyishness of his physical frame, the secluded nature of his cautious gaze in contrast to Mercy's physical maturity, the more forthright nature of her approach to the camera eye — well, maybe resigned, but that's consistent with Mercy's submissive nature. Yet this appearance of acquiesence, of composure, is somewhat unsettled by the slight bend in the vertical axis of her body, the feeling of strain that seems to mark her shoulder line, and the unravelling kilter of her neck.

I take this information back to the spell that Shields uses to cast Mercy at the outset. Wait a minute. This photographed Mercy is heavy-set, yes, but Daisy's recorded version invokes the macabre. Her mother's size, she insists, is "unorthodox" (5): Mercy is a "vault" of "flesh," with a "thick doughy neck," and "great loose breasts," that advance toward the "solid boulder of a stomach" (7). Well, the photograph is taken in 1902; Daisy's portrait comes three years later and Mercy is pregnant. There are some women, we know, whose bodies are held hostage by pregnancy, whose nine-month dimensions astound and mystify. Yet Mercy's growth has gone unnoticed. Even if her coordinates are simply rearranged by the pregnancy and her 1902 size correlates rather closely with her 1905 presence, Daisy's portrait alarms both daughter and reader: "Standing in her back kitchen, my mother's thighs, like soft white meat (veal or chicken or fatty pork come to mind) rub together under her cotton drawers — which are wet, she suddenly realizes, soaked through and through. There are double and triple ruffles of fat round her ankle and wrists, and these ridged extremities are slick with perspiration" (8).

Okay. Daisy's feelings about her mother are mixed. In fact, the dissonance between my sense of the Mercy emerging in the photograph and the scenes Daisy details seems more true of the fact that what we see is an act of choice, an expression of who we are. In contrast, I'm reminded of the "sweetness" of Mercy's face which captivates the "neat-bodied" (9) Mrs. Flett: "She loves Mercy, loves her ways, her solid concentration, though on the whole (it must be admitted) her love is churned from fascination, and also from pity — pity for that large, soft, slow-flowing body, the blurred flesh at the sides of Mercy's young face, and a blinking prettiness that shows itself in certain lights, in the curve of her upper lip or the tender spilt panic of her hazel eyes" (8-9). I find myself, as Shields knew I would, pulling the photograph in, reeling for a close-up, checking for sepia stains that survive the black and white reproduction, ranging through the vagueness of the interior, the well-educated backdrop with its Doric columns and period chair and then pushing back, seeking the consolation of distance, craning my own neck, as it were, so that I can accommodate disparate perspectives.

I sense the gap between Mercy and Cuyler much more in terms of temperament and role than of age, for I remember that there's but a two-year difference between them: in 1905 Mercy is thirty-one and Cuyler is twenty-nine. I understand Daisy's resentment because she's been so completely denied the mothering Mercy lavishes upon Cuyler as compensation for the unnatural rigidity of his biological parents. I seek the photographs again and again, using them as reality checks even as I appreciate their inauthenticity. I don't even remember whether I read the photographs before I started the novel or whether I happened on them by accident the first time I put the novel down. I can't reconstruct how or when they found me and I them. I think Daisy knows they are there but she doesn't explicitly refer to them. But perhaps I think that Daisy knows because her "think" and my own often become indistinguishable.

There's no way of grounding the text by verifying its credentials empirically. While Shields clarifies the origin of the photographs in a general way in the interview, I anticipate yet another ruse. And so, this photograph is and is not "'Cuyler and Mercy in 1902.'" These visuals so cleverly filed in the "Motherhood 1947" chapter relate to but are distinct from the fiction. Insofar as I know that the photographs pretend to be elements of the novel's life story, they are hypotheses that can disturb the narrative advance: much as Cousin Beverly's appearance and her tales of "dropping bombs" and the unlucky parachutist "falling through the sky" (176-77) so upset the status quo that Daisy, who "cannot bear [t]o be the cause of injury" (334), dishonourably discharges her niece. Daisy violates the very code of civility and good will she almost consistently feels compelled to embody. She exposes aspects of her own nature most of her acquaintances — those who find her unfailingly accommodating and domesticated — often cannot detect.

Like Daisy, the photographs sustain the illusions of both facsimile and artifact. Able to accommodate any number of paradoxes, they illustrate in the visual medium the open-endedness and indefiniteness of Daisy's account. This looseness finds its verbal correlative in the very description of the sound Mercy makes during labour: "The sound that comes from her lips is formless, loose, a wavy line of bewilderment" (4). Daisy too is bewildered. As the unexpected and abandoned expression of the "lovesickness" that committed Cuyler to Mercy, she wanders through feelings of admiration and contempt, longing and disconnection. While she admits her mother's artistry, she spares little when she considers the physical impact of Mercy's passion: "Eating was as close to heaven as my mother ever came" (1). Thrilled by the scene she envisions to mark the making of the Malvern pudding (2), impressed by her mother's devotion to a husband whose extravagant appreciation she can't quite comprehend, warmed by the love and generosity Mercy inspires in others, bewildered by her own desire to "surrender" like Clarentine "into the pale bulk of Mercy's neck, into Mercy's soft shoulders and curling brown hair" (10), Daisy is also given to loathing and condemnation.

Accordingly, Daisy's aversion to her mother's size affects many of the verbal portraits she presents. Clarentine believes in the "enchantment" of the love that exists between Cuyler and Mercy, and her "parlor picture" of the two of them after supper at the kitchen table takes off within Daisy's memory: "Light from the doorway fell on my mother's broad face, giving it a look of lustre. My father was lean-ing toward her, his hand covering hers. The two of them, Clarentine Flett thought, might have been the subject of a parlor picture, a watercolour done in tints of soft blues and grays" (17). Daisy's feelings of betrayal, her "illness" of "orphanhood" redistribute these composi-tional values. The Renoiresque is displaced by an Expressionist grotesquerie:

> My mother, as I have already said, was an extraordinarily obese woman, and with her jellylike features, she was rather plain, I'm afraid. It's true her neighbour, Mrs. Flett, glimpses a certain prettiness behind her squeezed eyes and pouched chin, but the one photograph I possess, her wedding portrait, tells me otherwise. My mother was large-bodied, heavy fleshed. My father, in contrast, was short of stature, small-boned and neat, with a look of mild incomprehension flitting across his face. It can perhaps be imagined that among the men of the commu-nity coarse jokes were made at his expense. (17)

Daisy argues that Clarentine's eye is shackled by the "cheap" romance novels she's read (17); she reminds us of the non-Harlequin "facts" that testify to the actual nature of events as critical as her own birth: "There lies my mother, Mercy Stone Goodwill, panting on the kitchen couch with its cheap, neat floral cover; she's on her side, as though someone has toppled her over, her large soft trunky knees drawn up, and her woman's parts exposed. Like seashells or a kind of squashed fruit" (23). The dissonance between Daisy's pictures resists reconcili-ation. In the next breath she argues:

> There's nothing ugly about this scene, whatever you may think, nothing unnatural that is, so why am I unable to look at it calmly? Because I long to bring symmetry to the various discor-dant elements, though I know before I begin that my efforts will seem a form of pleading. Blood and ignorance, what can be shaped from blood and ignorance? — and the pulsing, mindless, leaking jelly of my own just-hatched flesh, which I feel compelled

to transform into something clean and whole with a line of scrip-
ture running beneath it or possibly a Latin motto. (23)

I understand the need for order and the sense of outrage and so I
revise my portrait of Daisy, just as I return to the 1902 photograph
whose meaning is continually readjusted. The moment of the snapshot acquires a duration which defies the physical and biographical
conditions of its production in a world outside the novel. That is,
exposure to the novelistic resources of time and sequence secretes
layers of significance. I come to know this Mercy Stone soon-to-be-
Goodwill in the photograph even while I recognize that this photograph is not *really* Mercy Stone soon-to-be-Goodwill at all.

I am experiencing a correlative of the very "tricks of consciousness" Daisy herself accesses and which bring clarity and vividness to
events often blurred and circumspect. In these instances, the "narrative maze opens and permits her to pass through" (190). While Daisy
may only vaguely recall the disconcerting effect[2] of the man whose
coat sleeve grazed her own as she "stood gazing at Niagara Falls" during her maiden voyage toward Barker Flett, may in fact "be crowded
out of her own life — she knows this for a fact and has always known
it," she does possess, "as a compensatory gift, the startling ability to
draft alternate versions" (190). It becomes clear that Daisy simply
can't be relied upon to provide an unambiguous account. She's gifted,
and the gift tricks — distorts and clarifies, retracts and confirms,
thwarts and encourages discontinuities. A citizen of diverse time
zones, Daisy's representation must be taken with a "grain of salt, a
bushel of salt": "much of what she has to say is speculative, exagger-
ated, wildly unlikely," her "perspective is off," her leaps back and forth
through time cause "all manner of wavy distortion" (148). She's got a
vested interest and so insists "on showing herself in a sunny light," a
predilection the narrator laments: "And, oh dear, dear, she is cursed
with the lonely woman's romantic imagination and thus can support
only happy endings" (149).

In Brookner's *Hotel du Lac*, we also face a narrator who by her
own admission is unreliable: Edith Hope is thirty-nine, single, a
"householder, a ratepayer, a good plain cook" (8), a Londoner who

writes "romantic fiction" under the pseudonym Vanessa Wilde. Having alarmed and offended her friends by disposing of a perfectly reasonable offer of marriage to one perfectly respectable Geoffrey Long on the day of the wedding itself, Hope defers to their better judgment and agrees to endure, at least, a brief, one month exile to a comfortable Swiss hotel. Hope alludes mysteriously to these events at the outset of the novel, careful to assure us that her supposed gifts of observation and evaluation are both inadequate and misleading. And, just as we are reminded of the vulnerable nature of our dependency on Daisy — "hers is the only account there is, written on air, written with imagination's invisible ink" (*The Stone Diaries* 149) — so too, we must adapt as best we can to the inconsistencies which distinguish Edith's "false equations." The "Belgian confectioner's widow" in residence at the hotel (11), for example, re-establishes herself as Madame la Comtesse, an elderly deaf matron whose estranged son and self-serving daughter-in-law have banished her into permanent exile. The "charming tableau" of Iris and Jennifer Pusey as "mother and daughter entwined, their arms locked about each other, their rosy faces turned" (44) which so enchants Edith proves as troublesome as their ages, whose actual implications Edith barely comprehends. "Lady X" emerges neither as exotic dancer nor as poor tragedy nursing a "breakdown" or "bereavement," but rather as Monica, a sphinx from the ruling class with an eating disorder punished because she's failed to breed, a woman who "knows far more" than Edith can ascertain (71). Edith Hope/Vanessa Wilde must consistently adjust her assessments because her "famed powers, etc." (11) fail when they come into contact with human nature: "She could make up characters but she could not decipher those in real life. For the conduct of life she required an interpreter" (72).

Like Shields, Brookner finds an illusion that she can use to exploit the provisional nature of the truths revealed by her protagonist. Shields plays with the photograph as icon, displaced in relation to both the life outside and the art inside the novel; Brookner plays with the letter as a verbal idiom, as hypothetical direct speech, and presents a series of them to generate specific illusions of our exiled hero writing almost daily to her married lover in London, a lover who had quietly, perhaps reluctantly, made way for the marriage to Geoffrey Long that Edith almost achieved. These are illusions that are gradually and insistently undermined by the narrative facts themselves in much the same way that Shields's photographs respond provocatively but tangentially to the text.

Edith's first letter is written the day of her arrival. Borrowing from Eliot's "Journey of the Magi," she proceeds to satirize the more immediately laughable aspects of her own disgrace: "A cold coming I had of it . . ." (10). Typographically, the letter looks like a letter: "'My Dearest David' (she wrote)," (10); we see the traditional spacing between the address and the body of the letter though the "(she wrote)" is as problematic as it is reassuring: we are reminded equally that Edith is writing a letter and that Edith is not *really* writing a letter — we're just pretending she is. Edith's touch is light, sophisticated, desiring to amuse even when the more baleful aspects of her relocation are brought into focus. Her eyes well with tears, but her written composure is more or less assured. There are the telling awkward repetitions that belittle her "famed powers," the throwaway phrases that prevent her from lingering over disturbing emotions — "Anyway, I got over that," "In any event," "Nevertheless" (10-11) — and the banal observations which briefly mingle with charged revelations: "'I think about you all the time. I try to work out where you are, but this is rather difficult, surrounded as I am by the time change, minimal though it is, and the lingering effects of my pills, and all these sad cypresses. In a manner of speaking. But tomorrow is Friday, and when it begins to get dark I shall be able to imagine you getting in the car and driving to the cottage. And then, of course, the weekend, about which I try not to think." The letter loses its nerve: "'You cannot know . . .'" The ellipsis speaks *sub rosa* on behalf of the lament Edith has trained herself to swallow: "At this point she put down her pen and massaged her eyes briefly, sitting for a moment with her elbows on the table and her head bent into her hands. Then, blinking, she took up her pen again and continued her letter" (12). The unnamed narrator's vigilant eye fills in the blanks here by confirming the dislocations that identify the rhetorical situation. Edith gathers herself quickly following the gap and softens the tone by combining the solicitous and the sentimental:

"'Ridiculous to tell you to take care of yourself, because you never think of all the mild precautions that others take, and in any case there is nothing I can do to make you. My dear life, as my father used to call my mother, I miss you so much'"(12).

Orphaned like Daisy, raised by a fragile father and a tempestuous and complicated mother, Edith has acquired the same kind of "brooding but acquiescent" (22) approach to her own life and her relation to others. Recovering in the hospital, an eighty-year-old Daisy Flett is appreciated by staff primarily because she's obliging, so exquisitely mannered, despite the "tubes and wires," "The drugs. The dreams," the "pain and bewilderment" she suffers so bravely, "poor thing" (*Diaries* 314). While inside she dismisses the young chaplain, no longer willing to play her part, outside she hears herself say "'It's so good of you to come'" (314). And we are advised that we mustn't take her seriously, ruminate on the abuse: "Never mind, it means nothing; it's only Mrs. Flett going through the motions of being Mrs. Flett" (314). Edith's isolation leads to a correlative duality. She is both observer and participant, both the mild-mannered, seemingly abstracted, obedient and plain unmarried woman, demure confi-dante of those with more style and drive, cautious, and considerate, the "complaisant foil" (82); she is also Vanessa Wilde, successful writer of romance novels, aloof, irreverent, ironic, and daring.

Brookner blends first and third person perspectives to create an illusion richly comparable to the way in which Daisy lives "outside" and "inside" her story (123). Edith herself accepts the fact that "most of her life seems to go on at a subterranean level" (*Hotel* 92); she brack-ets dimensions of her personality and vocation, secludes them in her garden, her room, in her quiet affair with David. The letters exist in the first person. The writing of them is framed by a detached yet kindly pseudo-omniscience that brings to mind painful memories Edith attempts to evade. Thus the tongue-in-cheek and artful "write up," which constitutes a second letter, parades the assorted eccentricities of hotel guests and then stalls, choked by Edith's recollections of her parents' hopeless marriage, the defencelessness and humiliation Edith suffers in hiding behind a parlour chair, crying, assaulted by the "brutal sound" of a language she doesn't understand (46-50). Unable to sustain the letter, Edith carefully blots what she's made up thus far and turns to the current draft of her new novel, bending "her head obediently to her daily task of fantasy and obfuscation" (50).

While the reader initially assumes there is more "reality" and less "fantasy" in the letters, he or she comes to acknowledge that the letters depart equally from the "terrible" "facts of life" that Edith excludes from her fiction: there the tortoise rather than the hare wins, the meek inherit the earth, the wallflower enraptures the peacock. When her letters do come too close to the "too real circumstances over which she could exert no control" (66), Edith edits them as scrupulously as she has edited the anecdotes she's prepared to divert her lover. The elaborate description of Mrs. Pusey's seventy-ninth birthday party sours:

> Edith laid down her pen. This letter would have to be fin-
> ished later, and even possibly revised. Unsound elements
> seemed to have crept into her narrative; she was aware of
> exceeding her brief. And was then aware of the restrictions that
> that brief implied: to amuse, to divert, to relax — these had
> been her functions, and indeed her dedicated aim. But some-
> thing had gone wrong or was slipping out of control. What had
> been undertaken as an exercise in entertainment — for had not
> the situation seemed appropriate, tailor-made, for such an
> exercise? — had somehow accumulated elements of introspec-
> tion, of criticism, even of bitterness. (113-14)

In many ways the good form Edith hopes to maintain in the letter, the very sportiness and seriousness of her good show, parallels the good will Daisy struggles to exhibit. In an interview with John Haffenden, Brookner objects to his suggestion that her novel writing is "a function of maladaption" by insisting on the redemptive capacity of form: "'No, I'm not going to let you get away with that. It's a form of editing experience — getting it out in terms of form, because it is form that is going to save us all, I think, and the sooner we realize it the better'" (30).

It is not until the eleventh hour of the twelfth chapter that we are informed that Edith actually has not sent any of the letters that she's composed to David. Having accepted, albeit reluctantly, the offer of a marriage of convenience by one Mr. Philip Neville — in return for maintaining an image of fidelity, Edith may enjoy some personal power, the possibility of writing "better" novels, and Neville's impressive estate which contains, among other attractions, "a rather well-known collection of *famille rose* dishes" (164) — Edith writes to end the affair: "'This is the last letter that I shall ever write to you and the first one that I shall ever post'" (179). The expressions of pain and longing that Edith removed because they erred on the side of truth now constitute the main of this final communication. While she's been advised by her friends not to use phrases like "You are the breath of life to me," she insists on their applicability. She is able to interrogate David's neglect, his insensitivity, his capacity to be aroused by others. Misgivings she would not countenance find expression and, as artist as well as lover, she recovers her principles. For example, David reads Edith's fiction as primarily her expression of "satire and cynical detachment." Not so, Edith advises: "'You were wrong, I believed every word I wrote. And I still do'" (181). And finally, insofar as we believe this letter will be sent, we accept the *trompe l'oreille* — Edith is courageous enough to say *out loud* that she was "'the more willing'" partner of the two (181). While David exists primarily within the terms that Edith and her narrator provide, we believe that at least in this letter the less appealing though more authentic dimensions of both letter writer and letter reader exist.

This last communication on the eve of her departure with Neville has, then, more secure bearings. We believe that Edith has found the voice that she's censored in her earlier attempts, that she's integrated the compensatory aspects of her double identity, that she will achieve the maturity and honesty the affair with David does not provide. And then, in the midst of this series of promises, we are reminded of the context that frames the letter itself. Edith has just made the decision to enter into a loveless "partnership" with a man committed to his own "centrality" and invulnerability, a man who above all requires such obedience and impassivity that when Edith momentarily grieves the loss of David, he threatens: "'I cannot bear to see a woman cry; it makes me want to hit her'" (168). Brookner uses the letter to subdue the fears we may have felt for Edith's welfare, to show us to what extent we too may support the deception that any marriage is better than none at all.

Both Daisy and Edith are refugees and both carry the impact of legendary attachments. Fate intervenes to execute one suicidal and alcoholic Harold Hoad, thus conferring upon Daisy the special status of survivor of a "honeymoon tragedy" (123) which now combines with the exotic circumstances of her birth. Edith abandons her would-be husband Geoffrey Long as he waits enthusiastically for her chauffeured car to come to a sensible stop at the Registry Office. The notoriety and condemnation that ensues because of this "epic occurrence" leads to Edith's probation. (There had of course been the adventure of the affair with David, one which read like "her story come to life" (89): passionate though too infrequent episodes of lovemaking climaxed with "heroic fry-ups" (29).

Daisy, "powerless, anchorless, soft-tissued — a woman" accepts "whatever accident of fortune awaits her" in the form of Barker Flett (150), and so initiates another unrewarding series of events that demonstrate the extent to which she is "someone who is always learning and forgetting and obliged to learn again" (151). Edith's deliverance from an equally pernicious marriage occurs only by accident. Leaving her hotel room at dawn, letter to David in hand, Edith stumbles upon the shadow of Neville in his dressing gown emerging from Jennifer Pusey's boudoir. Aware that she would "turn to stone, to paste" as part of his "collection," Edith destroys the letter and exchanges it for a telegram to be sent to David's business address: "she wrote. 'Coming home.' But, after a moment, she thought that this was not entirely accurate and, crossing out the words 'Coming home,' wrote simply, 'Returning'" (184). We believe that this enigmatic document will at least find its way across the channel. The clichéd "Coming home" replaced by the more unattached "Returning" might imply Edith's reaffirmation of "the only life that I have ever wanted" (184), the "orgiastic" pleasure of the writing life within her "little house, so long her private domain, a shell for writing in, for sleeping in, silent and sunny in the deserted afternoons" (120).[3]

Of course, the story ends before the telegram is sent. Edith's awakening might have been another pseudo-diary entry like the letters unsent. The telegram another diversion. Perhaps the entire sequence of novelistic letters exists simply as notes for a new novel; or, perhaps we are to understand that all hierarchies within the novel collapse: there is no difference in kind between the "pretence" that Edith fitfully acknowledges distinguishes her edited story in its letter form to David and the seemingly more inclusive actuality of the story of exile that exists outside of the world the letters partially represent. Charades like those artfully contrived by the novelistic photographs that comprise the Daisy (Goodwill) Flett family album in *The Stone Diaries* dramatize the artifice of our own reading habits and identities just as effectively as they encourage the illusion of the autobiographical. We defer, if only for the moment, to those plastic and rhetorical forms whose extra-literary ontology is prepossessing and whose tricks of eye and ear engender most immediately the primary illusions of "actual" space, time, and identity.

Notes

1 Of course the reader so persists in conflating autobiographical and fictional representations that, over time and with repeated exposure, the photographs of the Downing and Taylor women conjugate wonderfully with Sally Soames's "author photograph" titled "Carol Shields . . . internationally known author," sitting on the inside of the novel's jacket cover-up.

2 In his analysis of the textual unconscious in *Hotel du Lac*, John Skinner studies those dimensions that "resist temptation" — moments of anxiety, silence, erratic shifts in focus, unexplained hauntings (76-83) that are as darkly present in parallel forms in Shields's novel.

3 In his discussion of the "terminal ambivalence" (75) he believes intrinsic to Brookner's handling of the love story, Skinner cites two comments by the author which relate to the ending's impact. In the interview with Haffenden in 1984, Brookner comments: "'coming home' would be coming back to domestic propriety: 'home' implies husband, children, order, regular meals, but 'Returning' is her more honest view of the situation. To that extent she does break through to a clearer vision" (29). In a later discussion noted in Olga Kenyon's *Women Writers' Talk*, Brookner suggests a seemingly different conception: "I simply wanted to write a love story in which something unexpected happened, and in which love really triumphed" (13). Perhaps Skinner's concept of "terminal ambivalence" relates as interestingly to our awareness of ambiguities essential to any metafictional reading experience.

Works Cited

Brookner, Anita. "A family and its good fortune." *The Spectator* 4 (September 1993): 28-29.

— . *Hotel du Lac*. London: Triad Grafton, 1984.

Haffenden, John. "Playing Straight." Interview with Anita Brookner. *The Literary Review* (September 1984): 25-31.

Kenyon, Olga. *Women Writers' Talk*. Oxford: Lennard Publishing, 1989.

Shields, Carol. *The Stone Diaries*. Toronto: Random House, 1993.

Skinner, John. *The Fictions of Anita Brookner: Illusions of Romance*. New York: St. Martin's Press, 1992.

Thomas, Joan. "The Golden Book." An Interview with Carol Shields. *Prairie Fire* 14.4 (Winter 1993-94): 56-62.

Leona Gom

Stone and Flowers

The Stone Diaries is a splendid book, and its protagonist, Daisy Goodwill Flett, is as challenging a character as Canadian literature has ever given us. What I would like to look at here are the two complex and interwoven image patterns that Shields uses to depict Daisy and the people around her.

Stone

is clearly the dominant image/symbol/theme running through the novel. Daisy is born of parents whose lives are significantly influenced by the stone quarries of Tyndall and Stonewall in Manitoba. Her mother, growing up at the Stonewall Orphans Home, of unknown parents, is given, as was the custom with such children, the surname Stone. Her father, Cuyler Goodwill, has a life almost totally defined by his work in the limestone quarries of Manitoba and, later, Indiana. This, then, is Daisy's birthright: stone, both literal and metaphorical.

Certainly Shields uses stone for its expected negative connotations: hard, lifeless, cold. The "old Jew" who is present at Daisy's birth and mother's death feels a curse of sadness, of anguish, hanging over the baby and feels, when he says to her, "Be happy," "as though he were blessing a stone" (26). Clarentine Flett, the kind neighbour who raises Daisy, is killed when struck by a cyclist and thrown against the corner stone, "sharp as a knife," of the Royal Bank Building in Winnipeg. When Daisy marries her unpleasant first husband, his home is described as a "stone castle," and even the house in Ottawa where she is happier is described as cold and ill-favoured with an "ugly limestone foundation." When Daisy's father suddenly becomes an articulate speaker he thinks of it as "the moment when the stone in his throat became dislodged" (84). At the end of the novel the images of gravestones, of Daisy lying on a "thick slab" with a stone pillow and a stone scroll across her feet, of Daisy even becoming stone, are unquestionably sad, even tragic.

But Shields doesn't make it that simple. Stone is just as often seen positively, as full of promise. While work in the stone quarries is hard, Shields spends considerable time speaking of Cuyler's joy in his work, of the "miracle" of the limestone and its properties, of what he calls "our great gift from the earth" (81). Nor, on a symbolic level, is Daisy some version of Laurence's unyielding stone angel, Hagar Shipley. Daisy is more complex and elusive. Cuyler, who becomes a rather maudlin public speaker once the stone is rolled from his tongue, nevertheless offers some insight into all their lives when he talks of the remarkable freestone that can be split in either direction, that has no natural bias:

> [T]hink of this . . . as the substance of your lives. You are the stone carver. The tools of intelligence are in your hand. . . . You can fail tragically or soar brilliantly. (116)

For Cuyler, to "soar brilliantly" means to use stone as a medium for art, and it is when he does this that he seems most fulfilled. When he builds Goodwill Tower in memory of his wife, it becomes a marvel for tourists. "Every piece of stone in the world has its own center with something imprisoned in it" (90), he tells Daisy. It is only when he commercializes his art, becomes a successful businessman, that his gift leaves him, his sensibility coarsens. Still, at a commencement address he is able to speak reverently of how "a rigid, inert mass can be lifted out of the ground and given wings" (114).

Flowers

As the novel progresses, the images of and importance of flowers increase. As with stone, however, Shields uses flowers in subtle and complex ways. Although they are often in counterpoint or opposition to stone they are not a simple antithesis. In fact, the most interesting portrayal of flowers occurs when Shields shows them having a similar function as limestone — as a means of earning a living.

It begins with Clarentine Flett, the neighbour who becomes a mother to Daisy. For Clarentine, selling sprays of wildflowers on the street in front of the CPR station in Winnipeg is the beginning of a new life, of independence. "City folks were fools for fresh flowers" (49), she thinks unsentimentally, and apparently she is right: her florist business thrives, and, when Daisy marries in 1927, Clarentine's son Barker sends her $10,000, the amount, plumped up by good investments, realized from the sale of the business. Every woman, Clarentine believed, should have money of her own, and $10,000 in the 1920s is a substantial inheritance for Daisy.

For Barker, too, it is flowers from which he makes a living. He becomes a botanist, a professor. His profession seems to choose him as much as he it early in his life:

> He can't recall when he learned the names of the plants in his mother's garden, but he remembers how the exactitude of nomenclature lulled him into comfort. Early on, he knew himself to be one of those who are morally unhoused and in need of specific notation, plants, animals, the starry constellations. Soon, besides his mother's domesticated flowers, he mastered the plantlife of the fields and woods. He had all of it quickly by heart, common names as well as Latin. Each time he was able to match a specimen with the illustration in *Spotton's Botanical Note Book* he experienced a spasm of strength. The green world with its varying forms brought out an exotic tolerance in him and kept him calm. The discovery at the age of twelve or thirteen that the whole of the natural world had been classified, that someone other than himself had guessed at the need for this ordering, struck him like a bolt of happiness. (142)

That Barker should eventually marry Daisy (her first husband having died on their honeymoon) seems almost inevitable, and it seems inevitable, too, that he should wish to classify her comfortably in his Linnaean world, as he had the western lady's-slipper, the flower on which he did his dissertation. "He loved this flower. . . . This delicate, frilled blossom was his. He had worked on it (her) for months, and now he possessed the whole of its folded silken parts" (45, 46). Daisy, of course, is not as easy to possess; "she sits far out at the end of one of the branches, laughing, calling to him" (143). In Barker's last letter to Daisy, shortly before his death, he acknowledges, in a moving metaphor, this awkwardness, this difference, between them. "I can recall," he says,

> the repugnance you felt for the lady's-slipper's morphology . . . , that an insect might enter therein easily but escape only with difficulty. . . . The memory . . . has, of course, led me into wondering whether you perhaps viewed our marriage in a similar way, as a trap from which there was no easy exit. (198)

This letter appears in the chapter titled, "Work," but it is not Barker's work that is chronicled here, exclusively in letters, but Daisy's, and it, too, involves flowers. Continuing the gardening column begun by Barker for the Ottawa *Recorder*, she becomes Mrs. Green Thumb. It is clear that she not only does this job well and diligently, but that she enjoys it a great deal. Perhaps it is the only time in her life she is really happy. When an opportunistic reporter takes the position away from her she is bitterly disappointed, and she falls into a profound depression for most of the next year, 1965.

For Daisy, flowers are of course not simply a means of making a living — she has, in any case, few financial worries in her life. Flowers for her seem to provide, increasingly, a spiritual sustenance, and Shields connects them with her in intriguing ways. When Barker asks what she did during her nine years of widowhood she simply shakes her head.

> "You must have done something with your time," he prods. "Charities? The Red Cross?"
> She looks blank, then brightens. "The garden," she says. "I looked after the garden." (154)

And so Barker buys for them a house "of stone and brick," "with a garden that has seen better days" (154). He buys for his wife something for her to do.

And does he do the right thing? It seems so. For Daisy, flowers and gardens give her the purest of pleasures, and the garden she grows at this house is described in rich and loving detail. Lilacs, crocuses, sweet william, bleeding heart, campanula, poppies, dahlias, European Alpine plants — it is hard not to quote at length from these passages. And does Daisy "understand the miracle she has brought into being in the city of Ottawa . . . in the middle years of the century? Yes, for once she understands fully" (195, 196). The garden is in some ways "her dearest child, the most beautiful of her offspring, obedient but possessing the fullness of its spaces, its stubborn vegetable will" (196).

If Daisy's garden is Edenic — and Shields does say of visitors that standing in the garden they "feel their hearts lock into place for an instant, and experience . . . Eden itself, paradise indeed" (196) — then what really is Daisy? Is she God? A kind of bewildered, troubled God, nurturing what she has been given and ignoring the rest? Well, why not? Clarentine sees the Christian God as "the petulant father blundering about in the garden, trampling on all her favourite flowers" (113). Daisy, the child Clarentine raises, learns to do a better job than that.

It's unlikely, of course, that Shields really intends for us to see Daisy as God, but certainly the novel is full of images of her as a caretaker of the garden, its advocate. Consider this scene with Harold, her first husband:

> "Don't do that with your stick," she said to him.
>
> Idly, he had been swinging a willow wand about in the air and lopping off the heads of delphiniums, sweet william, bachelor buttons, irises.
>
> "Who cares," he said, looking sideways at her, his big elastic face working.
>
> "I care," she said.
>
> He swung widely and took three blooms at once. Oriental poppies. The petals scattered on the asphalt path.
>
> "Stop that," she said, and he stopped. (116)

The scene works to give us an easy characterization of Harold, but we also see Daisy, usually so placid and agreeable, assert herself, not on her own behalf but on behalf of the flowers. And she wins. He stops. In the Orkney Islands, she offers to the struggling flowers a kind of prayer, a blessing. "Love!" she tells them. "Tenderness! Courage!" (197)

When Daisy's life shrivels to its end at the retirement home in Florida, we see it reflected in her diminished garden, a row of miniature geraniums on her balcony. Her dreams are of dead shrubbery, of trash strewn in flower beds. At her funeral she has pansies, a flower she loves, but no one thinks to bring daisies, the flower for which she is named. "Ah, well," says the last unnamed speaker. "Ah, well" — an ambiguous comment, but one Daisy might have made herself about her life.

Stones and Flowers

weave, then, richly and beautifully through the novel, and we can see them both literally and figuratively forming/informing Daisy's whole life. If stone is her legacy from her father (and from the mother who died birthing her), flowers are the legacy from Clarentine (and from Clarentine's son Barker). If we can see the two struggling in her for meaning and coherence, what we can also see in the closing of the novel, in the larger world around her, is an effort to reconcile these two elements.

One of these attempts at reconciliation comes when Daisy, with her great-niece Victoria and Victoria's professor, Lewis, visit the Orkney Islands. Victoria and Lewis come to research the hard rock and fossil formations of the island. Fossil remains of small sea animals abound, but they are looking for something more fragile and elusive: early plant life.

> Such a discovery, they had told her, would be enormous in its implications — it excited them just thinking about such enormity — but at the same time the proof of discovery could be held lightly in the palm of a hand, a small rock chip imprinted with the outline of a leaf. Or a primitive flower. (301)

Do they find the flower in rock? Apparently not. The quest, perhaps, is what matters. And what Victoria really finds in the Orkneys has little to do with fossils: she finds love, passionate and immediate. When Victoria sees a plaque at their hotel that says

> *Happiness*
> *grows at our own*
> *fireside and is*
> *not to be picked*
> *in strangers'*
> *gardens*
>
> (302)

she laughs. Daisy, she thinks, might endorse this sentiment, but she will not. Perhaps she has learned from Daisy that seeking happiness only at one's own stone fireside makes for too limiting a life; for women of Victoria's generation, life means exploring the gardens of strangers.

Another interesting flower-stone conjunction occurs in a kind of epiphany to Cuyler as he lies dying in his back yard. For the last ten years he has been building a scale model (in stone of course) of the Great Pyramid; but, unlike his earlier Goodwill Tower, which was a triumph, it has become to him a disappointment, a folly, growing more out of plumb as it progresses. And suddenly he can see what he must do: call a halt to it, have it bulldozed, get a truck to haul away the stone chips.

> Of course there would be a terrible scar left in the middle of the back lawn, but come fall he could plant one of those fast-growing ornamental cherries in its place. A thing of beauty. (277)

He dies, of course, before this can be done. But, as with Victoria, perhaps it has been his quest that matters — a quest begun in stone, ending in flowers.

And then there is Daisy and her death, her quest finally ended. What does she find? In some of the most moving and beautiful writing of the novel, Shields describes her last thoughts:

> Stone is how she finally sees herself, her living cells replaced by the insentience of mineral deposition. It's easy enough to let it claim her. She lies, in her last dreams, flat on her back on a thick slab. . . . Only minimal energy is required to call up her stone self and hold it in place. (358, 359)

And is that her monument, then — stone, not flowers? Is she not "gone to flowers," as song lyrics and common euphemisms have it, but gone to stone? Her obituary notice says, "Flowers gratefully declined," but another immediately below, written by whom we do not know, says, "Flowers gratefully accepted."

A paradox, therefore, as is much of Daisy's life. Several times in the novel Daisy speaks of the need for witnesses of our lives. "We need to be observed in our postures of extravagance or shame, we need attention paid to us. Our own memory is entirely too cherishing," she says. "Other accounts are required, other perspectives" (36, 37). That is our role, then, as readers, to witness her life. Recent, rather disquieting, research in physics shows that matter acquires characteristics only by observation, that particles don't even have a location until the experimenter decides to look for them in a specific place: subjectivity, it seems, is the fundamental basis of everything. So it may be with Daisy: as we witness her life, it assumes significance in the context of our own. That is what makes this novel so compelling. At the end of *Schindler's List,* each survivor comes with a stone and places it lovingly on Schindler's grave. Christians put flowers on graves. Jews put stones. Stones or flowers: it doesn't matter. We give them our own meanings.

Note

All references from *The Stone Diaries* (Toronto: Random House of Canada, 1993).

DAVE WILLIAMSON

Seven Steps to Point-of-View Perfection

One of the pleasures of being a book reviewer is that occasionally you stumble upon an unheralded first novel that turns out to be superb. Too often, the situation is the reverse: you hear so much about a particular book that you can't wait to get your hands on it and, when you read it, it proves to be disappointing. I like to choose an unknown work for review from time to time, and it is worth making my way through the mediocre ones to find that gem.

I had heard nothing of *Small Ceremonies* before I came upon it in the office of the *Winnipeg Free Press*'s literary editor. It was 1976, the year of Marian Engel's *Bear* and Brian Moore's *The Doctor's Wife*. I had never heard of Carol Shields. She had published two books of poetry and a small critical book on Susanna Moodie, but none of these was known to me at the time.

What attracted me to *Small Ceremonies* was its jacket illustration: a painting of a stylish-looking woman taking a sip of tea. It was not her long patterned skirt or her red blouse or her partially covered face that drew my attention, but the subdued, understated quality of the picture — its feeling of calm good taste. This, with the title, seemed to promise quality, a caring for language, a keen awareness of the nuances. There would be no melodrama in this book, no sensationalism.

Back home, I opened the book and saw that the first chapter was called "September." I flipped the pages to find that each chapter covered a month and the novel ended with "May." Nine months in the life of a woman named Judith Gill. The opening paragraph: "Sunday night. And the thought strikes me that I ought to be happier than I am."

There was a time when a writer would be taking a big risk to present a narrative in the present tense. It was regarded as a device used in only the most serious of literary novels. One of the things that made popular fiction popular was the casting of the narrative in the familiar story-telling past. But John Updike's *Rabbit* novels changed that; by 1976, there had been two of them (*Rabbit, Run* and *Rabbit Redux*) and both were written in the present tense and both sold well. Shields gives her discordant opening lines an immediacy, the feeling that we're there, now, watching the story unfold before our eyes.

Judith is a biographer, married to an English professor named Martin Gill. They have two children, Meredith, sixteen, and Richard, twelve. We find the family back to normal in "a small city" in Canada after a year in England. While dealing so well with the brief but obsessive concerns of the young and the fading hopes of the middle-aged, Shields offers us some excellent insights into married life, living abroad, and the problems facing the biographer. Here is one of Judith's many musings on the latter topic:

> It was Leon Edel, who should know about the problems of biography if anyone does, who said that biography is the least exact of the sciences. So much of a man's life is lived inside his own head, that it is impossible to encompass a personality. There is never never enough material. Sometimes I read in the newspaper that some university or library has bought hundreds and hundreds of boxes of letters and papers connected with some famous deceased person, and I know every time that it's never going to be enough. It's hopeless, so why even try?
>
> That was the question I found myself asking during the year we spent in England. My two biographies, although they had been somewhat successful, had left me dissatisfied. In the end, the personalities had eluded me. The expression in the voice, the concern in the eyes, the unspoken anxieties; none of these things could be gleaned from library research, no matter

how patient and painstaking. Characters from the past, heroic as they may have been, lie coldly on the page. (SC 53)

This is Judith, coming to grips with her dissatisfaction as she pursues her third major subject, Susanna Moodie. But it could also be Carol Shields, convincing herself that, having written an MA thesis on Moodie (published as *Susanna Moodie: Voice and Vision*), she prefers to write fiction.

The nature of biography has continued to be a preoccupation for Shields; it is dealt with even more effectively and cleverly in her two most ambitious works, *Swann* and the Governor-General's-Award-winning *The Stone Diaries*. And "library research" has been a strong part of her fiction-writing method, helping to give her narratives their wonderful authenticity.

Of course, a certain commercially successful novelist named Arthur Hailey was lauded for his research for books such as *Hotel* and *Airport*. But his characters are two-dimensional, used simply to act out Hailey's exposition. Shields creates the characters first, gives them occupations, then turns to research to familiarize herself with those occupations. When you learn, in her novel *The Republic of Love*, that Fay is a folklorist, you can be sure that you are going to find out what a folklorist does and, in Shields's hands, you are probably going to find mermaids as fascinating as Fay does. We do, after all, spend a huge portion of our lives at work, and Carol Shields has mastered the art of making people's everyday occupations sound interesting.

In her book on Moodie, Shields's observations lead one to think that that particular piece of research had a profound effect on the fiction she would write. "Apart from physical details Mrs. Moodie is an observant and sensitive reporter on the nuances between people" (SM 22). That could certainly be said of Shields. "The looseness of the form permits her to shift the narration when she chooses: sometimes she tells the story herself, sometimes a friend relates it, and sometimes the story is overheard" (SM 22). This kind of "looseness" of form helps give *The Stone Diaries* its tremendous appeal. ". . . sometimes the dialogue is set up formally as in an actual play" (SM 22). See the last section of *Swann*.

A more subtle effect that the Moodie work seems to have had is in Carol Shields's *pairing* of things and people. She refers to Moodie's "pairing of characters to point up personality" (SM 25). "The device of pairing personalities is used," she says, "to compare male weakness with female strength" (SM 44). She speaks of a "dichotomy" in female character (SM 30), of "two sides of masculinity" (SM 39), of various juxtapositions and contrasts. It is likely more than serendipitous, then, that Shields's first published books were a pair of poetry collections (*Others* and *Intersect*) and that her first two works of fiction were a pair of related novels. *The Box Garden,* her second novel, features Charleen Forrest, divorced sister of Judith Gill. Judith and Martin play supporting roles in this one, which is also told in the present tense, and Charleen's personality is best appreciated when we see it in contrast to her sister's.

Shields's next two novels, *Happenstance* and *A Fairly Conventional Woman,* are such a distinct pairing that the English publisher brought them out in a single volume called *Happenstance.* (The two books were recently released in the same way in North America — back to back, with each starting at one of the covers and ending at the middle of the volume. I find this packaging clever but regrettable, since one of my favourite Shields novels has lost its separate identity and its appropriate pun of a title; under the main title, *Happenstance,* the sections are subtitled "The Husband's Story" and "The Wife's Story.")

The first of the two novels tells us, in the third person and past tense, about a few days in the life of Jack Bowman, a forty-three-year-old historian employed by the Great Lakes Institute in Chicago. His wife, Brenda, is away at the National Handicrafts Exhibition in Philadelphia, and Jack must cope with a mid-life crisis and his two children, twelve-year-old Laurie and fourteen-year-old Rob (duality again). *A Fairly Conventional Woman* tells us what forty-year-old Brenda does at the exhibition, where she is displaying her latest quilting creation. (As luck would have it, though the two novels in their original form were published by different publishers and set in different type, each was 216 pages long.)

Pairing — contrasting personalities — is the very essence of Carol Shields's longest work, *The Republic of Love.* Here, the separate lives of two characters, Fay McLeod and Tom Avery, are told in alternating chapters. Once again, the author's research pays off, taking us into the completely dissimilar worlds of the mermaid expert and the late-night talk show host. As in the Judith/Charleen books and the Jack/Brenda novels, the Fay/Tom stories can be appreciated separately but they gain something — almost another dimension — when one is contrasted with the other, when one is looked at in the light of the other.

This alternating of points of view can build in a certain freshness and a kind of suspense; the author picks strategic points at which to switch from one character's story to the other. I am reminded of that 1962 classic, *One Hundred Dollar Misunderstanding*, by Robert Gover, with its alternating of two distinct voices, those of the thoroughly middle-class white college boy, J.C., and the fourteen-year-old black prostitute, Kitten.

It might be stretching a point to suggest that *Swann* and *The Stone Diaries* make another pair. Both reconstruct the life of someone who has died (Mary Swann, Daisy Goodwill); both raise issues related to biography; both use multiple points of view as a narrative device. One could find many ways in which they differ, but again it can be a fascinating exercise to juxtapose them.

What these two novels have in common with all the rest, of course, is a facility, a nimbleness, with language. Since Shields's characters are common folk in the workaday world, she must rely on something other than outrageous traits or dramatic deeds to lead the reader on. Some writers invent clever plots. Shields does not. She grabs our attention through her use of words, through *style*. In this, she can be compared with, say, John Updike or Anita Brookner.

The Box Garden might be regarded as having her best plot; she does build suspense, taking Charleen on a trip with a man friend, having her son go missing, raising questions about the real identity of her pen-pal, Brother Adam. But no less a critic than Barbara Amiel attacked the "smaller-than-life" heroine, leading off her review with "Ordinary people will be the undoing of contemporary literature." She found the plot predictable and the style a substituting of "the commonplace perceptions of uninteresting people for a perception of the human condition itself" (*Maclean's*, September 5, 1977, 54-6).

Amiel may only be happy reading about (and associating with) captains of industry. To dismiss *The Box Garden* is to deny the shrewdness of a capsule observation like this one: ". . . don't high school girls in love with their math teachers furtively seek out their houses so they can cycle by, half-drowning in the thrill of proximity" (BG 157). And Amiel would likely not appreciate the witty self-depre-cation: "I had dressed for this evening with deliberate déclassé non-chalance, aware that Bea expects me to contribute a faint whiff of bohemia to her parties; I wore a badly-cut gypsy skirt and black satin peasant blouse, both bought at an Anglican rummage sale. Fortunately Bea's expectations conform to what I can afford" (BG 64).

The Jack Bowman story, *Happenstance*, has a great potential for melodrama. He's losing interest in the book he's writing, a history of Indian trade practices. He finds out a woman named Harriet Post is about to publish a book on the same subject — and she just happens to be his first lover. His best friend splits up with his wife and comes to Jack for solace. His next-door neighbour attempts suicide. His son Rob goes on a hunger strike.

A lesser novelist would have killed the neighbour, given the friend a nervous breakdown, sent Jack to Harriet's bed. But Shields blends incident with intelligent discourse on many topics, especially the nature of history. At times, there is too much discourse — a lengthy swatch of philosophizing when a lively scene would have been preferable. But then comes some gentle comedy, lifelike dialogue or a quick but vivid characterization: "Hap Lewis had hairy legs and a coarse slamming way with a deck of cards and a rollicking aptitude for opinion-letting — she made a hobby of vivacity" (H 58).

Jack is no mover or shaker. He is a man to whom things happen; he does not start anything. Given such a main protagonist, the author has to depend on style to carry us through. This she does and does well.

A Fairly Conventional Woman is presented in the same con-trolled, understated and appealing prose that make the first three novels so enjoyable. It has the research ingredient — all you ever wanted to know about quilting — but it has something extra: scene after scene that both capture and satirize the typical convention. The keynote address, the party atmosphere, the delegates who never go to any of the sessions, the delegates who attempt to twist a meeting to their own "hidden agendas," the mix-ups over rooms, the new and intense but brief friendships — they are all here. Protagonist Brenda meets a likable Canadian man named Barry and he becomes a tempting alternative to her happy but mundane life of earnest fidelity.

The delicate and assured way in which Carol Shields handles this brief relationship is a triumph, one of my favourite sequences in all of the novels. What Brenda thinks, what she and Barry say, and what they do are absolutely *right*. And at the perfect moment, there is the counterbalancing image: "She felt herself stretched with happiness. Something fortunate was happening to her. Ten-thirty. Time to meet Barry in the lobby. She sniffed; the room smelled of cigarette smoke. Verna's zippered case smiled up at her with grinning metal teeth" (FCW 179).

Shields's 1987 novel, *Swann,* was subtitled *A Mystery,* which caused it to be reviewed by *The Globe and Mail*'s crime columnist, Margaret Cannon (September 26, 1987, C9). She erroneously referred to it as a first novel, but she did like it.

Shields was not the first serious Canadian novelist to venture into the crime genre. A year earlier, Timothy Findley published *The Telling of Lies,* also subtitled *A Mystery.* Ironically, Shields won the Canadian crime writers' Arthur Ellis Award, while Findley won the American crime fiction award, the Edgar, when his book appeared in the United States two years later.

Whether *Swann* is truly a mystery is for purists to decide (the American publisher dropped the subtitle). Any fear that the book might be somehow trivialized or downgraded by such an appellation, though, was dashed by the Governor-General's Award jury, which put it on the fiction short list.

This novel is concerned with Mary Swann, a rhyming poet from Nadeau, Ontario. Trapped in an unhappy marriage and a dreary life of hard work on an unproductive farm, Swann eased her pain by writing poems. On the very day that a collection of her poems was accepted for publication, she was murdered by her husband. All this happened twenty years before the present of the novel.

The book is broken into five sections, the first four being told from the viewpoint of four different people who have helped "discover" the poet and her posthumously published single collection of work, *Swann's Songs*. They are Sarah Maloney, a feminist writer and teacher from Chicago; Morton Jimroy, a biographer and English professor from Winnipeg; Rose Hindmarch, the Nadeau librarian who pretends to have known Swann well; and Frederic Cruzzi, the elderly publisher who first saw Swann's potential. All four prepare for the Swann Symposium, which is the subject of the last section.

As a mock-serious treatment of a brief and ordinary life, Swann is a direct descendant of Steven Millhauser's marvellous 1972 novel, *Edwin Mullhouse: The Life and Death of an American Writer 1943-1954*. As a fine satire of academic conferences, it rates a spot on the same shelf as *Small World*, by David Lodge, and *Mustang Sally*, by Edward Allen. Here is Sarah Maloney trying to justify Swann's rhyming:

> . . . no modern academic knows what to do with her rhymes, her awful moon/June/September/remember. It gives them a headache, makes them snort through their noses. What can be done, they say, with this rustic milkmaid in her Victorian velours!
>
> I tend to get unruly and defensive when it comes to those bloody rhymes. Except for the worst clinkers (giver/liver) they seem to me no more obtrusive than a foot tapped to music or a bell ringing in the distance. Besides, the lines trot along too fast to allow weight or breath to adhere to their endings. There's a busy breedingness about them. "A Swannian urgency" was how I put it in my first article on Mary. (S 18-19)

This bit of discourse, coming so early in the novel, helps set the tone for what is a very funny book. As the reader tries to put together a true picture of poor Mary Swann from the pompous academic criticism and the conflicting memories and the fabrications, the characters of those preoccupied with her come clear. Some papers go missing, giving rise to the only real "mystery," but the demands of plot do not interfere with the fun.

The final section, in which all the characters come together at the symposium in Toronto, is presented as a film script. In the sections leading up to this, Shields uses a variety of narrative techniques — first person, third person, letters, even a tourist brochure — but the script format, while allowing the author to economize on description, does not seem appropriate for a gathering of academics. But, by then, the novel has picked up such a momentum that the form is only a minor hindrance. *Swann* is a satirical triumph.

The charm of *The Republic of Love* lies in Carol Shields's devotion to detail in showing us the day-to-day lives of her two protagonists. Fay, attractive to men but unable to sustain a relationship, has never been married but dreads living alone. She has had three serious love affairs. Her breakup with her latest live-in lover is presented with wry humour; some of her casual encounters with men are hilarious. We meet all her relatives and friends and co-workers and they jump to life with distinctive personalities even when their appearances in the book are only brief. One example: her sister's lover Jake, a "professional Communist . . . who has remained unmoved by the crumbling of the Eastern bloc" (RL 115).

Tom, like Fay, has been unlucky in love. His three ex-wives still live in Winnipeg and we are treated to his recollections of their mannerisms, their idiosyncrasies, their sexual foibles. We meet his friends and relatives, the technician for his radio show, the women he half-heartedly tries to woo. There are some lovely moments at a singles club, where the co-ordinator gives talks on such "key coping strategies" as "bonding, rebonding and disbonding" (RL 61).

Making Tom a late-night talk show host allows Shields to introduce any number of insomniac voices expressing opinions on any number of topics, thus delightfully satirizing some contemporary preoccupations while also making fun of the kinds of things you hear on the radio. People phone in to talk on such topics as what they think about in the shower — "I've got one of those map-of-the-world shower curtains . . . and I'm telling you, the stuff I've learned. South America. Africa, too" (RL 47) — and whether or not the city should spray for mosquitoes — "Hey, let's think of another way to blitz the little rascals. Let's bore them to death with Michael Jackson" (RL 102).

Underlying these details of two lives is a thoughtful scrutiny of love. Shields makes the point that "love is not, anywhere, taken seriously. It's not respected. It's the one thing in the world that everybody wants . . . but for some reason people are obliged to pretend that love is trifling and foolish. . . . They smirk or roll their eyes at the mention of love. . . . no adult with any sense talks about love's richness and transcendence, that it actually happens, that it's happening right now" (RL 248).

In the light of this plea to take love seriously, it is ironic that some readers found it difficult to accept that Tom and Fay could fall for each other. Perhaps the author has so successfully created two individuals, incorporating the product of her research so convincingly into two separate lives, that it is hard to imagine how the two could intersect. What is more, their coming together is decidedly anticlimactic. But isn't that the way it is with love?

Good as her first six novels are, they might be regarded as warmup exercises for her seventh, *The Stone Diaries*. After experimenting with various kinds of points of view, Shields harnesses them to be strategically employed in what, for now, is her crowning achievement. So confident is she in her craft that she throws out the basic rules and lets a first-person narrator report another person's thoughts whenever it suits her. That the reader will accept this is a tribute to Shields's powers of persuasion — what Creative Writing teachers don't tell you until graduation day is that anything is possible if you can convince the reader of it.

Just as *Swann: A Mystery* is not a mystery, *The Stone Diaries* is not a diary. The Canadian edition has the stubby bulk of a diary but a look at the table of contents tells you it is more like a classical biography: the ten chapters are Birth, Childhood, Marriage, Love, Motherhood, Work, Sorrow, Ease, Illness and Decline, and Death. The whimsy we have come to expect in a Shields novel extends beyond the text here: there is an accompanying chart of the family tree as well as a collection of family photos, some of which were borrowed from Shields's own albums.

The opening chapters give us the background of Daisy Goodwill, whose mother, Mercy (née Stone), died in 1905 giving birth to Daisy. Her father, Cuyler, is a stone mason who works the quarries around Tyndall, Manitoba. The story of his courting and marrying the absurdly overweight Mercy is both funny and touching. Daisy is raised by a neighbour, Clarentine Flett, who moves her to Winnipeg where they share a home with Clarentine's son, Barker, a botany professor. As usual, Shields refines her research into intriguing exposition, and the reader learns something new about the wildly diverse worlds of stonemasonry and botany.

Daisy eventually moves with her father to Bloomington, Indiana, where he becomes a pillar of the business community. Daisy marries an American but he is accidentally killed on their honeymoon. She carries on a correspondence with Barker and eventually they meet again and marry. The narrative moves gracefully through the twentieth century; this is the first Shields novel to follow a character from birth to death.

A plot summary does not do the book justice, of course. No Shields novel relies on plot for its pace, least of all this one. Yet you move through it as if it were a thriller. The secret is Shields's perfect blend of language and viewpoint — her ear for the nuances of speech working with her wonderful variety of speakers and forms. And what is said is coloured by whatever era we are in at the time. You keep turning the pages to see what character will be heard from next, and, on any topic, such as what ails Daisy, we are likely to have a dozen different perspectives. Take for instance these reactions to Daisy's planned trip to the Orkney Islands when she is a seventy-two-year-old widow living in Florida:

> "The Orkney Islands!" her daughter Joan said during their customary Sunday telephone call. "But I thought you said you were going to come up to Portland this year, you said you'd stay with the girls so Ross and I could get away for a couple of days, they were looking forward to seeing Grandma. It's always Grandma this and Grandma that, and now you're talking about the Orkneys."

"Have you looked this place up on a map?" her son Warren said. "Do you even know where the Orkney Islands are?" . . .

"Frankly," said Marian McHenry, who lives in the condo across the hall, "I'd rather see my own country first instead of traipsing around over there. Have you seen Washington DC? I mean, really seen it?"

"No one needs inoculations any more for Europe," Dr. Neely told her, "but I'm going to write you a prescription for travelers' trots. Also one for constipation. . . ."

"For God's sake, don't stay in hotels over there. Because, listen, they've got these darling little bed and breakfast thingies all over the place, they're much more homey, and you get a real feel for the day-to-day life as it's really lived kind-of-thing." . . .

"Two small suitcases are better than one big one, that's the smartest thing I've ever been told."

"When we were in Canterbury —"

"The time I went up to the Lake District —" . . .

"— a little plastic case with your own soap because —"

(SD 284-6)

As the advice multiplies, the advice-givers become anonymous, and we understand exactly what an elderly woman must go through when she tries to make a travel plan.

Minor as this example is in the grand scheme of the book, it does, in its way, show the extent to which Carol Shields's talent for narrative point of view has developed. We have gone from the single cultured voice of Judith Gill in *Small Ceremonies* to an infinite variety of voices and perspectives in *The Stone Diaries*, and each of those voices rings true. While much has been made of this latest novel's concern with the nature of biography, for me the essence of its success lies in the use of point of view — at once boundless and beautifully controlled.

It is easy to see how Carol Shields's art has strengthened and matured and expanded from novel to novel. Given her command of technique and her sense of humour, it is tempting to say that even this latest celebrated novel is only a stepping stone toward something bolder.

Note: All page references are to Canadian first editions. Key to abbreviations of titles follows:

BG: *The Box Garden.* Toronto: McGraw-Hill Ryerson, 1977.

FCW: *A Fairly Conventional Woman.* Toronto: Macmillan, 1982.

H: *Happenstance.* Toronto: McGraw-Hill Ryerson, 1980.

RL: *The Republic of Love.* Toronto: Random House, 1992.

S: *Swann: A Mystery.* Toronto: Stoddart, 1987.

SC: *Small Ceremonies.* Toronto: McGraw-Hill Ryerson, 1976. Cover illustration by Alan Daniel.

SD: *The Stone Diaries.* Toronto: Random House, 1993.

SM: *Susanna Moodie: Voice and Vision.* Ottawa: Borealis Press, 1976.

SIMONE VAUTHIER

"'They say miracles are past' but they are wrong"

No testimony is sufficient to establish a miracle, unless the testimony be of such a kind, that its falsehood would be more miraculous than the fact which it endeavours to establish. — David Hume, *On Miracles*

Fragmentation, affirms Québecois writer André Carpentier, is the generating principle of the short story. "L'écriture nouvellière renvoie à l'hétérogène, et à l'écriture fragmentaire. A chaque nouvelle corre-spond une forme, un défi. A chaque nouvelle aussi son interruption" (38). Carpentier looks at the genre from the angle of short story col-lections since, as he claims, "la nouvelle ne vient jamais seule" (37, 40) and he is thinking in terms of the relation of parts to the whole. In this light, the writing and reading of short stories is a paradoxical activity, which involves a constant negotiation between discontinuity and continuity: "entrer par un modèle de continuité dans la discontinuité, entrer aussi dans un régime de résistance à l'augmentation" (40). His remarks would therefore readily provide a key to Carol Shields's *Various Miracles*, all the more so because this is a collection of the kind Carpentier clearly favours, not a collection of interrelated stories but one of those heterogeneous "recueils délinquants qui refusent de feindre un ordre" (45). What is more arresting, however, is that a sin-gle text, the title story as it happens, is built on the same principle.

Exploding the narrative line, it plays on a discontinuity which generates an enigmatic continuity. The protocol of reading advocated in the Québecois critical essay[1] is already implemented in "Various Miracles," which, being also the introductory text, programs our reception of the book.[2] My purpose, however, is not to study the ways in which the single story affects the reading of the collection, which would be the topic for another essay. More modestly, I propose to take a look at "Various Miracles" and, in particular, to investigate some of the aspects of the interaction between the heterogeneous and the homogeneous in the text. Such examination makes contradictory demands. It is necessary to dwell on the fragmentariness of a constantly interrupted narrative if one is to accept the short story writer's need to begin afresh, "se répéter — puisqu'il le faut — mais autrement" (Carpentier 40) and it is equally necessary to process the fragmentariness into a dynamic continuity and the plurality into unity, through perception of the search for form and of the elaboration of the themes. The negotiation between continuity and discontinuity must be an ongoing activity and must be pursued throughout. In a critical essay, however, it is not easy to keep a balance between the two approaches and, especially as I draw to the close of this paper, I will inevitably be tempted to present something of a totalizing view.

Heterogeneity. "Various Miracles" does not flaunt its fragmentariness, for it is typographically continuous, showing the breaks of paragraphs but no blanks or stars or any typographical mark of pause or rupture. It does, however, consist of six discontinuous units introduced by a short sentence. (The arrangement reflects within the confines of the part the short story sequence that makes up the whole, *Various Miracles* consisting of an introductory text, "Various Miracles," followed by twenty heterogeneous texts.) One hesitates to call these units fragments, insofar as the word might suggest that they are shards broken off from some pre-existing larger narrative(s) which the reader-archaeologist might eventually piece together. One may more appropriately call them segments or sections, since, though they are autonomous, their succession forms a sequence. "Une succession d'irréconciliables fait un ordre," as Quignard remarks (55). In this case, the order does not depend on any narrative line, however interrupted. There is no causal link between the six items which involve unconnected "actors," placed in wide-spread settings, Palo Alto, a Moroccan village, Exeter, Chicago, Tournus, Toronto, etc. Furthermore each segment begins afresh, and, with one exception, finds its own form, as though each belonged to a different sub-genre, was related to different intertexts.

Thus the first item is close to the journalistic news in brief, what the French call *fait divers,* and not simply because it is very short: "On the morning of January 3, seven women stood in line at a lingerie sale in Palo Alto, California, and by chance each of these women bore the Christian name Emily" (13).[3] Nothing more, nothing less. The unit reports a curious fact which provokes surprise ("il n'y a pas de fait divers sans *étonnement,*" Barthes 191); according to a familiar structure,[4] it is built on an antithetic juxtaposition, between the common — the banal event of women standing in line for a sale — and the uncommon — the coincidence of their all bearing a name which, if not rare, is at least less usual than, say, Mary. It also implies a second contrast between a core action — the women queue for a purpose — and an irrelevant detail — their name has nothing to do with the described action and the implied transaction. This text which involves no transformation and is limited to so few facts seems to resist not only expansion but narrativity. The second segment is fashioned in the same way and also relies on co-occurence, (four strangers on the number 10 bus in Cincinnati are reading a paperback copy of *Smiley's People*). Such repetition of a model creates the expectation of a series of similar incidents that is immediately frustrated, the departure of the third section from the anticipated model being then all the more conspicuous.

With the third segment, there is a complete change of scenery, atmosphere, and thematics; telling the story of a dream or rather two dreams, it jolts the reader into the sub-genre of the Eastern tale, complete with lemon tree and oil lamp, prose poetry and an implicit lesson on the human heart, while raising faint echoes of familiar myths, even if reversed, like that of Psyche. In a Moroccan mountain village a lathe operator dreams that a lemon falling into his open mouth causes him to choke and die. Awakening, he is "overjoyed at being still alive" and embraces his wife. But while "snoring" at his side she has been happily dreaming that a lemon tree has taken root in her stomach. "Leaves, blossoms and finally fruit fluttered in her every vein until she began to tremble in her sleep with happiness and intoxication" (13). Lighting an oil lamp, her husband watches her face, feeling "ignorant" of the "spring that nourished her life." "What he saw was a mask of happiness so intense it made him fear for his life" (ibid.). End of story. The structure of the tale is dual like that of the *fait divers* but it is definitely narrative, since, in spite of its brevity, several transformations occur. It is also, needless to say, much more complex in all respects. Although beginning and ending on a fear of death, the tale has a circular pattern, yet insofar as it unites and separates two polarities — the husband's, the wife's dreams — it operates a sort of exchange between the oneiric and the real, the known and the unknown, and opens out on a kind of suspensive irony.[5]

The fourth segment breaks away from the poetic world of the third and seems at first to make a return to the *fait divers* mode. Like the first two units, it reports an unusual event: English schoolgirls find a dead parrot in their playing field at Exeter. But the treatment of the *donnée* is altogether different. In the first place, the reporting is no longer congruent with the news-in-brief. The narrator no longer proceeds by condensation of the facts but by expansion. Details pile up. The parrot is described with its colours, defined by the science mistress as *Amazona ochrocephala,* and later given a history and a name; its owners, "weeping openly" over their loss (14), are also named, etc. In the second place, the really striking element of the segment is that the parrot's fate is duplicated: in Chicago, Miguel's "twin brother," Pete or Pietro, who belongs to an Italian violinist (whose career, though irrelevant to the bird's life, is briefly reported), falls sick and while Francesca looks for a vet in the Yellow Pages, dies in his cage after pronouncing what Francesca "believed were the words 'Ça ne fait rien'" (14). Thus the two-term structure inherent in the *fait divers* that is exemplified here first in the antitheses, death versus playfield, exoticism versus everydayness, etc., is itself doubled and expressed in very similar oppositions: death versus the banality of condensed milk and telephone books, and more strikingly in the opposition between the human being's practical concern and the non-human being's stoical philosophy, verbally expressed and in a foreign tongue, to boot. (The parrot's "Ça ne fait rien" really does something to the reader and is likely to linger disturbingly in his/her mind.) Each part taken alone would stand on its own because of this split structure. But the major element of surprise of the whole unit lies in the fact that the two parrots die on the same day — a relation of coincidence that epitomizes the nature of the *fait divers*. "Le fait divers ne commence que là où l'information se dédouble et comporte par là-même la certitude d'un rapport" (Barthes 190). Yet, unlike the first three units, the basic codes of which were immediately ascertainable, the fourth segment is a mixture of codes, which gives it its distinctive character.

The fifth segment — the longest of all — shifts gears again; and the reader may well identify it as a short story of the domestic kind which Carol Shields practises with such delicate skill. An ordinary couple in Billings, Montana — emblematic of American small towns — is wakened by a loud noise. "My God, we're being burgled," (14) Marjorie, the wife says. On the following morning, they discover that "their favourite little watercolor" has fallen off the living-room wall and bounced onto the cast-iron radiator. In terms of the *donnée*, one is again close to the *fait divers*. A domestic noise taken for a sound of burglary is almost a stereotype of the genre and, as it does here, the model rests on the deviation of a normal, unimportant cause into a frightening one; but such an incident becomes news only when the consequences of the association of the noise with the wrong cause are dramatic, which, in truth, happens often enough as in a recent news story of a father shooting his teenage daughter. Here we have, as it were, a deflating parody of that kind of story. And the narrator proceeds to show Carl patching the plaster and installing a new hook while remembering "how the picture had come into his possession" (15). So that we come to understand the Hallsburys' "deep sentimental attachment" to a picture "they no longer believe to be the work of a skilled artist" (15) and which indeed has been described as an attractive clichéd view of trees, winding road, and "the usual arched bridge" (14). What they know of the story of the watercolor is part of its charm for them — as is the secret they share about it. For Carl and Marjorie, who believe married couples should have no secrets, are the only ones who know it to be "stolen goods." Carl, liking the picture, took it from the St. Brieuc house in which he was quartered in 1944, and popped it into his knapsack, where it fitted with a snugness that seemed to "condone his theft" (15). "He was not a natural thief," explains the narrator, "but already he knew that life was mainly a matter of improvisation. Other returning soldiers brought home German helmets, strings of cartridge shells and flags of various sorts, but the little painting was Carl's only souvenir" (15). Seeing his chance, Carl has seized it and the unusualness of the theft, in the circumstances, lies in the nature of the thing appropriated, which is neither a weapon nor a valuable object. Ironically, the peaceful little watercolor, the "pale rural scene" (14), has turned into a cherished souvenir of a bloody war. By itself, the segment makes an interesting vignette, which like the preceding ones, seems to be "immanent" in Barthes's sense of the word and to provide all the information needed about the circumstances, the causes, the past (Barthes 189).

But here the narrator, who has so far devoted one paragraph to each item, turns a trick upon the reader. The new paragraph the reader now begins does not introduce a new "story," as might have been expected, but supplies very different information about the picture. "It was, in fact, painted by a twelve-year-old boy named Pierre Renaud who until 1943 had lived in the St. Brieuc house" (15). Having a gift for imitation, he had copied a postcard of a bridge, which his father had sent him from Burgundy, in an act, as he later realized, of "pathetic homage, almost a way of petitioning his father's love" (15). Then the reader is brought up to date with later developments in Pierre's life, until he is shown standing "on a small stone bridge not far from Tournus" (15) with Jean-Louis, "his companion of many years." "'This is it,' he announced excitedly, spreading his arms, like a boy, and not at all feeling sure of what he meant" (15-16). His companion teases him, aware of Pierre's "capacity for nostalgia" and the fact that he has never been in the place before. "'That's true,' Pierre said, 'you are right. But I feel, *here*,' — he pointed to his heart — 'that I've stood here before'" (16). In another life, Jean-Louis suggests. "No, no, no" and then, "well perhaps." "After that the two of them stood on the bridge for some minutes, regarding the water and thinking their separate thoughts" (16). Again everything necessary has been told us and we are free to make our interpretation of the anecdote, which could almost work on its own except for the transition that links it to the Billings picture: "It was in fact painted. . . ." The transition between the two incidents is a clue to their unity; what happens in Billings is indeed curious not in itself but because of what happens in Tournus on the same day, just as what happens in Tournus is more enigmatic because of what happens in Billings. Though, in the last analysis, neither incident is complete in itself, the completion they achieve is hardly one we could have anticipated. Retrospectively, everything seems to turn on the picture of the bridge — even if Pierre does not remember it — as if it had a responsibility in the coincidence. "L'objet s'abrite derrière son inertie de chose," claims Barthes — though here it breaks the law of inertia by leaving the wall, "bounc[ing]" and "ricochet[ing]" — "mais c'est en réalité pour mieux émettre une force causale, dont on ne sait bien si elle lui vient de lui-même ou d'ailleurs" (193). The mystery remains entire.

The last segment operates a new drastic shift. Veering towards "magic realism" and metafiction, it is from the first slyly placed, in the middle of a fairly long sentence, under the patronage of the South Americans, who have had so much influence on Canadian authors. The immediately-named heroine is "Camilla LaPorta, a Cuban-born writer now a Canadian citizen," living in Toronto (16-17).[6] And her story, though told in a definitely Shieldsian voice, contains parodic echoes of Borges and Cortázar. Camilla is bringing the manuscript of a novel to her publisher, who had criticized an earlier version for "rely[ing] too heavily on the artifice of coincidence" (16). She has carefully revised her work, "plucking apart the faulty tissue that joined one episode to another, and then, delicately, with the pains of a neurosurgeon, making new connections. The novel now rested on its own complex microcircuitry. Wherever fate, chance or happenstance had ruled, there now was logic, causality and science" (16). But unfortunately, as she waits on the corner of College and Spadina — which any reader a little familiar with Toronto will visualize — a gust of wind tears the manuscript from her hands. "In seconds the typed yellow sheets were tossed across the busy intersection" (ibid.). Passersby help her, "stopping and chasing the blowing papers" from all over. When she presents herself with her untidy manuscript, the publisher teases her: "Good God Almighty, don't tell me, Camilla, that you of all people have become a postmodernist and no longer believe in the logic of page numbers" (17). When they have put the manuscript back in order, it turns out that "astonishingly, only one page was missing. But it was a page Camilla insisted was pivotal, a keystone page, the page that explained everything else" (17). While she thinks that she will have to reconstruct it, the publisher, in a reversal of his former role, disagrees. "I truly believe, Camilla, that your novel stands up without the missing page. Sometimes it's better to let things be strange and represent nothing but themselves" (ibid.). Meanwhile the missing page is not lost at all: it has blown into the open doorway of a grocery "where a young woman in a red coat was buying a kilo of zucchini. She was beautiful though not in a conventional way" (ibid.). An actress out of work, she wants to make a batch of zucchini-oatmeal muffins to cheer herself up. Since she is "the kind of young woman who reads everything, South American novels, Russian folk tales, Persian poetry, the advertisements on the subway," etc. she very naturally picks up the yellow sheet and begins to read: "She read: *A woman in a red coat is standing in a grocery store buying a kilo of zucchini. She is beautiful, though not in a conventional way, and it happens that she is an actress who — .*" The dash on which the story ends suspended enhances the mirror effect[7] as it implies there is no need further to reproduce what we already know.[8] What with this triple *mise en abyme* of the narrated matter, the narrating act[9] and the narrative code, its cast of characters — writer, "actor" and reader — and its blurring of the boundary between reality and fiction, the story embodies much of the problematics of stories by Borges and Cortázar.[10] The diegetic woman in red has, ostentatiously, a double in Camilla's hypodiegetic woman.[11] Less obviously Camilla herself is a mirror reflection of her fictional character for whom "print is [the] way of entering and escaping the world" (16) and, of course she is also a double of the extradiegetic narrator since the story she writes coincides with the latter's story. And where does that leave the reader, entering the world and escaping it through the print of "Various Miracles"? As Borges put it in a famous essay, "Partial Magic in *The Quixote*": "Why does it disturb us that Don Quixote be a reader of *The Quixote* and Hamlet a spectator of *Hamlet*? I believe I have found the reason: these inversions suggest that if the characters of a fictional work can be readers or spectators, we, its readers or spectators, can be fictitious" (quoted in Waugh, 127). In Shields's hall of mirrors the dizziness itself is parodically multiplied. A reflexion on the function of the imagination and the act of writing/reading, "Various Miracles" more precisely reflects Carol Shields's own practice which often depends on coincidence and rests on a "complex microcircuitry" that remains for the reader to trace. In this case, the major thematic linkage is made pretty evident while other circuits require a more attentive reading. For instance, in each unit one may observe a common linguistic feature, the dissemination in the place names and proper names of the first two letters of the word "miracle": the letter m (in Emily, Smiley, Moroccan village, Miguel, Marseilles, Montana, Camilla) and i (Emily, California, Smiley, Cincinnati, Miguel, Pietro, Billings, St Brieuc, Pierre, Jean-Louis, Camilla, Spadina).[12] But I will be concerned in this paper not with such microcircuitry but rather with the macro-connections.[13]

The homogeneity of heterogeneity. The narrator's introductory statement to the narrative provides a frame in which all the random stories become related: "Several of the miracles that occurred this year have been unrecorded" (13). In fact, although the narrator is self-effacing (but revealed as a hidden I-narrator through the deictics "this") the control which she displays through her liminal assertion is maintained throughout and is a factor of homogeneity. She imposes her choice of a time scheme, "this year," whereas one may well suppose that miracles have gone unrecorded in other years; and she uses a temporal pattern to structure what she reports. All "miracles" are related in chronological order and all segments begin with a date from "On January 3" to "On October 31," an anaphora which tends to stress the formation of the unconnected segments into a series. (To break the systematic pattern, the succession ends when the year is almost over but not quite, thus suggesting that the series may be incomplete.) This use of temporality replaces at once narrative and narrational causality.

In spite of the shift in codes and moods between the items, the posture of the narrator remains similar. Quietly self-confident, she speaks from the first from a position of superior knowledge where she can be aware of "unrecorded" miracles. She prudently refrains from giving their number and contents herself with stating that there are "several." Nor does she pretend to record all of those; for her two first items begin with the mention "Example," which presupposes that there were others to choose from. And insofar as she juxtaposes them without transition, she suggests that she is simply providing a list. Throughout her narration, the narrator, who is also the major focalizer, is close to being what one used to call an omniscient narrator. For her selection of examples, she is free to roam through the world (mostly, but not only, Western) and report what occurred at the same time in very different places, even on different continents. She is familiar with the characters' pasts (Carl is "Purdue, 1939," Pierre Renaud "grew up to be not an artist but a partner in the family leather-goods business" [15]),[14] as well as with their innermost thoughts and feelings. She is aware of things no one else could be aware of. Being in possession of all the facts required, she even can, on occasion, correct the characters' misapprehensions: she tells that Miguel, "one of a pair of birds sold in an open market in Marseilles in the spring of 1958," is not twenty-two years old, as his owners believe, but twenty-five. She not only knows who painted the little watercolor but comments on the young artist's talent: "It was said that as a child he had a gift for painting and drawing; in fact, he had a gift merely for imitation" (15). The phrase "in fact" is one which recurs, signalling the precisions supplied by the knowledgeable narrator and the care with which she wants to record the "miracles." Viewing things from a distance, she never participates in what she narrates but reports events with a serene detachment that somehow combines neutrality with sympathy. Her manner of recording is so straightforward that the doubt that may seize the reader faced with her flat introduction and her first two humdrum examples is eventually displaced. In other words, one may be tempted to think at first that the narrator is being ironic, actually holding these two cases of miracles up to ridicule and therefore putting all others into question. But it seems to me that the irony is much more diffuse, or rather lies elsewhere. It is not to be found in the distance between the narrator and the narrated or in her ensuing relation to the narratee, but rather in the benign underhand-edness of the narrative and in the dialectic relation between the author's text and the reader, that is to say, in the double (or rather multi-layered) response we give to the story.

Of course a major device of continuity is the title, strengthened by the narrator's announcement that the segments all record mira-cles, both of which require us to look for a thematic linkage between the discontinuous. Though the units do not cohere into a unified nar-rative syntagm, the disparate anecdotes and stories form a paradigm. Indeed each case receives a supplement of credence from being included in the accumulation of examples. Again, however, the para-digm is not exactly what the reader may have anticipated since it excludes religious miracles or "the miracles of science." Nor do the units show "various miracles," in the sense of presenting different types of the category, since they all are concerned with coincidence: "the occurence of events simultaneously or consecutively in a striking manner but without any causal connection between them" (*Chambers English Dictionary*). Within its limits, to return for a moment to formal considerations, the paradigm gathers "various" examples of such occurrences. Moreover it is carefully constructed insofar as the suc-cession of the segments is not as arbitrary as may at first seem; for the series evinces a strong **incremental pattern.** Nor can the pattern be imputed to the narrator who is reporting events in the world as she knows it in the random order of chronology. Yet, curiously — is that another happy coincidence? the text's ineluctable self-transforma-tion? the hidden scriptor's decision? — the segments increase in length, as the short story unfolds, with the first section being three lines long and the last fifty-one;[15] and correspondingly they increase in complexity. It is as though, after resisting augmentation in the first two items in order to be as non-narrative as is possible in this kind of text, which is after all included in a book of fiction, the following segments could only renew themselves by yielding to expansion. The co-occurrence immediately stated in the first two examples is more and more narratively delayed in the following ones. The "actors" who are at first merely defined by their relation to the basic coincidence acquire more and more individual features, apart from their being involved in the "miracle," and become "characters" in the last two stories. The pivotal event itself exemplifies variations of coincidence that are more and more complex. In the first segments, people in the same place do the same thing (standing in line, reading on the bus) at the same time, and have one thing in common (their name, their book). In the third, a couple in the same bed have the same dream but it is valued dysphorically by the husband and euphorically by the wife and moreover the inverted co-occurence has consequences for the husband, which leaves the tale open. In segment four, a new element is introduced — distance in space; the coincidence of the parrots' dying at the same time is enhanced by the fact that they have been separated and lived in different places. In segment five, this element of distance is amplified, being both spatial and experiential: a heterosexual couple and a homosexual one, who have no knowledge of one another, have, on the same day, experiences that are entirely different but which in both cases involve the representation, whether they consciously recollect it or emotionally apprehend it, of the same locus. Besides, this major coincidence — a simultaneous occurrence — is made possible by the minor coincidence — a consecutive one — of adult Pierre's finding in "real" life the place whose postcard photograph meant a lot to him as a child, a place which he has never actually seen but knows in "his heart," at once recognizing the bridge ("this is it") and not recognizing it as the bridge on the postcard that he painted from. In the last section, coincidence rules in yet more compounded forms and at different levels: in the action, the missing fragment lands at the feet of the very person it describes, so that, in the universe of the story, the reading subject and the written one coincide, as it were, in both place and time. Whether the page that blows away is the key page of Camilla's novel, as she believes, or not, as the publisher demonstrates, it does turn out to be the keystone page where the whole segment is concerned; while the publisher inside the fictional world criticizes "the artifice of coincidence," the very artifice generates the story "Various Miracles" in the world out there. Even the doublings and dual structures entailed in coincidences tend to be more and more elaborate. In the *fait divers*, duality is intrinsic, as we have seen, but undeployed as such. In the Moroccan tale, two strands are woven into a story of great unity and concision whereas in the case of the parrots, the two strands are narratively split although we know them to be part of the same story. In the picture section, the two substories acquire more autonomy and interestingly, the one piece of information which renders the whole a coincidence to be marvelled at is tucked away in an incidental clause, "August 26 it was," in the middle of a fairly long sentence. In the last section the duplication of reality by fiction, which gives its point to the narrative, is delayed to the very end but meanwhile relayed by all sorts of mirrorings: internal as when some of the "*yellow* typed sheets" come to lie "on a heap of soaked *yellow leaves*" and one bears "the *black* herringbbone of tire *prints*" (16, italics mine) and external as when happenstance eventually determines the final shape of Camilla's book. Evidencing further the continuity within discontinuity, the series starts with the most banal, though remarkable, of coincidences and works its way towards the most fantastic.

Thus while each segment stands alone, the succession of segments strings them, in the reading act, into a meaningful continuum. "L'ordre de la succession bâtit une architecture qui aussitôt subjugue" says Quignard (25) of any sequence of fragments. Here the architecture is strengthened — or should I say burdened? — by the semantic anticipations created by both title and opening. We expect the contrasting unity of the miraculous. In fact, one's expectations are at once answered, deflated, and questioned.

The word "miracle," of course, has several meanings: 1) an effect or extraordinary event in the physical world that surpasses all known human or natural powers and is ascribed to a supernatural cause; 2) such an effect or event manifesting or considered as a work of God; 3) a wonder: a marvel; 4) a wonderful or surprising example of some quality (*Random House Dictionary*). The plural "Various Miracles," which tends to make the thing commonplace, might seem to indicate that the theological kind of miracle is not intended, but on the other hand, the statement that the miracles have been "unrecorded" carries a religious connotation since, for instance, the Lourdes miracles have to be officially recorded as a first step towards certification. Hesitating about the meaning to be assigned to the word, we look to the examples to enlighten us as to the narrator's conception of the thing. But the story is constructed in such a way as to keep us revising what is meant by "miracle" and constructing theories about miracles as such.

The heterogeneity of the homogeneous. As we come to the first two cases, we may decide that the narrator is using the word to mean simply some strange chance happenings. The occurrences she records are certainly striking but not truly miraculous. In fact, there is something banal in their extraordinariness, reminiscent of many such curious coincidences the reader may have observed in life; hence the suspicion that the narrator may be being ironic. At any rate, after two examples are offered, one comes to a provisional inference, which may be something of a letdown: so what she means by miracles is simply some collision of everyday events. Nevertheless, the fictional examples heighten the sense of disorientation which such happenings provoke in real life, and they perturb the reader's conception of causality.

The Moroccan tale, however, upsets one's easy conclusions and restores one's faith in the narrator's sense of the miracle as something surreal. The doubleness of the dream, the woman's at-oneness with the world of tree and fruit break away from the logic of rationality yet spring from the quotidian. The miraculous, however, affords no easy escape from the complexity of marital relationships, and the husband's "glimpse of chaos"[16] ironically counterbalances the wife's radiant moment. Might this be a mythic story, telling of the origins of the so-called war between men and women? In any case, the man's negative response cannot make us discount either the dream lemon tree or the woman's happiness. So the irony is not absolute and the miracle, though qualified, is not denied.

In contrast, the parrots' "miracle" is again restricted to simultaneous coincidence. The narration postpones, and for a time masks, the parallel between the two deaths by developing the differences between Miguel's and Pete's stories so that all their travelling about increases the final coincidence of their dying on the same day and at what I think, perhaps mistakenly, is an early age. (Perhaps *Amazona ochrocephala* are shorter lived than most parrots?) Yet the narration at once suggests an explanation for, and enhances the strangeness of, their concomitant deaths by implicitly relying on the widespread belief that there is a particular empathy between twins who often do not survive one another. Thus the explanation attenuates the miracle only to bring in other mysteries — the mystery of twinship, which has long exercised human imagination, the mystery of twin symbolism. Note, however, that it is made possible by the humorous assimilation of birds and humans: the narrator calls Pietro Miguel's "twin brother." Conversely, in mythology, twins "appear fairly often in the guise of animals," and singularly birds, says Cirlot (356) who sees in "the myth of oviparous human birth a parallel manifestation of this" (ibid.). In this case it is the narrator's anthropomorphization of the two parrots, together with Peter's fatalistic and timely pronouncement in French, which lifts the story out of the realistic mode of the first two examples and brings us closer to a mundane miraculousness. Faint as these resonances are, they are of course all the more easily perceived because they follow the almost mythic Moroccan tale. This is part of the "microcircuitry" of the text since the contiguity of discontinuous sections sets up interactions between them.

In turn, while built on a similar pattern, the watercolor story depends on a coincidence that is at once more mind-boggling yet is, in fact, of the same order. One might read the story as an illustration of the "butterfly effect": a butterfly flutters in Paris and there is a hurricane in Tokyo, a picture falls in Billings, Montana, and in Tournus, France, a Frenchman has a singular experience of true/untrue déjà vu. But the butterfly effect, at least in the Western common or garden version now current in the media, seems to rest on causality, albeit unpredictable — causality regarded as, say, a sequence of spreading vibrations. In Shields, the incident reminds one rather of Jungian **synchronicity**, which does away with ordinary causality:

The causal point of view tells a dramatic story about how D
came into existence: it took its origin from C, which existed
before D, and C in turn had a father, B, etc. The synchronistic
view on the other hand tries to produce an equally meaningful
picture of coincidence. How does it happen that A', B', C', D', etc.
appear all in the same moment and in the same place? It happens in the first place because the physical events A' and B' are
of the same quality as the psychic events C' and D', and further
because all are exponents of one and the same momentary situation. The situation is assumed to represent a legible or
understandable picture. (Jung's Foreword to the *I-Ching*, quoted in Smyth, 1986, 7).

There is no need here to go further into, or indeed accept, the basis of
Jung's theory which posits the Archetypes or its applications regarding the Unconscious. Like electricity, synchronicity, understood as
"meaningful coincidences, significantly related patterns of chance"
(Chetwyn) works even if you cannot explain it scientifically. In this
episode of "Various Miracles," the synchronistic view presents us with
physical events A' and B' in Montana (the falling and rehanging of the
watercolor) which are of the same quality as the psychic events C' and
D' in France (the recognition and the failure to pinpoint its source);
and it produces a "legible and understandable picture" of a situation
which involves . . . a fictional picture. Only since Western ideology has
biased us towards the causal point of view must the absence of
causality appear as miraculous inasmuch as miracles surpass the natural laws of cause and effect. Nor is "the picture" produced as legible
as all that. What do these meaningful coincidences mean exactly —
beyond the fact that they are meaningful? In short, the fifth section
amplifies the questions implicit in all the others. Surely all these curious happenings are signs, but of what? In its exemplarity the episode
also shows that synchronicity frees storytelling from the usual logic of
narrative but only to a limited extent. If one wants to go beyond the
terse statements of related patterns of chance, as exemplified in the
first two sections, one must resort to causality. Here the synchronistic
relation A' B' C' D' . . . is in fact established between two accounts in

which, independently, a causal relation A B C D . . . holds sway. Either ostensibly in the Billings part (because the hook has worked off the wall, the watercolor falls down; because it has fallen, Carl installs a new hook; while and because (*post hoc ergo propter hoc*) he is doing the repair, he remembers how he acquired the picture). Or more discreetly in the Tournus part (because he is "in pursuit of sunshine and good wine") Breton Pierre goes south for his holidays; because of that pursuit, he finds himself on a road in Burgundy, where he happens to see the bridge, which causes him not to reminisce like Carl but to have a subliminal memory of the postcard he "recopi(ed) in watercolors" (15). Thus to deal with the *coincidence* of events, the narrator must also describe the *sequence* of events. And for the reader, to describe the *coincidence* of events is to deal with their *sequence*.

As for the sixth section, it is a pyrotechnics of synchronicity and miraculousness which ends on the crowning piece of a character's reading about herself. But if chance rules even more dazzlingly than in the other sections, conversely synchronicity and causality are more closely interrelated. For all the chance events may be regarded as caused by the initial fortuitous blast of wind at the corner of College and Spadina. The actress's action is doubly determined, first by the happenstance of the page's blowing into the store, and then by the constant of the woman's reading habits. If you are an omnivorous reader, a glutton even for "the instructions and precautions on fire extinguishers" (17), you are certainly not going to let a typed stray sheet flutter by unread. Moreover, the scattering of the manuscript causally generates two series of chance events — at the publisher's and at the grocer's — which are then reconnected by a coincidence of another kind. In both cases, page 46[17] plays a prominent role but its value undergoes singular transformations. The absence of the lost page does not affect the publisher (who seems to have been converted to a more synchronistic critical stance[18]) and, what's more, chance fragmentation shapes the manuscript into a better novel. Conversely, the presence of the wind-blown sheet at the actress's feet provides her with fascinating reading matter and the fragment comes to stand for her whole life story — even though the narrator cuts it short. Perhaps because of the intricacy of the causal and the acausal, in this synchronistic "picture" of the situation, the relatedness of patterns of chance is displayed more clearly than in the preceding sections, thus tantalizing the reader with multiple possibilities of meaning over and beyond the intrinsic significance of synchronicity.

In particular, self-reflexiveness[19] and synchronicity interact. Metafictional elements rest on happenstance events. After Camilla has worked at restoring "logic and causality," and making "new connexions," the final version ultimately depends on *accident* and *discontinuity*. The publisher who was all for traditional narrative is suddenly convinced by chance that "Sometimes it's better to let things be strange and to represent nothing but themselves" (17). Such are the little ironies of the writing (and publishing) life. But conversely it is the whole context of writing, including the relation of continuity and discontinuity in narrative, which makes the accidental loss of a page "a meaningful chance." The "artifice of coincidence," which the publisher first deplored, is no mere narrative device since it is in keeping with the conditions of experience; for "fate, chance, or happenstance rule" in the world described in this short story, as they do in much of Carol Shields's fiction. Implicitly, the reliance on causation becomes as much of an artifice.

That the (fictional) fictive should coincide with the (fictional) real story is a (fictional) true miracle, for the chances of it happening are astronomical. Furthermore the repetition of the actress's description may lead to disquieting hypotheses. A character of Borges argues that as the number of experiences available to human beings is limited, "basta una sola repeticion para demostrar que el tiempo es un falacia" (*Ficciones* 152). Synchronicity can take us very far. Thus the last section is a fitting coda. It affords a climactic closure to the discontinuous series and it ensures the thematic continuity of the whole, while flaunting its dissonance in the treatment of the theme. The dissonance is such that after cavilling at occurrences that did not seem miraculous enough, suddenly I — or dare I say *we*? — balk at this, which, after all, is a marvellous realization of the realist's dream to capture reality, an illustration of *mimesis* as the ultimate, though in normal, non-miraculous circumstances inaccessible, goal of fiction. But self-reflexiveness, so much more important in the last section, creates interferences, raising the reader's consciousness. The metafictional comment, brief as it is, on what Camilla's fiction ought or ought not be, the framebreak within the narrative (the story within the story) etc., disturb the readers' sense of ontological levels and even threaten our sense of our own status, hence leading to an unsettling of what we conceive to be reality, as I have already suggested. This, in fact, might contribute to and not detract from the miraculous effect. But what is also unsettled is our response to the story itself: because of "the paradoxical relationship of 'framed' and 'unframed'" (Waugh 31), these devices are a strong reminder that the overall story is itself a frame, a structure of illusion. This frame, it must be noted, has shaped our response all along. For, although its fragmentariness, the brevity of the earlier segments and conversely the digressiveness in the later sections hinder the reader from making full use of familiar codes of reading (and why not, of the Barthesian codes of character, action, enigma?), nevertheless the very frame creates at least a sense of *processive expectations.*

The heterogeneity of homogeneity: irony. With awareness of illusion comes distance. In fact, the structure functions paradoxically. On the one hand, the narrative constructs the illusion that the narrator is dealing with real events that, incredible as they may appear, deserve the credibility which must be granted miracles. Making the miraculous the theme of the piece naturalizes, as it were, the suspension of disbelief, since one expects commonsense assumptions about the world to be overthrown. On the other hand, the narration shatters that very illusion by various strategies: its use of an omniscient narrator,[20] its juxtaposition of different codes (the Moroccan tale appears almost as a collage), its balancing the parrot story on the use of the phrase "twin brothers," the flagrant metafictionality of the last section — the intertextual echoes — all these draw attention to the linguistic construction of the universe described, to the story not as a mirror held to the world but as a verbal replacement of the world. The reader, who considers herself a detached observer, has been compelled by such contradictory manoeuvres to take different posts of observation, which compromises her freedom, and in the end she finds herself doubly the *complicit* victim of the text's irony.

When we discuss the insufficient miraculousness of some incidents, we are yielding to the mimetic illusion, taking the story at face value. But then the whole story mocks our desire for spectacular miracles by displaying in segment after segment the undramatic smallness of everyday synchronicities. On the other hand, when we are at last granted a more impressive miracle in the Camilla episode, however much we enjoy the narrational tricks, we nevertheless tend to dismiss it as a *fantasy* of continuity through disorder, on the grounds that it is all a fabrication in a game of words. But again this is a misprision; on this occasion we have been misled by the ludic illusion into forgetting that this is a "true lie," a game whose high stakes in the real must not be disregarded.

Some of the text's gentle irony is also directed against the narrator. But, someone may object, ignoring my earlier explanations, isn't she the original ironist, the debunker of miracles? Were it so, she still would be a demystifier demystified. It is ironical that she should be debunking a feat that only extends her own game of recording, for Camilla inscribes not the unrecorded past but the *unrecordable* present. Besides, when the narrator undermines the final miracle, which is a miracle of writing (pun intended), she is consequently undercutting her own accomplishment. Storytelling is a perilous activity for all concerned. In my precarious reading of the story,[21] there is no significant gap between what the narrator says and what she wants to suggest about miracles. Nevertheless her narration, and singularly the final segment, betrays *her* as a device of the writer, with no authority of her own to speak about miracles or indeed the world out there, so that the distance between what her narration reports and what the short story shows creates ironical effects. In its starkness, the opening statement evidences the narrator's desire to recover what has been unrecorded, lost. This is narrative's redemptive function: to *celebrate* (one of the meanings of "to record," *Chambers English Dictionary*) the uncelebrated. But it is precisely the redemptiveness of the record that is, if not denied, at least questioned.[22] Or, one could say that the redeeming is itself a miracle (of another sort) at once achieved through writing and deconstructed by writing and its doubleness. In short, while the existence of small miracles is posited, the very concept is destabilized, the meaning and the usual associations of the word are displaced. Where the narrator says "miracle," the reader understands coincidence, chance, synchronicity.

But this understanding is by no means reductive and the story's structure does invite the reader's *wonder.* The narrator's trust in her gathering of exempla is founded, whatever one calls them. The very accumulation of fragments of unrecorded life transcends the individual cases and builds up a *silent argument* that establishes invisible connections between the unconnected so that the whole is necessarily more convincing than the parts. In the individual stories, the synchronic pictures may only signify synchronicity. But in the series, the return of related chance happenings, exemplifying the universality of synchronicity, transforms signs into significance, however uncertain and undefinable, during the reading process. It seems to point to the existence of patterns in the fictional universe, which now and then flash through the opaque randomness of reality. The story fictionalizes what Carol Shields elsewhere calls "the accidental *collision* of certain events. It produces those moments when we do feel or sense the order of the universe beneath that daily chaos" (Wachtel 43). Interestingly, in "Various Miracles" only Pierre has a sense of the irrational in his experience although one may presume that the actress in red has an even stronger shock. Only Carl understands that "life [is] mainly a matter of improvisation" (15) because it is so chancy. But the characters are all unaware of the world-scale patterns in which they are involved. Neither, the narrator assumes, are her narratees alert enough to the possibilities of miracles, their ignorance requiring her gesture of recovery. Synchronicity has to be *revealed* even if, or because, it is part of dailiness, just as most of us would know of no miracles were it not for the mediation of language. When the story is over, it seems fitting that all these coincidences should have been presented under the blanket word "miracles" — all the more so because they are, with the exception of the Moroccan tale, which is ambivalent, positive (or at best, neutral) phenomena.[23] "Various Miracles" illustrates a form of "generative irony," "one in which the gaps and discontinuities of twentieth-century literature, heretofore the mark of absence or negation, become instead the sign of a not yet constituted presence" (Wilde 186).

If the miraculous slips into the synchronistic, the synchronistic is a postmodernistic form of the miraculous. Carol Shields, though, is a postmodernist of the middle ground, who holds that language games are not an end in themselves.[24] "Print is her way of entering and escaping the *world*," she says of one of her characters (emphasis added). This applies to the author (and the reader as well) in a general manner of speaking. But the statement has a particular relevance to "Various Miracles": writing about the miraculous is a way of both entering and escaping the world, engaging directly with the experience of mystery and synchronicity and metaphorically with some of today's philosophical issues, while escaping the real through the surreal. "The entering and escaping the world" presupposes that there is some sort of coincidence, or could one say overlapping, between fiction and life. The fictional characters hold a commonsense view of the world that is challenged by the synchronistic view of the narrator, itself questioned by the tension between fiction and reality.

The fictional use of "miracles" enables Carol Shields to work a double row. First, she dismantles the conventions of causal plot, continuous narration and, to some extent, that of verisimilitude, which were adequate to render an integrated or deterministic view of the world but are no longer apt to render the "daily chaos" and confusion of our world. Thus she allows new effects, discovers new sequences and connections, and plays with the fragmentariness of improvisations, thereby demonstrating that avowed linguistic constructions may yet be clues to amorphous reality.[25] By one of those paradoxes which are so numerous in "Various Miracles," fragmentariness, instead of increasing, to some extent attenuates a difficulty inherent in the genre of the short story. As Pierre Tibi (28) has remarked, in the short story, the world lacks the time to acquire an "aspect of tangible evidence" ("aspect d'évidence palpable") and of "systematic organization." "Various Miracles" does not seek to create such a fictional universe. It plays on the fusion of the *countable* fragments of evidence provided by the *fait divers* and of the *invisible* evidence of the miraculous in the shape of universal synchronicity to suggest, rather than having to shape, a systematic organization of the world, which yet can never be asserted outright.

And, secondly, Carol Shields finds a language of reconciliation, oxymoronic in the sense that it brings together the extremes of the strange suspension of causality which is regarded as a natural law, and the ongoing banality of everyday life. "At bottom, the ordinary is not ordinary; it is extra-ordinary": no, I am not quoting fiction-writer Carol Shields but philosopher Martin Heidegger whose statement is a summing-up of many of her stories and novels (quoted in Smyth, 136). In "Various Miracles," Shields celebrates the mystery of the ordinary, the numinous exceptions to the world's disarray, creating a sense of order that yet accepts the contingent, and paradoxically positing through "generative irony" "anironic enclaves of value in the face of — but not in place of — a meaningless universe," as Wilde (148) says of some American postmodernists. Some of the miracles that language can accomplish are thus being performed under our own eyes. The story, for instance, not only records the diegetic miracles but embodies the miracle of make-believe that is the fictional recording/reporting/inventing of reality. But on this let Aritha van Herk, herself an adept practitioner of the tricks of narration, "extrapolate": "a miracle, the miracle of language, a recognition that the real miracle is that there are miracles, themselves miraculous. Carol Shields knows this: she writes with one eye on the miracle of language and another on the miracle of miracles" (107-108).

When we finally stop negotiating between discontinuity and continuity, fiction and reality, our universe has been expanded by the quiet, luminous, upbeat art of Carol Shields: we understand more about miracles, about stories, about our lives and ourselves. "Various Miracles" intimates that causality and logic are insufficient answers to the problem of narrating since it uses *fait divers* to question causality and fragmentation to question logic. It tolerantly mocks our romantic expectations, our ready-made ideas. It even suggests that all patterning may be a matter of language. Nevertheless, by offering us miracles in everydayness, showing the extraordinary in the ordinary, it wonderfully restores trust in a life which is less determined and less chaotic than it may appear, where improvisation therefore has a place, and it restores faith in language, too, since it allows us to talk, however obliquely, of mystery. And of course we now understand the title. "Various Miracles" displays miracles galore. "Various: varied, different, several, unlike each other, changeable, uncertain, variegated" (*Chambers English Dictionary*) — the miracles worked in the story and by the story in turn illustrate all these predicates with a miraculous — what else? — lightness of touch.

Notes

1   Carpentier's essay is grounded in his own work and in that of contemporary francophone practitioners.

2   According to a review of the English edition of *Various Miracles*, the collection opens not with "Various Miracles" but with a story that appeared in Shields's later collection, *The Orange Fish*. The difference must shape a different book.

3   Barthes has shown the kinship between the *fait divers* and the short story or tale which are "immanent" forms: "au niveau de la lecture, tout est donné dans un fait divers; ses circonstances, ses causes, son passé, son issue; sans durée et sans contexte, il constitue un être immédiat, total qui ne renvoie, du moins formellement, à rien d'implicite; c'est en cela qu'il s'apparente à la nouvelle et au conte, et non plus au roman. C'est son immanence qui définit le fait divers" (189).

4   "Ainsi tout fait divers comporte au moins deux termes, ou si l'on préfère deux notations" (Barthes 190).

5   Needless to say, in "Various Miracles," irony does not involve a full inversion of the first posited meaning; rather its mode is close to what Allen Wilde (10) calls suspensive irony, a form which he connects with postmodernism: "a vision of multiplicity, randomness, contingency," "a low-keyed engagement with a world of perplexities and uncertainties, in which one can hope, at best, to achieve what Forster calls 'the smaller pleasures of life' and Stanley Elkin its 'small satisfactions'" — and Carol Shields its "small ceremonies," if I may add to Wilde's quotations the title of one of Shields's early novels. "Generative irony," of which more later, is a variety of suspensive irony.

6   LaPorta combines French (la porte) and Spanish (la puerta) with in both cases door associations. It is a gate through which we may enter the story — it is also the door through which we leave it.

7   The dash suspending the new story also opens out the whole structure and ends the short story on another voice — Camilla's — which in a sense relegates the overall narrator's voice to the background yet also paradoxically foregrounds it, since it repeats the same words as the extradiegetic narrator and in the same tone.

8   The ending is more striking than my summary implies because of the use of tenses in the two almost identical statements. The preterite is used for the description of the young woman, who in terms of the fictional world of "Various Miracles" is "real," therefore present, while the present is used for the young woman created by Camilla, who must needs be fictive in terms of the world of "Various Miracles" and whose absence is signified by the shift to the present.

9   There is of course a shift in narrators without which the final statement would be simple duplication and not *mise en abyme*. There is also a shift in the typeprint codes since the last description is italicized.

10 One thinks in particular of Cortázar's "Continuidad de los parques," in which the reader of a novel is murdered at the end by a character in the story he is reading.

11 After Gérard Genette, I use "diegetic" in the sense of belonging to the space-time universe of the story. For the level below the diegesis, Mieke Bal, Shlomith Rimmon-Kennan etc. prefer the term "hypodiegetic" rather than Genette's "metadiegetic," the prefix of which, they rightly think, can be a source of confusion.

12 Not systematically present in the proper names of all segments, the other letters of the word can still be found in most sections (the r in Ramsay, Francesca, Carl, Hallsbury, Marjorie, Pierre, Renaud, Burgundy, LaPorta, Toronto, the a in Palo Alto, California, Marseilles, Netherlands, Chicago, Carl, Hallsbury, Marjorie, Jean-Louis and with a vengeance in Camilla LaPorta, the less ubiquitous C in Carl, Francesca, Camilla, the l in Palo Alto, California, Billings, Marseilles, Netherlands, LaPorta, the e in Exeter, Marseilles, Francesca, Netherlands, Purdue, Pierre, Renaud, Jean-Louis, Marjorie).

13 I cannot resist another example of microcircuitry: the text plays with the polyglossic form of Peter (Pete or Pietro, and Pierre, section 4 and 5) which can be linked through etymology to the "stone bridge" (section 5) and the "keystone page" (section 6). Thematic echoes also abound: the unobtrusive mentions of happiness in several sections, the acceptance of chance or fate (the parrot's, "ça ne fait rien," the theft of the picture, the lost page).

14 That piece of information, digressive as it may seem, raises characteristic doubts. Is that "leather-goods business" a random and innocent choice? or does it connect, in a tiny microcircuit, with Pierre's homosexuality? In Carol Shields's texts, even apparently irrelevant notations thus often question the reader who is afraid either of reading too many connections or of missing the subtlety of the web Shields is weaving.

15 As could be expected, the pattern is broken once so that it is not mechanical: item one has 3 lines, item two 4, item three 16, item four 27, item five with its 60 lines marks a peak, from which item six declines slightly (51 lines).

16 I borrow the phrase from Carol Shields's interview with Eleanor Wachtel. She then opposed the "glimpses of chaos" and "those other, equally rare, transcendental moments when you suddenly feel that everything makes sense and you perceive the pattern of the universe. I think we all get a few of those minutes. I'm very interested in looking for those and recording them and finding language for recording them" (39).

17 Was the page number chosen at random? In some systems four signifies "the orderly arrangement of what is separate," six is "expressive of dualism" and ten (4 + 6) "a return to unity." But has it some other special significance?

18 Camilla revised her work so that "where fate, chance, or happenstance had ruled, there was now logic, causality, and science" (16). These qualities are presumably those the publisher wanted. The juxtaposition of three terms in the comparison between the two versions invites us to regard logic as the antithesis of fate, causality of chance and science of happenstance. The conception of narrative thus defined is clearly ironic and condemns the causal narrative as too abstract, like science.

19 The metafictional aspects of "Various Miracles" would deserve a treatment of their own, which cannot be attempted here.

20 I am not claiming, of course, that omniscience in a narrator is necessarily destructive of the referential illusion, merely that it is in this case.

21 The story may generate different interpretations, since, given its ironic bias, it invites readers who will construct double meanings and, filling in an absence, will add something of their own to the narrative — an operation which is not without risks both to the interpreter and to the text.

22 Further ironies: Wishing to transcribe some invisible ruptures in the real, the narrator is compelled to rely on the linear visibility of written language and the intrinsic duplicity of storytelling. The fragmentariness which enables her to account for the fact that miracles are isolated phenomena has to be sutured in the reading act.

23 In this context, the subject of Smiley's People, a spy story by John Le Carré, matters less than the signifier Smiley. It is to be noted, too, that Various Miracles includes one or two stories in which coincidence is more dysphoric (see "Accidents" and also, though it relies less on coincidence, "Fragility").

24 In the interview with Eleanor Wachtel, Carol Shields defines her position. She accepts the postmodernist idea of "playing with language to make a point — and I don't think it pointless. Some postmodernists think there is no point beyond the language game, but I think there can be — and I don't know why we

have to talk about these two forms of fiction. Why can't we have something in the middle — which is, I suppose, what I'm trying to do. Because postmodernist ideas do allow you to do things that you can't do as a naturalist" (44-45).

25 The novels of Carol Shields, before *Various Miracles,* were much less exploratory in form. The short stories seem to have liberated the author for her more experimental novels, *Swann: A Mystery* or *The Stone Diaries.*

Works Cited

Barthes, Roland. "Structure du Fait Divers" in *Essais Critiques.* Paris: Seuil, 1964.

Borges, Jorge Luis. *Ficciones.* Barcelona: Planeta, 1979.

Carpentier, André. "Commencer et finir souvent, Rupture fragmentaire et brièveté discontinue dans l'écriture nouvellière," in Whitfield, Agnès and Jacques Cotnam, *La nouvelle: écriture(s) et lecture(s).* Montréal: XYZ éditeur, 1993.

Chetwynd, Tom. *A Dictionary of Symbols.* London: Granada Publishing Ltd, 1984.

Cirlot, J.E. *A Dictionary of Symbols.* Translated from the Spanish by Jack Sage, N.Y.: Philosophical Library, 1971.

Genette, Gérard, *Figures III.* Paris: Seuil, 1972.

Quignard, Pascal. "Une gêne technique à l'égard des fragments," *Furor,* 11 (1984): 3-32.

Room of One's Own. Special Issue on Carol Shields, Vol. 13, Nos. 1 and 2 (1989).

Shields, Carol. *Various Miracles.* Toronto: Stoddart, 1985.

— , *The Orange Fish.* Toronto: Random House, 1989.

— , *Swann: A Mystery.* Toronto: Stoddart, 1987.

— , *The Stone Diaries.* London, Fourth Estate, 1993.

Smyth, Donna E. *Subversive Elements.* Toronto: The Women's Press, 1986.

Smyth, Donna E. "Shields's Swann" in *Room of One's Own.* Special Issue on Carol Shields, Vol. 13, Nos. 1 and 2 (1989): 136-146.

Tibi, Pierre. "La Nouvelle, Essai de Compréhension d'un genre," *Cahiers de l'Université de Perpignan, Aspects de la nouvelle* 4 (Printemps 1988): 7-62.

van Herk, Aritha. "Extrapolations from Miracles," in *Room of One's Own.* Special Issue on Carol Shields, Vol. 13, Nos. 1 and 2 (1989): 99-108.

Wachtel, Eleanor. "An Interview with Carol Shields," in *Room of One's Own.* Special Issue on Carol Shields, Vol. 13, Nos. 1 and 2 (1989): 5-45.

Waugh, Patricia. *Metafiction, Theory and Practice of Self-conscious Fiction.* London: Methuen, 1984.

Wilde, Allen. *Horizons of Assent, Modernism, Post-modernism and the Ironic Imagination.* Philadelphia: University of Pennsylvania Press, 1987.

BRIAN JOHNSON

Necessary Illusions: Foucault's Author Function in Carol Shields's *Swann*

"The charm of falsehood is not that it distorts reality, but that it creates reality afresh." (*Swann* 163)

The detective game of Carol Shields's *Swann: A Mystery* centres not upon the discovery of Mary Swann's killer, as one of Agatha Christie's readers might expect, but rather upon the discovery of Swann, the author herself. The relentless search for the dead woman "behind" the work firmly locates the disappearance of the author as the text's central mystery and suggests ways in which Shields's novel addresses the debate about authority in contemporary criticism, inaugurated by Roland Barthes's 1968 eulogy for the author in which he attacks "the image of literature to be found in contemporary culture [that] is tyrannically centered on the author" (50). Barthes's "murder" of the author at least makes room for a community of readers who infinitely re-imagine texts, thus privileging an endless proliferation of meanings over more traditionally conservative approaches to authorship that "close" texts and limit signification.

In terms of this poststructuralist ethos of the open text, the literary ethic of *Swann*'s detectives seems to manifest itself in precisely the opposite way. Although the novel and its characters often display an acute awareness of contemporary literary theory, individual approaches to solving the riddle of the author's identity seem remarkably parochial, more in keeping with the Romantic tradition of imagining the author as a nourishing presence that explains and fixes meaning in a text. Sarah Maloney's quest to protect the "true" Mary Swann from the dogs of contemporary criticism is one such attempt to recover the writer's authority over the work. Similarly, Morton Jimroy's biography of the poet as "Mother Soul," or Rose Hindmarch's readings of the poems as confessions of a person named Mary Swann, show how critics can present an image of the author as a brake on meaning. Each of these examples, however, suggests that the authority of the critic also depends upon a particular definition, or circumscription, of the poet's life, a strategy epitomized in the question that resonates throughout the pages of Shields's text: "Who is Mary Swann?" (128). Taking as its model the *roman à clef, Swann* ostensibly sets out to account for the disappearance of the author using a theological paradigm of detection that, like Rose's espionage novels, presupposes the possibility of a series of clues cohering to furnish incontrovertible truths. Adapting the traditions of the classic whodunit to "A Literary Mystery," *Swann* seems to present itself as the form's literary counterpart: the whowroteit.

However, the formal coherence expected of "a literary mystery" breaks down as Shields's text deconstructs itself, denying the moment of final closure that defines the mystery genre. *Swann*'s total subversion of the traditional detective story plot through its failure to answer conclusively its primary question, "Who is Mary Swann?", dramatically undercuts the theoretical assumptions of *Swann*'s literary detectives, suggesting ways in which any attempt to uncover the objectively "real" author is fundamentally misguided — a red herring of the critic's own devising. Significantly, the novel's ironic subversion of the detective story's formal aspects replays itself on the level of character as well: Sarah Maloney is no Miss Marple and Cruzzi is no Poirot. On the contrary, as characters manufacture or destroy evidence to support their own solutions to the mystery of Swann's identity, the novel begins to raise very different questions about power and appropriation which suggest that the author's role in *Swann* is a good deal more complex than their detective game implies.

If *Swann* moves toward a theoretical paradigm of authorial absence that leaves discourse open to appropriation, detective games are still insufficient as a means of accounting for the author in the novel. This absence raises new problems as well. Although Mary Swann may be absent from the text of *Swann's Songs*, she is so powerfully present in the text of Shields's novel that one critic refers to her as "the major character who is missing," acknowledging that "[f]or someone not there, she seems very real" (Smyth 145). The apparent simplicity of the question "Who is Mary Swann?" resonates with irony as the reader is left in the uncomfortable position of having to account for the simultaneity of the author's absence/presence. As Michel Foucault suggests in "What Is an Author" (1969; trans. 1972): "it is not enough . . . to repeat the empty affirmation that the author has disappeared . . . Instead, we must locate the space left empty by the author's disappearance, follow the distribution of gaps and breaches, and watch for the openings that this disappearance uncovers" (266). Foucault shows how, despite our supposed acceptance of the author's "transcendental anonymity," we impose an image of the author onto the text of our own making. This "author-function," as Foucault calls it, precisely describes the process of author construction — traditional criticism's so-called "rediscovery" of the author — that underlies the readings of each of *Swann*'s detectives, since "[the] aspects of an individual which we designate as making him an author are only a projection, in more or less psychologizing terms, of the operations we force texts to undergo, the connections that we make, the traits that we establish as pertinent, the continuities that we recognize, or the exclusions that we practise" (269). Unsatisfied with the simplicity of Barthes's installation of the reader in the place of the author, Foucault explores the author as "a certain functional principle by which, in our culture, one limits, excludes, and chooses; in short, by which one impedes the free circulation, the free manipulation, the free composition, decomposition, and recomposition of fiction . . . The author is, therefore, the ideological figure by which one marks the manner in which we fear the proliferation of meaning" (274). As a form of restraint, the author function is therefore involved with silencing apocryphal discourses by displacing them with other, "authorized" versions.

It is through this relation of the author's death to the notions of power associated with his persistent "classificatory" function of "manifest[ing] the appearance of a certain discursive set and indicat[ing] the status of this discourse within a society and culture" (267), that Foucault articulates a paradigm of authorship that may be interrogated as a narratological model for reading *Swann*. I would argue that *Swann* dramatizes the full progress of Foucault's argument, beginning with the Barthesian premise of the dead author and his subsequent re-examination of "the privileges of the subject" (274) through his notion of the author function as it guides and limits Sarah, Jimroy and Rose's respective readings of the Swann poems. Just as Foucault exposes the author as a social construct whose "ideological" status enables a discursive system of critical domination over the work and audience alike, so *Swann* parodies and undercuts the pretensions of its critics, revealing an academic power-play that manifests itself at several textual levels in recurring acts of appropriation. At the broadest level, the author function in *Swann* produces a paradigm shift which reframes the question of "Who is Mary Swann?" to implicitly accommodate the more complex problems of authorship that Foucault identifies in "What Is an Author?"

In order to understand the workings of this paradigm shift and the way it is achieved, it is vital to recognize that *Swann*, like Foucault, begins with the premise of Barthes's dead author — a premise exemplified by Mary Swann, the novel's quintessential dead author. Sarah, commenting on her readerly attraction to the poet, identifies the most salient aspect of her character on the very first page of the novel: "And Mary Swann. Also dead. Exceedingly dead" (11). This brief obituary is not isolated but is foregrounded throughout the text as Sarah later reminds us when she first visits the Swann house: "At that time Mary Swann had been dead for more than fifteen years" (17), and then proceeds to visit the cemetery where Swann is buried. For Sarah, Swann is more compelling, more "useful," dead than alive: first, there is her mortal lesson to Sarah, who confides that by "reading Mary Swann [she discovered] how a human life can be silently snuffed out" (20); but there is also her ontological lesson to the critic who may celebrate Swann's Songs as a living testament, the "famous last words" of the poet, but who in fact relies on a radical absence of the person as the condition of her own critical authority. Although it is significant that the reader is never allowed to forget the literal and metaphorical fact of Swann's death, the nature of the death itself suggests other ways in which Mary Swann's murder becomes emblematic of Barthes's primary claim that "once a fact is recounted . . . [a] gap appears, the voice loses its origin, the author enters into his own death, writing begins" (49).

Swann's affinity with Barthes's dead author is also suggested by the horrific dismemberment that follows Mary Swann's murder in its echo of Barthes's authorial disembodiment. Just as Mary Swann's husband "shot her in the head at close range, . . . pounded her face with a hammer, dismembered her body, crudely, with an axe, and hid the bloodied parts in a silo" (223), so Barthes's argument implicitly disembodies the authorial voice, asserting that "his hand, detached from any voice, borne by a pure gesture of inscription (and not of expression), traces a field without origin" (52). Despite their seemingly parallel construction of authorship, however, the sheer extravagance of Swann's murder points to ways in which Barthes's wholesale eradication of the author might be somewhat overzealous. Where Barthes simply cuts off a hand, Swann's husband "put a bullet right through her head and chopped her up into little pieces" (43). The unnecessary violence of the beating and the dismemberment that follows the murder itself convey a powerful sense of overkill, the excess of which points directly to the exaggeration of parody. Viewing Mary Swann's murder as a parodic metaphor for Barthes's treatment of the author calls for a radically different way of imagining authorship within the text. If *Swann* suggests that Barthes's total eradication of the author is too severe, and, as we shall see, ultimately inadequate as a means of dealing with the author's lingering pseudo-presence, it also suggests ways in which a new theory of authorship must somehow accommodate the issues of power and appropriation that are intimately linked to Swann herself throughout the novel.

The relation of appropriation to authorship is most vividly suggested by Sarah's conversation with the woman in the fur coat during a bus ride in the final section of the novel:

Sarah: She wrote these poems. Not many, just over a hundred, but they're . . . there's nothing else like them.
Fur Coat: Is she still writing?
Bus Driver: (calling out) Harbourview.
Sarah: Oh, I get off here. She's dead. Since 1965. Her husband finally —
Fur Coat: Her husband finally what?

(Sarah hurriedly gathers her things together. The two women start to shake hands, then embrace quickly. Sarah gets off the bus, turns and waves.)

Fur Coat: (shouting through the open window) Her husband finally what?
Sarah: (shouting from the pavement in front of the revolving doors) Shut her up.
Fur Coat: Did what?
Sarah: (waving and shouting as the bus starts to pull away) He shut her up. For good. He — (250)

Rather than tell the woman that Swann was murdered by her husband, Sarah substitutes the act of silencing for the killing itself, suggesting that the two are virtually interchangeable; "He shut her up" becomes, as Jimroy has earlier suggested, "a miniature act of murder" (110).

In effect, the silencing of the poet plays itself out as a prototypical drama of appropriation in which Swann's husband asserts his murderous will over the discourse of his wife and thereby silences her "for good." This primary discursive displacement is hardly unique. The author's death (equated with silence) becomes the underlying theoretical basis for the machinations of all of Swann's critics, enabling a continuing legacy of appropriation. The drama of the murder suggests that, although Mary Swann may certainly be seen as a Barthesian author (albeit an ironic one), the implications of her death demand further consideration as they relate to Foucault's declaration that "all discourses are objects of appropriation" (268), or to the notion that one discourse inevitably displaces another. Building upon Barthes's notion of the silent author and the "neuter" text (49) by imagining Mary Swann's work in terms of Foucault's notion of discourse as it engenders the "activity of the author function" (273), we might more readily explain the questions of power and appropriation that surround Swann's writing and the meta-texts of Swann's critics.

Sarah Maloney's accidental discovery of Mary Swann places her in the unusual critical position of reading Swann's text before it acquires an author function and, as such, provides a dramatic glimpse at the way in which the author function is embroiled in issues of power, even at its most primary level. The narrative details that accompany Sarah's first discovery of *Swann's Songs* constantly emphasize its physical marginality: "[in] a cottage on a lonely Wisconsin lake," "toward the end of the month, at the end of a shelf, I discovered an odd little book of poems written by a woman named Mary Swann. The title of the book was *Swann's Songs*" (17). Like so many other instances in Shields's novel, physical relations resonate with metaphorical value. The fact that Mary Swann's "odd little book" (actually a "stapled pamphlet") is not discovered in an urban centre but on a "lonely" and unnamed Wisconsin lake emphatically conveys a sense of the book's peripheral social value. As Sarah notices, it is "[a] case of obscurity seeking obscurity." From these details, it is apparent that Mary Swann begins in the position of Foucault's writer, deprived of an author function that "manifests the appearance of a certain discursive set and indicates the status of this discourse within a society and a culture" (267). Because she is "a woman," an "unknown poet," with no power or privilege in literary discourse, Mary Swann is dismissed by the majority of academia as a *poète naïf*. Sarah's project then becomes one of valorizing Swann's work and winning her the "recognition" from which she's been "cheated" (18). In short, Sarah begins "a complex operation which constructs a certain rational being that we call 'author'" (Foucault 269).

Sarah, however, does not view her involvement with Mary Swann in terms that even remotely resemble Foucault's notion of author construction. Ostensibly, she sets out to discover the "real" Mary Swann, embarking upon a vigorous biographical investigation that takes her to Nadeau, Ontario where she tries to reconstruct the poet's life in order to discover "[w]here in those bleak Ontario acres, that littered farmyard, [she found] the sparks that converted emblematic substance into rolling poetry?" (31). Her motives, she assures us, are pure:

> My own responsibility toward Mary Swann, as I see it, is custodial. If Olaf Thorkelson hadn't badgered me into near breakdown and driven me into the refuge of northern Wisconsin where Mary Swann's neglected book of poems fell like a bouquet into my hands, I would never have become Swann's watchwoman, her literary executor, her defender and loving caretaker. (31)

All of Sarah's roles emphasize her intention to steer clear of tampering with Mary Swann in any way. She will take care of her, she will watch her, she will look out for her interests and she will defend her, but she will in no way violate what Clara Thomas calls "the tenuous reality of the woman behind the poems" (113). In fact, Sarah sets herself up in contrast to those who would do so:

> Willard Lang, swine incarnate, is capable of violating her for his own gain, and so is the absent-minded, paranoid, and feckless Buswell in Ottawa. Morton Jimroy means well, poor sap, but he'll try to catch her out or bend her into God's messenger or the handmaiden of Emily Dickinson . . . (31)

Sarah self-righteously condemns these unscrupulous critics who "violate" and "bend" Mary Swann for their own self-interested purposes, appropriating and distorting her text only to further their own careers.

Because Sarah describes the distortions other critics perform on Swann's text in terms that are both Romantic and Foucauldian, her own critical position is open to contradiction. While she implies the presence of an Author-God whose meaning can be violated in the same way as her physical body, the sheer brutality of her metaphors simultaneously invokes the implicit violence that Foucault identifies in readers who "force texts to undergo" operations of their own construction. That is, Foucault's argument implies a certain violence that readers do to texts in their merciless drive to constrain their (implicitly natural state of) copious signification by creating an "author" whose name persistently "mark[s] off the edges of the text" (267). Because this being is an unnatural "projection," the reader can only create him or her by forcing the text to yield only certain predetermined meanings that are bound up in the critic's own schemes and desires. As Sarah explains, "[a] man like Morton Jimroy wouldn't be bothering with her if he didn't think that she was going to take off. Willard Lang wouldn't be wasting his time organizing a symposium if he didn't believe her reputation was ripe for the picking. These guys are greedy. They would eat her up inch by inch. Scavengers. Brutes. This is a wicked world, and the innocent need protection" (32).

While she is acutely aware of the ways in which literary critics appropriate discourse, as the plucking of Mary Swann's reputation and the image of prey-birds devouring her textual remains vividly suggest, Sarah makes the remarkable claim that she can somehow step outside of discourse and protect the "real" Mary Swann. However, Foucault's contention that everything is discourse might seriously question any such manoeuvre. Sarah's Romantic claims for the authority of genius are repeatedly undercut as she practices the same "exclusions" and makes the same selective connections for which she condemns her fellow "scavengers." Sarah's hypocrisy, however, is not a "violation" — that is her term. Her very creation of an author function for Mary Swann is only possible because, contrary to Thomas's argument, there is no "tenuous reality of the woman behind the poems"; Sarah's Swann, like that of all the other critics, can only be a pure construction.

The extent to which Sarah is guilty of such construction, no matter how good her intentions, is profoundly apparent in her treatment of the evidence she does come across during her biographical investigation. In particular, her disposal of Mary Swann's rhyming dictionary suggests that Sarah fabricates an image of the author that will allow "a limitation of the cancerous and dangerous proliferation of significations" that threaten to undermine her project of refuting those critics who dismiss Swann as a *poète naïf* and assuring her a place in the literary canon (Foucault 274):

> Mary Swann's rhyming dictionary and notebook rested on the seat. I could reach out and touch them as I drove along. My thoughts were riveted on the notebook and what its contents would soon reveal to me, but the dictionary kept drawing my eye, distracting me with its overly bright cover. It began after a few miles to seem ominous and to lend a certain unreality to the notebook beside it.
> I stopped at the first roadside litter box and dropped it in. (45-6)

The danger posed by *Spratt's New Improved Rhyming Dictionary for Practising Poets* is precisely that it seems to substantiate the critical view that Sarah opposes. It implies that the achievement of Swann's poetry may merely be the accidental projection of signification onto her naïve text by critics like herself and, as such, must be destroyed. The incident of the rhyming dictionary brings into sharp focus the nature of the conflict between the two competing discourses that attempt to define Mary Swann in opposing ways. Sarah's actions cut through her rhetoric and make it clear that her interest in Mary Swann's ontological status as either a rustic genius or a *poète naïf* is not motivated by a concern for "truth." The disturbing and violent selectivity of Sarah's methods (she does not merely ignore, but actively destroys evidence) dramatically undercuts her claim that she is acting solely as Swann's caretaker and forces the reader to re-evaluate her motives altogether.

Upon closer inspection, Sarah's creation of an author function reveals that her interest in "protecting" Mary Swann is not purely selfless. As Catherine Addison slyly suggests, "[e]ach of the main characters [including Sarah Maloney] . . . has a vested interest in the reconstruction of the poet's life and work" (159). What Addison so accurately points to here, and what Sarah has already recognized, is the fact that Swann's critics are not only involved in securing the "authority" of Swann's discourse through their creation of an author function for her, they are also interested in securing the authority of their own critical discourse as well. Consequently, Sarah's own personal ambitions profoundly shape the ways in which her reconstruction of "Mary Swann" takes place, and what that final construct will be. As she lays out her relative position within the system of academic authority, Sarah, perhaps inadvertently, exposes her true motives for "protecting" Swann:

> Better just say I discovered Mary Swann. Even Willard Lang admits (officially, too) that I am more or less — he is endlessly equivocal in the best scholarly tradition — *more or less* the discoverer of Swann's work. He has even committed this fact to print in a short footnote on page six of his 1983 paper "Swann's Synthesis," naming me, Sarah Maloney of Chicago, the one "most responsible for bringing the poet Mary Swann to public attention." This mention on Willard's part is an academic courtesy and no more. (30)

Sarah's own discourse, relegated to "a short footnote on page six," sounds strangely like Mary Swann's, discovered "toward the end of the month, at the end of a shelf . . . [in] a cottage on a lonely Wisconsin lake." The possibility that her hostility toward Lang, "swine incarnate," is the result of professional jealously is even further suggested by Sarah's intense awareness of the marginalization of her own discourse, consequent to the authorizing of Lang's. Mary Swann isn't the only one who has been "cheated . . . of recognition" (18):

> Ah, but Willard Lang's kind of courtesy amounts to a professional sawing off, a token coin dropped in a bank to permit future withdrawals. Willard Lang's nod in my direction — "S. Maloney must be cited as the one who" — is a simple declaration of frontier barriers between authority and discovery, Willard Lang being the authority, while S. Maloney (me) is given the smaller, slightly less distinguished role of discoverer. (30)

Particularly significant is Lang's appropriation of Sarah's discourse in the form of "withdrawals" from her academic piggybank. It not only sets up a parallel between Sarah and Mary Swann, but also points to the larger power struggle that is being waged over academic owner-ship of Swann's discourse. Indeed, Sarah's own construction of Mary Swann is dependent upon a sense of ownership that is precisely in keeping with Foucault's notion that "discourses are objects of appro-priation." Her feeling that she somehow owns the "rights" to Swann's material, is ironically suggested by her periodic possessive references to "[m]y Mary" (18); her rejection of Jimroy's request that she share the Swann notebook with him: "Mary Swann's notebook is mine" (28); and finally by her declaration that for the time being, the poems are hers as well: "my toys, if you like, little wooden beads I can manipu-late on a cord" (54). All these examples expose the appropriative act as a necessary and integral part of the author function in cultural dis-course — one that will be replayed with increasing intensity through-out the novel.

As Swann's literary biographer, Jimroy begins like Sarah with the claim that he is objectively unearthing the "real" Mary Swann with the expectation that once completed, his biography will "expose the key to Swann's genius" (111). Like Sarah, Jimroy declares that his pri-mary motive is simply to expose the pre-existing condition of Swann's genius and to insert her into the canon of Canadian Literature by proving that she is not the *poète naif* contemporary crit-icism makes her: "Marvellous Swann, paradoxical Swann. He would take revenge for her. Make the world stand up and applaud. It would happen . . . Here was Mother Soul. Here was intelligence masked by colloquial roughness" (87). According to Jimroy's formulation of the problem, the process of validating Mary Swann's poems depends upon resolving the Romantic paradox of her simultaneous genius and colloquial roughness by showing that the latter is merely a pose, a "modest" mask that obscures the former. However, confronted with the terrifying ordinariness of the poet's life at every turn, Jimroy finds that the paradox seems unshakable:

> The fact is, the poems and the life of Mary Swann do not meld, and Jimroy, one morning, working in the garden, spreads his handwritten notes in the December sunshine and begins to despair. . . . He is not such a fool, he tells himself, as to believe

that poets and artists and musicians possess an integrity of spirit greater than other people. No, of course he has never gone in for that kind of nonsense. What an absurdity is that critical term *unity of vision* for instance — as though anyone in this universe ever possessed such a thing, or would want to.

And yet . . . how is he to connect Mary Swann's biographical greyness with the achieved splendour of *Swann's Songs?* (108)

The heavy irony of this passage suggests that, on the contrary, Jimroy very much does believe in, or at least desires a *unity of vision* in Mary Swann's life and work that is simply not present. Unwilling to accept the "defeat" of a "long article" (109) that this rupture would produce, Jimroy embarks upon a detailed process of creating an author function for Mary Swann that imagines her precisely in terms of what Foucault identifies as classic criticism's method of "construct[ing] the figure of the author beginning with existing texts and discourses" which was "derived from the manner in which Christian tradition authenticated (or rejected) the texts at its disposal" (269).

Jimroy, engaged in the process of turning Swann's life into a text that will justify his interpretation of her work, subverts his own claim, by working backwards from text to life, that he is simply "discovering" and "recording" her biography so that her poems might "open out and become clear" (111). In the absence of detailed evidence about Swann's life, Jimroy's primary biographical focus becomes an extrapolation of influences — the most obvious choice for a biographer whose formalist concern is really with the text itself:

Of course he can surmise certain things, influences for instance. He is almost sure she came in contact with the work of Emily Dickinson, regardless of what Frances Moore says. He intends to mention, to comment extensively in fact, on the Dickinsonian influence, and sees no point, really, in taking up the Edna Ferber influence; it is too ludicrous. (110)

Here is Jimroy's version of author construction at its most intense. Like Sarah, Jimroy rejects any detail that does not fit into his version of Swann, going so far as to totally ignore "the Edna Ferber influence" that has been reported not only by Mary Swann's daughter, but by Rose Hindmarch as well. In order to combat the image of the *poète naïf* that is always looming behind the evidence Jimroy assembles, he constructs the image of an author steeped in the works of already valorized literary women such as Emily Dickinson. Unable to justify his "exclusions," as Foucault calls them, Jimroy simply dismisses Edna Ferber as "too ludicrous," sweeping it into the trash beside Sarah's rhyming dictionary.

A similar story of overt fabrication can be found in "the Jane Austen influence." During his interview with Frances Moore when Jimroy first learns that Mary Swann was particularly fond of Edna Ferber, "Jimroy makes a noise that signifies regret and writes it down in his notebook. Of course he is disappointed. Has he foolishly hoped for Jane Austen? Yes, though he knows better" (93). As Frances goes on to regale Jimroy with "the Mother Goose influence" and "the *Bobbsey Twins* influence," Jimroy's situation becomes increasingly desperate as conflicting information threatens to totally undermine his goal of creating a coherent, intellectual Mary Swann. If Mary Swann is to be salvaged as a serious poet at all, her history of influences must be entirely rewritten. In fact, this is precisely what Jimroy does months later as he sits in his garden on Christmas day, "going over some notes covering Mary Swann's middle period (1940-1955) and making a few additions to the notations with a freshly sharpened pencil. *It is highly probable that Swann read Jane Austen during this period because...*" (118). Thus, Jimroy's biography ironically shapes up as a book of literary analysis of Swann's poems that masquerades as objective reportage. As one of his colleagues at the symposium puts it, "[t]he bugger should have been a novelist, not a bloody biographer" (272).

Jimroy's biographical fiction, however, is not simply a case of imagining a presence in the space left empty by the author's disappearance. Rather, it manifests itself in Jimroy's mind as a power struggle between himself and the poet in which Jimroy appropriates both her text and her life as text for his own self-serving purposes. For example, his admission that "for the moment at least, Mary Swann has defeated him" (110) leads directly into his strategy of author construction in which he infers her literary influences from the text itself, just a few lines later. The fact that Jimroy "triumphs" by asserting his will over her text, appropriating it like her husband did by "burying Swann's grainy likeness, keeping her out of sight and shutting her up" (110), emphatically suggests that he has something to gain by doing so. In fact, Jimroy's claims on Swann are both personal and professional. On the one hand, Jimroy has a vested interest in preserving a sophisticated image of the poet who "had rescued him from emotional bankruptcy" in the wake of his wife's departure and the moral failure of his books on Starmann and Pound: "and, at first, he *had* loved her" (87). As this love gives way to distrust, however, Jimroy's misogyny asserts itself as a power trip in which he makes Mary Swann into a pseudo-sexual plaything, finding that "he is in the embrace of happiness" fabricating the story of her existence (119). On a more professional level, the successful appropriation of Swann's discourse will also advance his career, establishing him as the authority on Swann's life. Although Jimroy may be more overtly appropriative than Sarah, as his theft of Mary Swann's pen and photograph dramatically reveals, the two critics differ more in degree than in kind.

As the novel progresses, the issues of power and appropriation that were submerged in Sarah's narrative and only slightly more obvious in Jimroy's become increasingly blatant. In Rose's and Cruzzi's sections, for instance, the novel's treatment of the author function is overtly focussed on appropriation. Rose explicitly appropriates the unwritten text of Mary Swann's life and writes herself into it in a way that is obviously self-serving:

> She felt a happy, porous sense of usefulness, as though joined for once to something that mattered. *Slim-shouldered Rose Hindmarch, local expert on Mary Swann, a woman with an extraordinary memory and a gift for detail, able to remember whole conversations word for word, able to put precise dates on ... episodes that were years in the past ... and ...* (151)

Rose's self-construction through her appropriation of Swann's life-text is only a more overt instance of the very process in which Sarah and

Jimroy are already engaged. While Rose pretends to honesty and integrity in her reports of Mary Swann's life, she is only interested in establishing her own power and authority as a "local expert" on Mary Swann. As Rose later admits in church, in the most explicit confession of the novel, "The two of them had *not* gone for long walks together. They had *not* discussed — not even once — the books Mary Swann borrowed from the library. . . . None of this had taken place. . . . Forgive me, forgive me. Forgive me the sin of untruthfulness" (152). Although Rose is the only character to admit explicitly that her author function is untrue, the implication that she is making a more general comment upon author functions in the novel is taken up by the glib Foucauldian generalization by the narrator that "the charm of falsehood is not that it distorts reality, but that it creates reality afresh" (163).

Where Rose appropriates the life, Cruzzi appropriates the work. The revelation that Swann's editor has in fact literally rewritten Swann's entire ruined manuscript with the help of his wife, herself an aspiring poet, after it is almost destroyed by being drenched in fish guts, literalizes the metaphor of appropriation. While Cruzzi and Hildë set about "guess[ing]" at and "invent[ing]" the parts of Swann's poems that have been obliterated, however, the language of this section is loaded with self-justification: "At one point, Hildë, supplying missing lines and even the greater part of a missing stanza, said she could feel what the inside of Mary Swann's head must look like. She seemed to be inhabiting, she said, another woman's body" (223). Although Hildë uses this temporary embodiment of Mary Swann as a justification for the lengths of her own "transcription," it might more accurately be seen as the bodily equivalent of the textual appropriation she enacts by inventing.

The most vivid example of Cruzzi and Hildë's textual appropriation centres upon the blood poem, which has already been the subject of considerable critical speculation:

Blood pronounces my name
Blisters the day with shame
Spends what little I own,
Robbing the hour, rubbing the bone. (51, 148)

For Sarah, this poem is the emotional core of Swann's work that "turns on the inescapable perseverance of blood ties, particularly those between mothers and daughters" (50-51). Jimroy too is fascinated by the poem, but reads it into an entirely different context: "This seems to be — now you may disagree — but to me it's a pretty direct reference to the sacrament of holy communion. Or perhaps, and this is my point, perhaps to a more elemental sort of blood covenant, the eating of the Godhead, that sort of thing" (148). Rose's own response to Jimroy's reading suggests yet a third possibility, although "[s]he was unable to utter the word menstruation" (148). It can be no accident that all of these readings succeed in revealing more about the characters themselves than they do about Mary Swann's elusive poetic intent. Sarah's concern over her relationship with her own mother, Jimroy's desire to discover Mary Swann as "Mother Soul," Rose's own bleeding, all suggest the extent to which their readings appropriate the blood poem as it reflects their psychological states of mind at a discrete moment in time, utterly removed from Swann herself.

Against this backdrop of textual appropriation on a metaphysical level, Cruzzi's revelation concerning the circumstances of poetic reconstruction peels back yet another layer of appropriation at work in the blood poem:

> The last poem, and the most severely damaged, began: "Blood pronounces my name." Or was it "Blood renounces my name"? The second line could be read in either of two ways: "Brightens the day with shame," or "Blisters the day with shame." They decided on *blisters*. The third line, "Spends what little I own" might just as easily be transcribed, "Bends what little I own," but they wrote *Spends* because — though they didn't say so — they liked it better. (223)

Cruzzi's reconstruction of the poem is particularly significant as it dramatizes the creation of a new discourse that replaces a previous one in which readers are literally figured as authors who actively rewrite texts to their own specifications. Their new manuscript, which epitomizes discursive appropriation, then becomes the ironic center of a whole tradition of displacement. As Thomas notices, "there never was a text of Mary Swann's poems authentic to her own words" (120), and this fact undercuts, not only confirms, the author's textual death, even as it suggests that the entire novel is made up of a series of displacements in which discourses perpetually vie for the position of authority.

The Swann Symposium brings the issue of appropriation to a head in the novel's final section. The Symposium itself, embodying the social and cultural institution that establishes author functions and validates or rejects authors, would seem to present itself as a veritable nexus of appropriation. As all of Swann's critics stand assembled, one expects the power struggle for academic authority to reach a fever-pitch as the competing versions of Mary Swann and their authors come head to head. In fact, the opposite is true. The question of appropriation is perhaps most vividly parodied in this section by Brownie, whose shadowy presence has haunted the entire book, although, like Mary Swann herself, he never appears. Nevertheless, his narrative absence does not prevent him from stealing every existing copy of *Swann's Songs*, in what Addison cites as a parody of the other characters' "sense of ownership, or guardianship of Swann" (159). Most significant, however, is the fact that Brownie, by appropriating every last trace of Swann's material remains, forces the critics to re-evaluate their own positions with respect to the appropriations of which they themselves are guilty.

This, in fact, has been the theme of the entire conference. Rose's public declaration that "Mrs. Swann liked a good story. For example, Pearl Buck. I remember she liked Pearl Buck real well. And Edna Ferber —" (260) totally disrupts the scholarly proceedings as Jimroy presents his paper and "order break[s] down" in the conference room. Rose's relinquishment of Mary Swann's text provides Jimroy with the opportunity to come clean as well. Abandoning his self-interested pretensions, if just for the moment, he publicly acknowledges the information he had previously suppressed: "Mrs. Swann's daughter, whom I have interviewed in depth in recent months, has confided that her mother was familiar with that genre of verse commonly known as Mother Goose —" (261). Sarah admits that the notebook that was supposed to hold the key to Mary Swann's poems was nothing more than "shopping lists" and Cruzzi himself confesses to Sarah that "Mary Swann, in my judgement, *was* an ordinary woman" (276). Ultimately, then, the power struggle in *Swann* gives way to a relinquishing of power in which the critics temporarily cease their furious and self-interested author construction.

If power is ultimately relinquished in Shields's text, where does this leave the argument about inevitable appropriation in discursive practice? In fact, the conclusions of Shields's novel and Foucault's essay are strikingly similar. Just as *Swann*'s architects abandon their projects of appropriation that attempt to contain meanings for their own purposes, Foucault looks forward to a time when "the author function will disappear, and in such a manner that fiction and its polysemous texts will once again function according to another mode" (275). "The Director's Final Note" reveals precisely this disappearance as

> The faces of the actors have been subtly transformed. They are seen joined in a ceremonial act of reconstruction, perhaps even an act of creation. There need be no suggestion that any one of them will become less selfish in the future, less cranky, less consumed with thoughts of tenure and academic glory, but each of them has, for the moment at least, transcended personal concerns. (311)

According to Donna E. Smyth, "what really matters in *Swann* is the group of academics who have become for the moment, a loving community as they piece together *Swann's Songs*. In the end, this mystery reveals itself as a kind of existentialist divine comedy" (144). This is particularly true from a Foucauldian perspective as one glimpses an almost "absolutely free state, in which fiction would be put at the disposal of everyone and would develop without passing through something like a necessary or constraining figure" (Foucault 274). The critics' re-membering of Swann's text as each supplies a line of the poem "Lost Things" seems to locate us firmly in the realm of Barthes's community of readers, the poststructural promised land that Foucault also returns to at the end of his essay. By the end of *Swann*, the author has been disposed of in all of her guises . . . or has she? The poem "Lost Things" does not allow us to do away with the "constraining figure" of the author altogether. The characters' ascription "by Mary Swann" that appears innocuously under the title ironically emphasizes the persistence, as Foucault says, of "the necessary" figure of constraint that underlies and validates our culture's entire system of discourse. At the end of it all, the author still functions.

Works Cited

Addison, Catherine. "Lost Things." *Canadian Literature* 121 (Summer 1989): 158-60.

Barthes, Roland. "The Death of the Author." 1968. Trans. Richard Howard. *The Rustle of Language.* Berkeley: University of California Press, 1989: 49-55.

Foucault, Michel. "What Is an Author?" *Contemporary Literary Criticism.* Ed. Robert Con Davis and Roland Schleifer. New York: Longman, 1989. 263-75.

Shields, Carol. *Swann: A Mystery.* Toronto: Stoddart, 1987.

Smyth, Donna E. "Shields's *Swann.*" *Room of One's Own* 13 (1989): 136-46.

Thomas, Clara. "'A Slight Parodic Edge': *Swann: A Mystery.*" *Room of One's Own* 13 (1989): 109-22.

KATHARINE NICHOLSON INGS

Illuminating the Moment: Verbal Tableaux in Carol Shields's Poetry

If there is one characteristic that has been a defining feature of Carol Shields's poetic vision these past twenty years, it is her ability to create visual moments of almost epiphanic clarity through which she reveals subtle insights about humanity that are both disconcerting and reaffirming. These moments are verbal tableaux — pictures painted through language — which give each poem a sense of immediacy that dissolves the paper medium between reader and poem, allowing the reader to enter the scene. Yet the tableaux also carry the weight of an implied past and future, assuming an air of familiarity that suggests to the reader that she is an insider, that she has been privy to something prior to the poetic moment. They begin *in medias res* — especially evident in titles such as "Getting Born," "Learning to Read," and "Remembering," all written in the present progressive tense that includes the reader in the processes of getting, learning, or remembering. Carol Shields accomplishes this sense of inclusiveness and belonging by creating a self-contained poetic world, one capable of evoking a heightened awareness in the reader, but also of being a potential point of criticism. For the reader to enter the tableaux, to participate fully in the poems, she must give herself over to the moral codes of Shields's world; the poems do not so much invite as assume that the reader shall do so.

Such an assumption may be too smothering for some readers, however, and if a reader does resist Shields's world, she may indeed find herself too distanced from the poem to experience its impact — the medium may act as a barrier. And granted, there may be reason to resist Shields's poetry at first glance. Readers who bring their personal political views to bear on poetry may not immediately find something to latch onto because Shields's poetry is not obviously written for a politically aware audience. Or is it? Indeed, much of Carol Shields's material is familiar, even mundane — friends, family, people she has observed, or traditions. But in Shields's hands, this material transcends the sentimental, perhaps clichéd approaches that might be considered more "appropriate" for it, or at least more expected. In *Coming to Canada,* for instance, the section entitled "New Poems" critiques those societal events and traditions held dear to many people — weddings, class reunions, or sending out Christmas cards — to expose the terror, the masquerade, and the rote behaviour devoid of feeling that often accompanies acts of seeming goodwill. In "Wedding" Shields juxtaposes a picture-perfect bride standing in "white / fullness on the church steps" with violent descriptions of the day's events: when an "afternoon of sentiment" is "suddenly unfurled" the bride's "bafflement" and "blinked-back surprise" suggests she flinches from an attack and that her more conventional feelings of "joy" and "sunshine" are overwhelmed. With a "blue fixed / shock of hurt in her eyes," this bride is far from blushing

> when she looks up and sees
> storms of confetti hurled
> with such precision, such fury that
> she must freeze and ask herself what
> it means and if it ever stops

Transported out of the realm of fantasies and traditions, the wedding day becomes a visual assault that may or may not be a prelude to what marriage will unleash.

When Shields visits another persona at a tenth-year reunion, a validating, comforting refrain — *"you're looking just the same!"* — rings hollow as the friends examine their ten-year-old photographic images:

The camera brings resolve
and reason, a hard
focus on a bright wall,
the image that we came
here for, but can't afford

("Tenth Reunion")

The moment captures the dissolution of a fantasy, one sustainable only through the collusion of others, but inherently flawed because the conspirators know they are uttering false security to each other. From the need to be reassured comes the act of reassuring, and so the friends have an unspoken agreement to lie — "you're looking just the same." Shields takes social insincerities one step further in "Season's Greetings," exposing the lack of true sentiment in people's yearly Christmas card ritual. Prompted only by "the reckoning of calendars" to send out cards that deliver "not / knowledge or good cheer or love" but "indistinct / messages scratched and signed," the act of mailing holiday cards is revealed as only an act, a performance, but one maintained because it is too difficult not to go through the motions.

In such poems, Shields paints the precise moment when a tradition is exploded or a fantasy is revealed as just that, yet the poems do not revel in this epiphany; rather, they suggest a profound disappointment that society has come to this state of automaton-like behaviour. For Shields has great expectations for human beings and a definite moral framework she would like people to live within — one that will accept only a sincere emotional response, not a programmed reaction to a planned event or a prescribed time of year. Shields demands honesty from her personae and her poems.

Nor does Shields celebrate political correctness in her poetry. Her ironic dismissal of the characters from the "Dick and Jane" primer — "They were boring and middleclass and, worse, / they were stereotypes — there's nothing worse than that" — marks the opening stanza of "Learning to Read" (from the "Coming to Canada" sequence), a poem which rails against literary and cultural revisionists who refuse to accept a story about an impossibly perfect white family as the primary reading material for children from multicultural and varied class backgrounds. Dick and Jane's politically correct replacements, "second rate / kids with shouting mothers and fathers, and token / yellows and blacks, and folks who are overweight," may more appropriately represent the population of North America, implies Shields, but they are not "healthy" role models. When we sacrifice idealism for literalism, she suggests, we are also sacrificing children's minds. Although Shields's words valiantly ring of striving for the best — after all, a human's reach should exceed his or her grasp — this is one of those poems a reader could easily resist: Dick and Jane, emblematic of the way things never were (for was there ever a family like theirs?), are revised as "brave" cultural heroes in the face of a more inclusive literature.

And here lies the paradox in Shields's poetic universe: she demands both honesty and idealism. Yet she knows the two are not always compatible, because she is well aware that the whitewashed American Dream Dick and Jane represent is at odds with the reality of the homeless, parentless, or otherwise dysfunctional families that live in this country. Significantly, then, her volume *Others* bears as a title the label commonly given to non-white, non-middle class folk who need to be distinguished (by the white middle class) from the so-called norm. Generally not a complimentary term, "other" suggests one who is alienated from mainstream society — certainly not an ideal person, practically a social and political non-entity. Is Shields aligning her personae in this volume with those less desirable folk? First published in 1972, *Others* arrived too early to coincide with the canon wars, a battle waged on the foundations of literary history that had the aggressors — people of colour and women — demanding not to be "othered"; that is, to be represented in the anthologies and in the classrooms as influential, legitimate authors. Shields's poems have no immediate truck with this debate, but read twenty years later through a lens that has been trained to be suspicious of the term "other," the poems reclaim the term *for* the other, through their non-judgmental innocence and intimacy. There are no demonized others here, just common folk whose moments of epiphany, pain, or familiarity are not commonly explored, hence the book's title. "The New Mothers," for example, takes place in a hospital within the quiet blanket of time between the bustle of eating dinner and showing off newborn babies to visitors. Having finished their meals, now pregnant with expectancy, the new mothers

> bunch at the frosted windows
> in quilted trios
> watching the parking lot where

> pair after pair
> the yellow headlights arc
> through blowing snow —
> the fathers
>   are coming.

A moment of no eventful importance — the event, a performance of parenthood, begins when the fathers arrive — becomes a moment of exciting tranquility. In fact, Shields transforms the mothers' waiting into the event itself, one so warm and cozy and full of loving anticipation and pride that the arrival of the fathers can only be anticlimactic.

In "John," however, Shields reworks an unexpected event into something inevitable, cleverly equating the "other" with the "norm." "John" depicts a revelatory moment when a young boy realizes that the pilot of a passing airplane does not know he is eating an egg for lunch. John appears "shocked, / just as if he'd never known / nor suspected he was locked / in, from the beginning, alone." Previously believing himself to be connected with the world, John undergoes a rite of passage before our eyes, developing from child to man as he utters the words that both note and activate his separation from the pilot. By ending the poem on the word "alone," Shields lets the reader feel its weight, its finality, and because the boy did not anticipate that being alone was his destiny, the poem ends on a note of "otherness": John is other than he thought, other from the world around him. He will not be a permanent Wordsworthian child who delights in his communion with nature but will be a man, and that requires being on his own. Here is where "other" becomes "not-other," for the poem suggests that the child's being alone is a natural phase of development, his realization of it a jarring initiation into adulthood that neither he nor anyone else can escape.

Shields further indicates that otherness is a necessary part of the human condition in the titles to her poems. Many include the strong presence of the author, with her use of "we" or "our," in poems such as "An Old Lady We Saw," "Our Old Professor," or "A Friend of Ours Who Knits." While the titles can read as maddeningly self-contained — the poet Christopher Levenson grumbles about their "stifling coziness" — they are also optimistically inclusive: the "other" is one with "us." As both voyeur and participant in Shields's tableaux, the reader both sees and experiences the "other" as someone not detached from society, but as one who fully partakes. Indeed, by not distinguishing many of the "other" characters as singular (as she does in *Intersect*, for example, with "Daughter," "Mother," and "Professor"), but as attached to other humans' lives, Shields bridges the gap (one that is widely felt in the 1990s) between self and other.

Although Shields's most recent volume comes almost two decades after its predecessor, Shields bridges the gap there too, for the poems in all three volumes, *Others* (1972), *Intersect* (1974) and *Coming to Canada* (1992), demand to be read together. Although each poem is a whole unto itself, it is also part of a larger poetic vision, one that requires an honest interconnection of its poems as much as it did of its various characters. The poems intersect as moments do: they complement, repudiate, or confirm each other, but they need each other to complete the vision. For instance, the new poem "Season's Greetings" picks up the outrage voiced at social convention in the earlier "An Old Lady We Saw" where a persona catches herself in a double bind: she later scolds herself for offering a fallen woman "clockwork sympathy," but also admonishes the woman for not having "cursed / the deceitful ice, the murderous cold," and for having said "the wrong thing, the worst / thing, thank you, thank you." "Radio Announcer" and "Old Men," both from *Intersect*, play off one another: the radio announcer's verbal skills span oceans and continents, his throat "a piece of sculpture / designed for ultimate resonance," but the old men know well the "disabling treachery / of language," uttered in "hoarse phrases that catch / in folded throats." And "Spring," another new poem, suggests the solitary adult that the boy "John" may grow into:

We're older this year
and as for spring we love
it less   violets, new leaves,
the tender unfolded air

mean not renewal but heaviness,
a coldness at the core,
like ourselves, honest, sober,
whom we also love less

Yet Shields directs the reader not only to juxtapose moments in
different poems; she also maintains a certain tension within individual poems that forces the reader to contend with the unexpected. In
"Anne at the Symphony," a musical instrument becomes a nightmar-
ish medical instrument for Anne, who

. . . listens like someone submitting
to surgery;
and at twelve she's quiet
under the knife,

stilled in ether, permitting
an alien clarinet
to scoop out an injury
we can't even imagine.

And in "Voices," a "round porcelain" Greek vase hums next to a
Chinese woman's shoe, "screaming" inside a glass case. Both poems
illustrate Shields's skillful balance of not only subject matter but of
emotional and visual tension: perfect control and total abandon
coexist in every image. There is no outpouring of excess emotion, no
sprawling lines, but a clean spareness that matter-of-factly expresses
both the familiar and the shocking. Thus a symphony can represent a
graphic operation. And a shoe can be contained safely within the
sanctity of a museum's glass case, yet it can simultaneously be shriek-
ing in the tortured voice of the woman whose bound foot it once
painfully encased. This careful balance allows Shields to create
tableaux that are at once tidy and contained, but also bursting with

the possibility of breaking out of those neat boundaries set both by the poet and society.

Perhaps the poem that reveals most about Carol Shields the poet, her craft, and her poetic vision, is the possibly autobiographical "I/Myself." The poem begins in a "moment of no importance" with the persona, a three-year-old girl, playing and thinking "here I am, three years old / swinging on the gate." She cannot control her thoughts because "consciousness is a bold / weed, it grows where it wants, / sees what it wants to see," and it sees "a moment within / a moment, a voice / outside a voice / saying: here I am, three / years old, swinging on a gate." This moment of no (seeming) importance is exemplary of many of Shields's tableaux: familiar, even throwaway moments take on a profundity that belies their apparent simplicity when their visual details are so cleanly drawn. Here Shields depicts the young poet watching herself at work, creating a tableau within a tableau. The visual double layer is evocative of how Shields's poems function as individual pieces, but the girl's acute self-awareness takes the visual image to a higher level as one picture resonates with the other, complicating the moment. That the girl's consciousness is uncontrollable, that it thinks seemingly without the permission of the girl, speaks to the abandon that simmers in Shields's poetry; restrained by the frame of the tableau, it nevertheless threatens to spill over. But it does not, and the tension between containment and eruption, the familiar and the unusual, the realism and the artifice of the visual image are what distinguish Shields's poetry. It is her keen perception of the human condition, however, that ultimately separates her poetry from others': she understands that

> the best of what we know
> is randomly given
> carried on difficult journeys
> and lightly worn
>
> ("Accident")

Carol Shields gives her readers the best of what she knows. And it is enough.

Works Cited

Shields, Carol. *Intersect.* Ottawa: Borealis, 1974.

—. *Others.* Ottawa, Borealis, 1972.

—. *Coming to Canada.* Ottawa: Carleton University Press, 1991.

JACQUELINE REID-WALSH

Tracing the Arcs of Jane Austen's Life

The suitability of Carol Shields to be the author selected for a "writer's" biography of Jane Austen has often been remarked upon. Shields works largely in the same genre of domestic fiction that Austen helped forge and accordingly has suffered some of the same critical misconceptions regarding size and scope as Austen did. While writing biography is necessarily a more restrictive project than writing fiction, this task has allowed Shields to explore in the cognate genre of domestic biography her belief that "art lives from constraints" (Hollenberg 344). At the same time, the undertaking has enabled her to explore more fully her ideas about the art of writing and share these with readers both of Jane Austen and of Carol Shields.

Shields has remarked that one overriding plot that fascinates her is the "arc of the human life" — "the processes of aging, growing, and the shadowy end of life, illness and eventual death." She has also noted that as she ages she has become more interested in "writing about writing" (Wachtel). In this essay, I examine Shields's biography of Jane Austen in light of these twin fascinations: the presentation of the arcs of Austen's life as a writer and a historical person, with a focus on Austen's youth, and the discussion of Austen's writing, with a focus on the mature Austen. In so doing, I hope to illuminate Shields's unique contributions to Austen biographical scholarship as a writer and as a critic.

Shields begins by stating the bald fact that "today Jane Austen belongs to the nearly unreachable past" with no documents to "prove" many aspects of her daily life such as a diary, or photograph, or even portrait (5). The resultant "opacity" of her life, despite the presence of a set of chatty letters pruned carefully by her beloved sister Cassandra, presents a challenge to the biographer. To circumvent this difficulty, Shields asserts that the aim of literary biography is not the impossible task of prying into the crevices of a person's life but rather to illuminate the writer's texts. While one of the difficulties of creating a biography of a figure from an earlier period is that it "throw[s] a profile of theory against a text" . . . "that had no immediate knowledge [of] literary theory (10)," the focus on Austen's literary compositions, not intimate details, is important to remember. Shields describes the task of the traditional Austen biographer in order to set her approach in opposition to this: a "nail[ing] together" of the established facts of Austen's life with "speculation gleaned from the novels" with the presumption being that "fiction flows directly from a novelist's experience rather than from her imagination" (11).

In contrast, Shields suggests that the relation between life and text is more complex and indirect. For example, she notes how the period during which Austen wrote her most optimistic novel, *Pride and Prejudice*, was one of the sadder times in her personal life — leading Shields to propose that the novel can be seen as a "palimpsest" with Austen's own life "engraved roughly, enigmatically, beneath its surface"(69). This image of the palimpsest, where one layer of writing partly erases the other but leaves traces underneath, evokes an impression of multiple surfaces and layers of inscription, and introduces the idea of poststructuralist literary theory into the discussion.

Implicitly, Shields distinguishes the technique of using literary theory, a modern invention itself, from what may first appear to be a similar interpretive technique sometimes used by biographers whereby the past is judged against the standards of the present and found lacking. This assumption is part of a larger problem that historical literary scholars call "presentism" (Beer), the arrogance and solipsistic belief of the present day to assume that the current interpretation is not only correct but also the only way to understand earlier beliefs and attitudes. As an instance of this, Shields cites the idea of using current sociological views of the family to understand Austen's family, and thereby to label it as dysfunctional (11). The differences between the methods are partly in attitude, for in the latter the past is found wanting, and partly in focus, for in this form of literary interpretation the emphasis remains on the texts as entities distinct from the author.

Shields asserts that in order to try and understand the difference in periods between the late eighteenth century and our own she has attempted "to read into [her] own resistance instead of seeking proof in the fiction"(11). Accordingly, her method combines what she calls an "impressionistic response" to Austen's writings (2) with a questioning or interrogating approach. This approach is informed by a women-centred perspective on the development of the novel and by feminist reading theories that present women as active and resistant readers of the male-dominated canon. Shields calls her technique a "close textual inspection"(18) of various texts at hand — ranging from fiction to poetry to letters to notes to biographical information — all separated out from one another. At times, in her range and depth of imaginative rendering of the personality of Austen, expressed by her use of the phrase "it can be imagined . . .", Shields appears to be a type of biographical "imaginist" like Austen's character Emma, full of "speculation and foresight" (160) as she, as a woman writer, tries to imagine herself back into the mind of Austen at key stages and times of her life from early childhood onwards.

Some ideas of Virginia Woolf's provide a useful context with which to approach Shields's presentation of Austen. Woolf appreciated the lack of knowledge about Austen's life and the corresponding challenge this represents to biographers, famously comparing Austen to Shakespeare: ". . . when people compare Shakespeare and Jane Austen, they may mean that the minds of both had consumed all impediments; and for that reason we do not know Jane Austen and we do not know Shakespeare, and for that reason Jane Austen pervades every word that she wrote, and so does Shakespeare" (*Room of One's Own* 73). Shields expresses a similar perception when she states that since Austen's life is largely opaque due to lack of primary historical documentation, perhaps the only authentic record that traces the "genuine arc of a human life" is that which is presented in fiction because it respects the "human trajectory"(10-11).

Shields provides a brief historical context of the emerging genre of the novel by comparing its impact on literate eighteenth-century households of the middling classes to that of the television in the 1950s (24). This analogy stresses how the novel was a popular form, not an elite form, and it helps us to understand what it might have been like to read for the first time about the texture of daily life, and encounter recognizable men and women who thought and felt and endured the vicissitudes of existence. It is an aspect of the "almost unreachable past" for us today to appreciate that in the 1740s when the novel began to flourish there were no fixed novel types and even the form the novel itself would take, such as epistolary, or narrative, was still in question. In the development of this messy but vital form, due to the coincidence of widespread literacy among women, the novel is the only genre in which women played a full role from the outset (26), unlike their involvement with the genres of poetry or drama.

As keen novel readers, members of the Austen family can per-haps be seen as unconventional in their wide reading of fiction, just as they were in their wide appreciation for drama, a form they both read and performed. From childhood on, then, Jane Austen was exposed to this broad range of literature in an uncensored way, and since children's literature was in its infancy as well, she began reading adult books very early on. Since the Reverend Austen had five hun-dred books when they left Steventon, his was a substantial library for her to forage in.

Shields's presentation of the trajectory of Jane Austen's writing life begins with Austen's reading in early years, before her writing of juvenilia, for she states that "[e]ven as a child Jane Austen seemed to be thinking of herself as a future novelist" (24) and thereby read nov-els critically, self-consciously and with laughter. Shields refers to Austen's ironic comments as an adult about the absurd adventure of Mary Brunton's heroine of *Self-Control* (1811) when she says "[my] Heroine shall not merely be wafted down an American river in a boat by herself, she shall cross the Atlantic in the same way, and never stop until she reaches Gravesend" (24) and uses them as inspiration for her depiction of Austen's self-directed method of reading. For instance, Shields suggests that Austen may have thought of her beloved *The History of Sir Charles Grandison* (1751) by Samuel Richardson as a "kind of fantasy rather than an imprint of the world's 'reality'" (27). She considers that the young Austen would have been "provoked to laughter by Richardson's melodramatic effects" and that she would have "rea[d] *against* the Richardson tradition, and unconsciously form[ed] her own idea of the 'realistic' novel and of what material she might include when her time came" (28).

By invoking the idea of the resistant reader, one who reads "against the grain" of the text, Shields is employing ideas from feminist reading theory. Judith Fetterly, for instance, proposed that when faced with reading a male canon, women must resist the temptation to identify with the hero and read against the grain of the dominant discourse and use ideological inconsistencies to read on behalf of feminism (in Eagleton 119-34). Shields adapts these concepts to her own purposes to construct a portrayal of the young Jane Austen in her self-directed program as a novelist-in-training.

Shields links this account of Austen as a young reader to her subsequent production of satirical juvenilia, asking "[w]hat makes a child of twelve or thirteen a satirist?" (29). She proposes some answers by presenting Austen's output as a performance for a select group of readers — her family — and relating it to her self-directed writer's education. Thereby, the juvenile texts can be seen as extensions of "a deliberate and inventive misreading" that may have helped form her "vision" of the possibilities of what the novel form could do when "fortified with irony and structure" (30). By referring to Austen's response of laughter to the excesses of the novel form and by relating this to her sometimes outrageous early writings, Shields evokes Virginia Woolf's famous account of the young Austen where Woolf asks in her discussion of the juvenilia, "but what is this note which never merges in the rest, which sounds distantly and penetratingly all through the volume? It is the sound of laughter. The girl of fifteen is laughing, in her corner, at the world" (*Common Reader* 135). By her approach, Shields adds a current feminist edge to this view and focuses on the continuity between the juvenilia and the mature work (35).

In this way, Shields develops as the foreground of her book a tracing of the arc of Austen's life as an emergent writer. In the background, she is able to give secondary attention to tracing the arc of the historical figure of Austen based upon a close reading of primary documents composed by Austen, documents written by her family, and available biographies. This second line interweaves with the first arc but also provides a context for it. Here again Shields emphasizes an unconventional childhood that, with the exception of two short periods away at boarding school, was one that possessed freedoms of education and play outside the normal range of well-brought-up girls (20). In her account of Austen's later childhood and young womanhood she creates an equally attractive account of a vital (teenage) girls' culture centred on Austen, Cassandra and their female neighbours: "Girlish talk held sway: clothes, books, dance steps, neighbourhood gossip; giddy expeditions were planned: long walks or trips into Basingstoke" (40). Here, Shields appears to be utilizing insights of feminist cultural studies theorists, such as Angela McRobbie, who have presented positive images of girls' domestic culture in our current period, and adapting these images to a representation of eighteenth-century girlhood.

Throughout her biography, Shields is able to draw upon her extensive "inside" knowledge as a writer to provide an informed commentary on writers and on the process of writing. In this aspect, Shields engages less in a gendered or women-centred approach to focus more on the presentation of Austen as an author and what she considers necessary in order for a writer to be productive. In this way, she can interpret events in Austen's life differently, even though they have been examined many times before, and interpret gaps in new ways by illuminating them from a different angle.

Notably, by possessing this angle of vision, Shields can provide a thoughtful interpretation of Austen's long silence during the first decade of the nineteenth century. Shields counters what has been understood as the typical view since it was first articulated by Austen's nephew James Edward Austen-Leigh, that the busy life in Bath should have been stimulating to her creative faculties. Instead, Shields quotes Virginia Woolf's insights to propose the opposite: "A writer, she [Woolf] maintains, does not need stimulation, but the opposite of stimulation. A writer needs regularity, the same books around her, and the same walls. A writer needs self ordered patterns of time, her own desk, and day after profitable day in order to do her best work" (103). Based on this, Shields can argue that it is this dislocation and change of scene that unsettled the frame of Austen's creativity during the long writing gap in which she only produced the unfinished "The Watsons," halted around the time of her father's death.

This writer's insight enables Shields to pull together different types of silences in Austen's life, such as the lack of commentary on her presumably disabled brother George, on her mother's temperament, on a proposal of marriage accepted and then immediately refused in 1802, and on the non-response of the publisher Crosby about "Susan" (*Northanger Abbey*) to ultimately emphasize the writer's needs over all else. Shields states: "Novelists do not write into a void. They require an answering response, an audience of readers outside the family circle, and they also need the approval that professional publication brings" (110). Accordingly she posits that it was the combination of a sequence of discouraging events that conspired to silence Austen in the middle years of her life.

This writer's need for a settled home and an established routine, then, also accounts for the sudden reflowering of activity when Austen and her family settle in Chawton, where Austen produces a yearly succession of novels. Shields interprets the tone of a slight poem about Chawton, written before they have even moved, to be prescient of the conditions necessary for Austen's emergence as a published writer:

Our Chawton Home, how much we feel
Already in it, to our mind;
And how convinced, that when complete
It will all other Houses beat
That have ever been made or mended,
With rooms concise, or rooms distended.

You'll find us very snug next year,
Perhaps with Charles & Fanny near . . . (134)

Indeed, it was in one these "concise" rooms with a community of family and friends around her that Austen's masterpieces would be composed.

In chapter 15 Shields digresses from her chronological account to write insightfully about how a novelist needs to achieve a "delicate balance" between being alone and being with others, and how this requirement is different for each writer. She observes that since Austen wrote extremely social novels, she was obviously a very sociable being, drawing attention to how key moments in the fiction often occur not in solitary meditation but in social groups (119-20). This insight allows Shields to reinterpret the fact that Jane Austen "composed" in a common sitting room, covering her writing when someone entered, and to puncture the established view of this as being solely a detriment. Rather, Shields discusses the positive and negative aspects of this lifelong lack of solitude and the pressure of domestic duties, citing Austen's famous complaint: "[c]omposition seems to me impossible with a head full of joints of mutton & doses of rhubarb" (123). At the same time, she notes how the idea and practice of friendship were exceptionally strong in Austen's period, and how lifelong friendships nourished Austen immeasurably.

In chapter 17 Shields provides a nuanced description of the positive and negative features of Austen's reading community. The positive dimension was that she had a reliable audience who possessed a wide cross-section of taste (139). They were knowledgeable insiders in terms of their long (in some cases lifelong) relationship with her, and personally sympathetic in their listening and interpreting. Although not writers themselves, their close relationship with her made them part of the process she underwent in order to become a published author. Shields considers them in some ways to be an "ideal audience": attached to Jane Austen and to the emergent novel form, they were both "critically alert" and "emotionally attuned," participating in the process of writing through "communal consultation" (140-141).

Both of these features of reception, the social community and their special or inside knowledge of Austen's circumstances, suggest one ideal situation of readership and present the major initial context for Austen's work. At the same time, as Shields reiterates, Austen was an aspiring and later published writer who was also writing for an audience wider than both her family circle and similar demographic circles. Apart from reading the rare review in contemporary magazines, such as the excerpt Shields provides from the *Critical Review* about *Sense and Sensibility* — "the incidents are probable, and highly pleasing, and interesting; the conclusion such as the reader must wish it should be, and the whole is just long enough to interest without fatiguing" (146) — Austen had little sense of how her books were received. Shields states that Austen doubted whether the Prince Regent actually had read her novels when he expressed the wish that *Emma* be dedicated to him, and points out as well that Scott's private tribute was not published until after her death (164-66). The sales figures available then, which gratifyingly gave some indication of readership, probably did not include the majority of readers who used circulating libraries. Austen, due to her restricted life and anonymity, had little knowledge of what general readers thought of her work. This lack of knowledge of audience reception outside her community may suggest why she felt impelled to canvass her circle for opinions of *Mansfield Park* and *Emma*.

The lack of wider reception in terms of readership is the flip side of the positive aspects of Austen's tightly knit reading community and can be connected to what Shields considers to be more grievous a lack: how Austen's writing life occurred in isolation from other writers so that she was unable to partake in any writers' community. Shields observes that James Edward Austen-Leigh understood this lack. He states that his aunt never met any contemporary authors, and probably never even met any intellects to match her own. Consequently, "her powers never could have been sharpened by collision with superior intellects, nor her imagination aided by their casual suggestions. Whatever she produced was a home-made article" (142). Shields seizes on the phrase "home-made article" and meditates on what this might have signified in the early days of the English novel when "working at a stern[] forge" they were exploring "the dimensions of fictional belief and disbelief" (142). She draws attention to how in a state of absolute writer's isolation Austen took the architecture of the eighteenth-century novel, and "made it new, clean and rational, just as though she'd taken a broom to the old fussiness of plot and action" (143). With her domestic image of the isolated woman and her broom, Shields animates her perception of how the two arcs of Austen's life interconnect. Shields privileges the writing life over the historical life, yet brings them together in a homely image.

In the latter chapters, the pace of Shields's writing quickens considerably, beginning at the end of chapter 17 with her account of the acceptance by a London publisher of *Sense and Sensibility* late in 1810. The style of these short chapters, one about each of the published novels, is brisk, and the tone captures the contained excitement of Austen becoming an author that only another author can relate to. When we read these chapters, we can sense the energy and excitement of publication at second hand and become caught up in the drama of Austen's late success. Similarly, while reading about *Persuasion* in chapter 22 we experience almost palpably the pathos of premature ending of Austen's life.

If we were to stand back and consider Shields's overall presentation of the two arcs of Jane Austen's life — her writing life and her historical life, and observe them in terms of the patterns they create — the arcs could almost be plotted on graph paper. Let us imagine a chart where the vertical axis represents the affective or emotional dimensions of Austen's life and the horizontal axis represents the chronological lifeline. If the arc of Austen's writing life were to be mapped, this arc would be plotted high on the page at an early age, and then experience a long gap in the middle with only a single point ("The Watsons" at mid level). Then the line would return to a high level with a rapid rise for each published novel, achieve a peak with the writing of *Emma*, and be cut off suddenly in *Persuasion*. It is interesting to note that if the arc of Jane Austen's physical life were to be plotted, it would also be plotted high on the page at an early age, experience a few high points, including romantic encounters, then fall off to a level line interrupted with the same long gap in the middle. The final part of the arc would return to a level line, offsetting the rapidly rising line of the writing life.

Carol Shields's biography *Jane Austen* introduces Austen to new audiences, such as the literate but non-specialist general reader, or "common reader," a phrase coined by Samuel Johnson, and used to great effect by Virginia Woolf. It also provides a theoretically informed "writerly" perspective on Austen and on the art of reading and writing that would be appealing to both aficionados of Jane Austen and of Carol Shields. The book's brevity and accessible style lend themselves to a pleasurable few hours — indeed it could be read in one long sitting. If a second edition were to be issued, some factual errors would have to be corrected, but more importantly, some scholarly apparatus would be useful. A table of contents, name and subject index, and reference list would enable this study to be both pleasurable and useful for readers of literature, biography, Jane Austen and Carol Shields. The book is an elegant and incisively rendered tribute to both authors, and the relationship between Carol Shields as a reader of Jane Austen and writer of her biography is fascinating to deduce. Indeed, if Shields's observation that writing is a "palimpsest," with the author's own life being "engraved roughly, enigmatically, beneath its surface," is applied to her own text, we can detect lineaments of the image of Carol Shields underneath.

Works Cited

Beer, Gillian. *Arguing with the Past: Essays in Narrative from Woolf to Sidney.* London: Routledge, 1989.

Eagleton, Mary. *Working With Feminist Criticism.* Oxford: Blackwell, 1996.

Hollenberg, Donna Krolik. "An Interview with Carol Shields." *Contemporary Literature* 39.3 (1998): 339-55.

McRobbie, Angela. *Feminism and Youth Culture: From "Jackie" to "Just Seventeen."* Houndmills: Macmillan, 1991.

Shields, Carol. *Jane Austen.* A Penguin Life. New York: Penguin Putnam, 2001.

Wachtel, Eleanor. "Interview with Carol Shields." *Writers and Company.* Toronto: CBC Radio (September 21, 1997).

Woolf, Virginia. *The Common Reader.* First Series (1925). Ed. Andrew McNeillie. San Diego: Harvest Books, 1984.

— . *A Room of One's Own* (1929). New York: Harcourt Brace Jovanovich, 1991.

CHRIS JOHNSON

Ordinary Pleasures (and Terrors): The Plays of Carol Shields

At their best, the full-length plays of Carol Shields illuminate ordinary pleasures: eavesdropping in an airport, playing cards with old friends, living in a family, watching kids grow up. At their very best, the plays counterpoint these pleasures with ordinary doubts and terrors: the departure of friends and children, loneliness, mortality. A dog howls in the distance.

In performance, the plays thrive on a strong sense of familiarity; an audience of "ordinary people" owns the material in a way that encourages them to accept the absence of a linear plot as well as quirky leaps in style and scale. On the other hand, critics, dramaturges, and academics often call attention to what they regard as shortcomings in the plays (their sentimentality, their generalizations, their dependence on vignette structure) or dismiss them entirely as lightweight; Kevin Longfield's qualified admiration for *Thirteen Hands* is quite typical: "It's very good for what it is, but I'm not sure that it is a play. It's theatrical without being dramatic" (*Theatrum* 33, 42). In a recent e-mail exchange, a colleague in a British Columbia university-college writes: "They [Shields's plays] seem competent enough and occasionally interesting but I find they don't plumb deep enough into character or situation; they feel more like exercises in playwriting." But the reservations, some of which I share myself, must always be placed in the context of the fact that these plays speak to a non-specialist audience, the "ordinary people" for whom as well as about which they were written, in a way seldom matched by other recent Prairie plays. Ultimately, I'm more interested in what the plays do than in what they don't.

I first encountered Carol Shields, playwright, not as an audience member but as a stage director, directing the first full production of *Departures and Arrivals* for the University of Manitoba's Black Hole Theatre in 1984, with help from Vic Cowie, Kathy France, Denise Brown and Sue Matheson, and a cast which included, among others, Yvette Nolan, Mike Gottli, Gerry Akman, Jocelyn Thorvaldsen, Peter Spencer, Robert Taylor, Donna Lewis, Wes Crealock, Margo Wilson, and Mike Lawrenchuk. Like the many other universities and colleges that followed in producing the play, we used many actors to play the many characters, although they can be presented, with doubling, by only six performers. *Departures and Arrivals* is a drama teacher's dream, its twenty-two vignettes not only offering many parts, but many good parts, good opportunities for student actors.

I had wonderful times exploring Shields's airport, her "public place . . . as a venue for the theatrical sense that enlarges ordinary lives" ("Introduction"). Again, part of the attraction is plentitude, a fullness made of fragments, glimpses of many lives. But the glimpses, though brief, are for the most part also penetrating; the economy with which characters are fleshed out, provided with sub-text and a crisis before being whisked away and replaced, is remarkable. The compression is organic, scene after scene propelled forward by the urgency of imminent departure, or by the heightened emotional, para-theatrical demands of arrival; while an airport may not really be a theatre, coming down the arrivals escalator at Winnipeg International often feels like making an entrance, indeed often involves entering a scene, "social theatre," when friends are waiting below. Frannie and Richard, divorced for eight years, meet accidentally; while exchanging pleasantries, they fence, fish for information, find together some common ground, memories funny only to them. Suddenly, Richard blurts "I loved the backs of your knees" (79). If he wants to see the backs of those knees ever again, he's got to work fast, and inventively, for this is, after all, a public place. Taking advantage of nostalgia and tentatively recaptured tenderness, Richard persuades Frannie to bend over to return her book to her bag, thus hitching up her skirt, while he bends over, pretending to tie his shoe. Glorious moment, simultaneously tender, wry, and very funny.

Such scenes, such moments, dense, emotionally complex, revealing, are found throughout the play. Two women buy flight insurance for their departing husbands, exchange somewhat embarrassed reassurances, slide almost imperceptibly into a discussion of contingency plans, into which creep small freedom fantasies, which in their turn crescendo to a full-throated duet of longing for a new, husbandless life, the nasty corollary, "I wish he were dead," present at some level and in some part of the mind, clear but never explicitly acknowledged. Similar sub-surface nastiness enriches a deliciously protracted and archaically phrased monologue from the elderly Mrs. Kitchell of Rosy Rapids. It emerges that Mrs. Kitchell is on her way to England to meet her new grandson, that her daughter married an Arab, that she has hidden her grandson's name, Mohammed, from the neighbours, that she is regretful and frightened: "But I didn't think this, that she'd marry . . . Susan says he's real modern though, doesn't wear the cloth thing on his head" (51). The scene provoked strong debate at the university, with easy condemnation of racism (purportedly in the play) pitted against an acknowledgement of the complex veracity of Shields's portrait of bigotry coexisting with the otherwise charming attributes of an elderly, rural Manitoban; some even saw the human cause of this particular xenophobia, Mrs. Kitchell's loss of her daughter to the unknown, an ordinary terror after all. I was sorry when Shields softened the contradictions slightly in the published version of the play. We lost, for example, "I hope he isn't too dark, the baby I mean" (1984 production script, 42). I valued the provocative and truthful power of the original.

The theatrical experience of the whole is further enriched by Shields's sudden shifts in tone and style from scene to scene. The wistful sweetness of elderly strangers meeting through a companion wanted ad in *The Rose Lover's Quarterly* is exquisitely undercut by the ghostly appearance and tart comments of their dead former spouses, a moment our audience clearly thought was one of the funniest things they'd ever seen in the theatre. Interior realities invade exterior realities, as when a family attempts several "takes" of their airport reunion, striving for the emotional intensity Hollywood tells us should be normal, theatricalizing the common contemporary sensation that we are all, somehow, on camera, that all lives, even ordinary ones, are movies.

Not all the scenes in *Departures and Arrivals* work as well, particularly those which are free from the pressure of either departure or arrival, or in which the inherent theatricality of the latter is overwhelmed or neutralized by a forced, overt theatricality. Lacking this pressure, we get static comment from two-dimensional characters; here Shields apparently cannot muster a sympathetic understanding of the characters (the reporters, the movie star, the poet, the basketball players), or does not have sufficient understanding of or affection for the form she attempts to parody. The single ongoing story, the true romance contretemps between pilot and flight attendant, gave me the biggest directorial headaches, partly because it treats sexual harassment lightly, and without the contextualizing that serves to interrogate similarly explosive material in the Mrs. Kitchell monologue, partly because Shields doesn't sufficiently understand or acknowledge the (admittedly tawdry) power of soap opera, a factor exacerbated in the Black Hole production by the fact that I didn't either. These problems are addressed but not entirely solved by the rewrites for the published version.

Paul Thompson has said of the episodic and anecdotal structure of Theatre Passe Muraille's *The Farm Show* that it resembles "a Canadian Sunday School or Christmas Concert where one person does a recitation, another sings a song, a third acts out a skit, etc." ("Introduction," *The Farm Show*). While *Departures and Arrivals* is the work of a single author rather than a collectively created piece, and while its tone is considerably more urbane than that of *The Farm Show*, the same, I think, can be said of Shields's first play, especially the earlier, Black Hole Theatre production version in which song and dance played a considerable part. The apparent informality of the structure (which Shields, in her introduction, gives directors permission to play with further still, rearranging scenes to suit particular productions), the effect of a sequence of "turns" is for me part of its charm, and, further, an effective theatrical model of the random nature of eavesdropping in an airport or other public place, an activity of which I myself am extremely fond.

Thirteen Hands is similarly episodic and anecdotal, its thirteen scenes giving us vignettes from the lives of the members of the "Clara Circle," a group of women who meet weekly, ostensibly to play bridge. In her introduction to the Blizzard edition of 1993, Shields says her intent is to valorize the lives of women caught between "movements," the suffragist movement and the current feminist project. She goes on to say that "Two principal patterns of human behaviour play against each other: continuity and replacement" (Playwright's Note). The group, sustained by the social needs it fulfills and its own history, continues, while death and departure require the replacement of individuals, old friends by new friends, mothers by daughters and granddaughters as the play moves through the current century. Again, scenes are presented through widely differing conventions, including song, and again, shifts between styles and realities are part of the effect and meaning of the whole. Again, Shields explicitly gives directors permission to "reshuffle," and again, it is suggested that many actors could be used to play the parts rather than the four who doubled their way through the many characters in the premiere at Prairie Theatre Exchange in the winter of 1993.

As in the case of *Departures and Arrivals,* some observers were disdainful of the "vignette" structure, but here too I don't think that that in itself is a problem, for again the structure serves as a model of the experience of "departures and arrivals." This structural dimension, introduced early in the piece by Clara Wesley's monologue about the first death in the group, is extended over a longer time-frame and put at the mercy of a randomness unregulated even by airlines schedules. The characters East, North and South become, in some respects, interchangeable, and I think Marlene Moser is closer to putting her finger on what may be a matter of real concern: "We are encouraged to listen for the sounds of unheard voices: at times dialogue is accelerated, or voices switch from the inner to the outer. Unfortunately, this polyvocity is never quite realized: a universalizing impulse in the play inevitably subsumes the individual into the whole" (*Canadian Theatre Review* 79/80, 164). The characters in their comings and goings are not as sharply individualized as are the personae of the earlier play. As individuals (rather than components of a group, participants in an ongoing ritual) they come perilously close to the invisibility they themselves explicitly fear in their lives away from the bridge table; as North puts it: "I could feel people looking right past me, looking for someone more attractive, looking for someone more interesting to talk to" (27, 28).

The exception is Clara/West, an original member of the group who survives throughout the play to become the great grandmother playing bridge with three generations of descendants in a scene near its conclusion. Clara stays, and the actor playing her (in the Prairie Theatre Exchange production, Nancy Drake) stays in that role most of the play, seeming to give it a centre and raising the expectations that go with a play that has a centre: we want to learn more about Clara than we do, and I suppose we want Clara to learn more about herself than she apparently does, or to put words to the insights on whose brink she hovers — she does see that the gathering is not "just a game," and in the penultimate scene justifies a life which some might see as banal to the (unfortunately abstract) interrogator on the bicycle by identifying some of the gifts members of this community of women gave to each other, the bridge game "a little planet we'd put together and it was us who'd written the rules" (59). But finally, Clara (and perhaps Shields) retreats into nostalgia.

These reservations were apparently not shared by most of the people attending the premiere production; a large contingent of bridge-players evidently enjoyed the play as much as playing bridge, in itself an important accolade. I did note that by and large, women responded more warmly to the play than did men, and that much of the pleasure seemed to arise from a kind of validation, a recognition of emotions, situations, womanly communication and social custom not commonly seen on stage: the witty Gilbert and Sullivan acknowledgement that winning is fun (however "unfeminine" the admission); the scene of self-doubting, sometimes caustic spoken sub-text; the reworked freedom fantasies similar to those seen before in the insurance scene from *Departures and Arrivals*; the discussion of mothers. In its emphasis on matrilineality (biological and spiritual), and its politically conscious departure from "patriarchal," Aristotelean dramatic structure, *Thirteen Hands* is, among other things, a liberal feminist statement, valorizing not only the women portrayed but the liberal feminist women (not all of whom would be comfortable with that description) who saw in the play ordinary experiences and values important to them but largely ignored by the cultural establishment, despite the fact that that group is strongly represented in the Canadian theatregoing public in general, the Prairie Theatre Exchange audience in particular.

That liberal feminist vision is not likely to find favour with patriarchs on one hand, radical or materialist feminists on the other, but it is the vision which informs Shields's latest play, "Fashion Power Guilt and the Charity of Families," co-written with daughter Catherine, and I believe at least some of the response, positive and negative, will therefore be overtly political. There is obviously a danger in expecting Shields to conform to a hegemony from which she feels distinct, but there is also a perhaps less obvious danger in asking her to assume a stance more radical than the one with which she feels comfortable and which is therefore inconsistent with the vision of the world she has been realizing. A word of caution here: my response to "Fashion . . ." is based on the script (a rewrite) submitted to Prairie Theatre Exchange September 6, 1994.

As its title suggests, the play is an exploration of family, ideas about family, doubts about family. It functions on two levels of reality: a bureaucratic investigation of social organization, and scenes from the life of a particular nuclear family (father, mother, daughter, son); occasionally the two intersect, as in the family's monthly meeting with the fret-and-worry consultant, and there are side excursions into song and other stylistic heightenings in the manner of earlier Shields plays. While there is a stronger through-line than in either of the earlier plays, there are the signature digressions and commentary, the use of the more or less self-contained scene as the basic structural unit; to head off the "this is not a play" response, let's call "Fashion . . ." a revue, an intelligent theatrical revue on the themes of family and family politics.

There is in this revue something of the TV family sitcom, and a parody of that cultural icon, but also something of the realistic, domestic drama fathered (I use the word advisedly) by Ibsen, with its unacknowledged family secrets and suppressed individual desires, and again, comment on same. The characters feel obliged to be content, but nonetheless experience loneliness, hear a dog howling in the distance. The house is both refuge and trap.

There is much to admire in this script. The New Age, supportive Scrabble game is hilarious. The family fashion show will be a *coup de theatre*, wittily superimposing Euro-pop garment jargon on changing family roles: "G-I-R-L, she's *here*. She's checked in. Trans-avant-garde screen on her *chest*. She's retro-fitted. Her industrial construction shows through — each line a *connector*. She can spell *kinetic*" (Act 2, 1). (I think this is one of the points in the script where I can hear Catherine's voice.) The "typical day" sequence will provide the basis for a lovely vaudeville turn. The intrusion of loneliness and of painful memory is often very moving.

But I have trouble with the bureaucrats, not so much with the idea of this level of the play as with the bureaucrats as written. Shields brings to all her scripts her fine gift for language, and here we have evidence of her ear for the absurdities of officialese and her talent for parody, but reading the script at least, I get no sense that people are saying these words, that a person is playing this official role, wearing, for whatever reason, this mask, and probably holding an opinion about wearing the mask and saying these words. In this lack, these characters remind me of the flight attendant in *Departures and Arrivals* and the young woman who interrogates Clara in *Thirteen Hands*. Instead, we get overt editorial comment. In turn, this seems to me to be part of a still larger pattern: I'm not convinced that Shields always comes to terms with the idea that the characters in her plays, as opposed to the characters in her novels, will eventually be inhabited by living, breathing, creative human beings, actors. The result is sometimes awkwardnesses such as those just described, sometimes stasis when the theatrical eye/ear is slowed (or narrowed) to the pace (or scope) of the reading eye, sometimes scenes not faulty as they are, but thinner than they need be, missing opportunities by not allowing enough room for creative contribution from the actors, or by not giving them enough to do, to act.

Nonetheless, "Fashion Power Guilt and the Charity of Families," like *Departures and Arrivals* and *Thirteen Hands* before it, will speak to its audience and will include many in its moments of recognition, often guilty and rueful recognition. While many people no longer live within a "traditional" family, many do, and, no longer able to take the stability of the institution for granted nor the "rightness" of this way of life, are more than ever before conscious of the contradictions, compromises and difficulties of living in this way. For this group of people, a sizeable proportion of the theatregoing public, "Fashion . . ." will offer the witty and insightful takes on ordinary pleasures and ordinary terrors that we've come go expect from her work. The Scrabble game turns "fun" into "function" into "functional" into "dysfunctional," and as so often in Shields, a word game encapsulates the meaning and movement of the work as a whole. These family lives are full of "typical days," but, as in the earlier plays, surface ordinariness is often deceptive. At night, a dog howls somewhere in the neighbourhood; members of the family, and the audience, hear different things: "A big loud wild bark that says — it says everything. Like it doesn't leave one single thing out, it's the greatest" (Act I, 44) or ". . . just a bark, your regular standard neighbourhood dog bark, but this particular dog is, like, talking? Oh my God, it's awful what he's saying. He's saying (using tiny voice) *help me, help me*" (Act I, 46).

Notes

Except where the 1984 production script is specified, quotations from *Departures and Arrivals* are from the 1990 Blizzard edition.

"Fashion Power Guilt and the Charity of Families" had its premiere at Prairie Theatre Exchange in Winnipeg on March 9, 1995.

CAROL SHIELDS

About Writing

I heard somewhere that actors must never lose their stage fright, since stage fright keeps them agile and edgy and just enough in awe of their project to support their necessary torment.

In much the same way I cling to my self-consciousness about being a writer. I'm not really a writer (minor toe scuffing here) but just someone who now and then sits down and commits (too strong a word, cross that out) — a woman who now and then sits down and attempts to make with her two hands an artifact of sorts.

Some writers feel differently about their chosen medium, but for me words can shape themselves into poetry or fiction or drama or essay, as long as there are sentences to be constructed and words, that, by their rhythm and rightness, bring a sense of perfect consolation. Consolation? For what?

At times I feel guilty about this. Sitting upstairs in an old sewing room and making up stories does not always feel like an appropriate occupation for a grown woman. But a Winnipeg friend of mine reminded me once that "we also serve, who only sit and think." Think, and write down our thoughts, she might have added.

From the beginning there is the problem of how we write and what we write *about* — the subject, the materials that furnish the narrative. Are they worthy of a reader's time? Is Muriel Spark right when she says that the only fit subjects for literature are good and evil? I have never been able to work this puzzle out. There is writing itself, and then there is what we write about.

Language has always mattered more to me than the "aboutness" of fiction — this is Nabokov's term, and I believe he uses it somewhat derisively. As human beings we carry patterns of language and experience, and these patterns are what I find myself trying to bring together. You can see that this involves a good deal of trust, the trust that the readers' patterns will, somehow, match up with the writer's.

I continue to worry about my chosen subject of home and family, always imagining it might be read as a retreat from real issues. Nevertheless, over a lifetime I have convinced myself — on good days, at least — that we all possess a domestic space, and that it is mainly within this domestic arc that we express the greater part of our consciousness. My faith in this idea comes and goes, rallies and subsides, but I want, above all else, to be allowed to stare at the question seriously.

I hesitate to use the term *literary writing* or *serious writing*, but let me say what I have discovered through the acts of reading and writing. It is simply this: that language that carries weight in our culture is very often fuelled by a search for home, our rather piteous human groping toward that metaphorical place where we can be most truly ourselves, where we can evolve and create, and where we can reach out and touch and heal each other's lonely heart.

A Shields Chronology

1935   Carol Warner born in Oak Park, Illinois to Robert and Inez
            Warner. Sister Barbara and brother Robert (twins) born 1933.

1940-48   Nathaniel Hawthorne School (1940-43) and Ralph Waldo
            Emerson School (1943-48) in Oak Park.

1948-53   Oak Park High School.

1953-57   Hanover College, Hanover, Indiana.

1955-56   Exchange student, University of Exeter, Exeter, England.

1957   Graduates with MA from Hanover College. Marries Donald
            Hugh Shields; the couple moves to Vancouver, then Toronto.

1958-60   Son John (1958) and daughter Anne (1959) are born in Toronto.

1960-63   Family moves to Manchester, England (1960-63); daughter
            Catherine is born in 1962; Carol publishes first short stories.

1964   Family returns to Toronto; daughter Margaret is born.

1965   Shields is a winner in the CBC Young Writers Competition for
            poetry.

1967   Family moves to Ottawa; daughter Sara is born (1968).

1971   Shields becomes a Canadian citizen.

1972   *Others* (book of poems) published (Borealis).

1973-75   Editor of *Canadian Slavonic Papers* (Carleton University).
            Intersect (book of poems) published (Borealis, 1974).

1975   MA (English), University of Ottawa; thesis on Susanna
            Moodie's writing.

1975-76   Shields spends year in France, returns to Ottawa.

1976   *Susanna Moodie: Voice and Vision* (critical study based on master's thesis) published (Borealis); first novel, *Small Ceremonies*, published (McGraw-Hill Ryerson).

1976-77   Lecturer in the Department of English, University of Ottawa. *The Box Garden* (novel) published (McGraw-Hill Ryerson, 1977). Shields wins Canadian Authors Association Award for best novel of 1976 for *Small Ceremonies*.

1977-78   Shields teaches Creative Writing at the University of Ottawa.

1978   Moves to Vancouver (1978-1980); Shields teaches Creative Writing at the University of British Columbia, 1978-79.

1980   *Happenstance* (novel) published (McGraw-Hill Ryerson); Shields moves to Winnipeg and begins teaching at the University of Manitoba.

1981-92   Assistant Professor of English, University of Manitoba.

1982   *A Fairly Conventional Woman* (novel) published (MacMillan).

1983   "Women Waiting" (radio drama) wins First Prize, CBC annual literary competition.

1985   *Various Miracles* (short stories) published (Stoddart); "Mrs. Turner Cutting the Grass" wins National Magazine Award. Documentary film *Carol Shields* aired on Access Network.

1986   Shields is Writer-in-Residence (short term) in Kingston, Ontario, then spends year in France (1986-87).

1987   *Swann: A Mystery* (novel) published (Stoddart).

1988   *Swann* wins Arthur Ellis Award for Best Canadian Mystery; Shields is Writer-in-Residence at the University of Winnipeg and (short term) at Douglas College, New Westminster, BC.

1989   *The Orange Fish* (short stories) published (Random House); *Room of One's Own* (Vol. 13, Nos. 1 & 2) devotes special issue to Shields's work, *The Carol Shields Issue*. Shields is Writer-in-Residence at the University of Ottawa.

1990   *Departures and Arrivals* (play) published (Blizzard). Shields wins the Marian Engel Award; *The Christian Science Monitor* chooses *The Orange Fish* as one of the two best books of short fiction of the year.

1991   *A Celibate Season* (novel, with Blanche Howard) published (Coteau).

1992-95   Associate Professor of English, University of Manitoba.

1992   *The Republic of Love* (novel) published (Random House); *Coming to Canada* (book of poems) published (Carleton University Press).

1993   *The Stone Diaries* (novel) published (Random House); wins the Governor General's Award for fiction.

1994   *The Stone Diaries* wins the McNally Robinson Award for Manitoba Book of the Year and the Canadian Booksellers' Association Prize.

1994-95   The Shields spend a sabbatical year in Berkeley, California.

1995   *The Stone Diaries* wins the National Critics' Circle Prize and the Pulitzer Prize for fiction. "Fashion Power Guilt and the Charity of Families," a play written with Catherine Shields, opens in Winnipeg. *Prairie Fire* publishes a Carol Shields special issue (Vol. 16, No. 1, Spring, 1995). Honorary degree conferred, University of Ottawa.

1995-99   Professor of English, University of Manitoba.

1996   Shields is named Chancellor of the University of Winnipeg. Honorary degrees conferred: Doctor of Humane Letters, Hanover College; Doctor of Laws, Queen's University; Doctor of Letters, University of Winnipeg; Doctor of Literature, University of British Columbia.

1997   *Larry's Party* (novel) published (Random House); wins Orange Prize.

1998   Shields is appointed Officer of the Order of Canada (investiture April 1999) and becomes a Fellow of the Royal Society of Canada. Honorary degrees conferred: Doctor of Letters,

University of Toronto; Doctor of Laws, Concordia University; Doctor of Letters, University of Western Ontario. *Anniversary* (drama, with Dave Williamson) published (Blizzard).

1999   Shields is awarded a Guggenheim Fellowship and the Shields move to England for a year. The first Carol Shields Winnipeg Book Award is won by Gordon Sinclair, Jr. Shields made Professor Emerita at the University of Manitoba.

2000   The Shields move to Victoria, BC. *Dressing Up for the Carnival* (short stories) published (Random House). Shields appointed Chancellor Emerita at the University of Winnipeg. Honorary degrees conferred: Doctor of Literature, Carleton University; Doctor of Literature, Wilfrid Laurier University.

2001   *Jane Austen* (biography) published (Penguin/Viking); *Dropped Threads: What We Aren't Told* (essays, ed. Shields and Marjorie Anderson) published (Random House/Vintage); *Thirteen Hands and other Plays* (drama) published (Vintage). The musical "Larry's Party" premieres in Toronto. Shields awarded the Order of Manitoba and named Winnipeg Citizen of the Year. "Life and Times" biography of Shields aired on CBC Television. Honorary degrees conferred: Doctor of Letters, Lakehead University; Doctor of Letters, University of Victoria; Doctor of Laws, University of Calgary.

2002   *Unless* (novel) published (Random House). Shields appointed to the Order of Canada and receives Queen Elizabeth Golden Jubilee Medal. Bust of Shields sculpted by Eva Stubbs mounted on its plinth in Assiniboine Park, Winnipeg. Red River College's first Carol Shields Creative Writing Award, co-sponsored by the Manitoba Writers' Guild, is awarded.

2003   Honorary degree conferred: Doctor of Letters, University of Manitoba.

Contributors

MARJORIE ANDERSON taught literature, writing, and communication at the University of Manitoba for close to twenty years. She and Carol met there in the English Department and have maintained a close friendship, which in 2001 blossomed into a creative partnership with their book *Dropped Threads*. The second volume will be out in April, 2003. Marjorie lives in Winnipeg with her husband Gary and a bevy of children and grandchildren.

WARREN CARIOU has published a book of novellas entitled *The Exalted Company of Roadside Martyrs* and a memoir called *Lake of the Prairies,* and he is now at work on a novel. He also writes criticism of First Nations literature and culture, and he teaches in the English Department at the University of Manitoba.

MARTA DVORAK is a professor at the Sorbonne Nouvelle. She is the author of *Ernest Buckler: Rediscovery and Reassessment,* published by Wilfrid Laurier University Press. Among the books she has edited are two collections of essays on Margaret Atwood, and a book on Nancy Huston is forthcoming (University of Ottawa Press). She is currently organizing a conference on Carol Shields in collaboration with Manina Jones and Aritha van Herk.

MAGGIE DWYER was born in Stratford, raised in southern Ontario towns and Toronto, and spent twenty interesting years in Winnipeg before moving to Vancouver Island with her second husband in 1998. She published a short fiction collection, *Misplaced Love,* in 2001 with Turnstone Press and is now writing a novel.

ANNE GIARDINI is one of Carol Shields's five children. She is a lawyer and writer, and is working on her first novel.

LEONA GOM has published six books of poetry and seven novels and has won both the Canadian Authors' Association Award for her poetry collection *Land of the Peace* and the Ethel Wilson Fiction Prize for her novel *Housebroken.* She taught for many years at Douglas/Kwantlen College, where she edited the award-winning magazine *Event,* and also at the Universities of Alberta and British Columbia. She has held writer-in-residencies at the Universities of Alberta, Lethbridge, and Winnipeg. Her work has been included in over fifty anthologies, and five of her books have been translated into other languages. Her latest novel is *Hating Gladys* (Sumach Press, 2002).

BLANCHE HOWARD collaborated with Carol Shields in writing the novel *A Celibate Season,* and a play she adapted from the novel was produced in 1990 in North Vancouver. Prior to that she had three novels published, one of which, *The Manipulator,* won the Canadian Booksellers' Award. A number of short stories and essays have appeared in literary magazines, and in 2000 *Penelope's Way* was published. She has just completed a new novel, "So Long Judas."

A native of Prince Edward Island, KATHARINE NICHOLSON INGS is assistant professor of American literature, gender studies, and journalism at Manchester College, Indiana. She is also a freelance copyeditor for W.W. Norton. Ings is revising her manuscript on how white women wrote romantic fiction about interracial romance during the Civil War.

BRIAN JOHNSON is a doctoral candidate in postcolonial literature and theory at Dalhousie University. His dissertation concerns the role of nomads and nomadism in contemporary discourse. His articles on Alice Munro, Thomas King, Martha Ostenso, and the history of word balloons have appeared in recent issues of *The Dalhousie Review, Studies in Canadian Literature, Wascana Review,* and *Rutgers Art Review.*

CHRIS JOHNSON teaches Theatre at the University of Manitoba, and directs plays for the University of Manitoba's Black Hole Theatre. In 1984, he directed the premiere production of *Departures and Arrivals,* and this year directed a staged reading of the play for the Manitoba Association of Playwrights' tribute to Carol. He has published numerous articles about Canadian theatre, and recently published a book about George F. Walker.

Lorraine McMullen is Professor Emerita, University of Ottawa. She is retired and lives in Victoria. For a while she was an Adjunct Professor in the Department of English at the University of Victoria. Professor McMullen has written extensively about women in Canadian literature. She supervised Carol Shields's MA thesis on Susanna Moodie.

William Neville is a Winnipeg-based academic, writer and broadcaster and is currently head of the Department of Political Studies at the University of Manitoba. He has written on politics and other public issues for a number of Canadian newspapers, including the *Winnipeg Free Press* where he has been a regular columnist since 1989. His writing has also appeared in two volumes of *Manitoba 125*, as well as *Manitoba History* and *The Beaver*.

Perry Nodelman, a professor of English at the University of Winnipeg, has written two books about children's literature and about a hundred or so articles, also mostly on various aspects of children's literature. He has also written three novels for young adults, all set in the republic of Winnipeg, and, in collaboration with Carol Matas, a four-novel series of fantasies. He is currently working on a novel about ghosts and a theoretical book about the generic characteristics of children's fiction.

Jacqueline Reid-Walsh is a long-time reader and admirer of Jane Austen and a more recent one of Carol Shields. She does research in the area of late eighteenth- to early nineteenth-century women writers, eighteenth-century cultural practice, and children's literature and popular culture. She teaches at several Montreal area universities: McGill, Bishop's and Concordia.

Wendy Roy has a PhD from McGill University and is currently a postdoctoral research fellow at the University of British Columbia, where she is researching women's travel writing in Canada. She first became interested in Carol Shields's writing during work on her master's thesis. She has since published an essay on autobiographical form and theory in *The Stone Diaries*.

DEBORAH SCHNITZER teaches at the University of Winnipeg and is excited by inter-arts analysis as well as community- and arts-based education. She has contributed to projects like *Children of the Shoah* and *Dropped Threads*. With Neil Besner and Alden Turner, she co-edited *Uncommonwealth: An Anthology of Poetry in English*. Most recently, she and Deborah Keahey have gathered Canadian women's writing into *The Madwoman in the Academy: 43 Women Boldly Take On the Ivory Tower* (University of Calgary Press 2003). She welcomes this new book on Carol Shields and its participation in the continuing exploration of her creativity.

CLARA THOMAS's engagement with Canadian literature began in 1939 at the University of Western Ontario. Her first book was published in 1946 and she began teaching in 1947. She is Professor Emerita at York University, Toronto.

JOAN THOMAS was co-editor (with Heidi Harms) of *Turn of the Story: Canadian Short Fiction on the Eve of the Millennium* (House of Anansi Press, 1999). She was a contributing reviewer for *The Globe and Mail* for many years. She lives in Winnipeg and is currently working for the Manitoba Arts Council.

SIMONE VAUTHIER, who is Professor Emerita at the University Marc Bloch, Strasbourg, is one of the best-known European critics writing on the English Canadian short story. Her book *Reverberations: Explorations in the Canadian Short Story* was published in 1993 by Anansi.

DAVE WILLIAMSON is the author of four novels, *The Bad Life, Shandy, Running Out,* and *Weddings,* and a collection of short stories, *Accountable Advances.* His 2000 memoir, *Author! Author! Encounters with Famous Writers,* includes a chapter about his collaborating with Carol Shields on the play *Anniversary.* For many years Dean of Business and Applied Arts at Red River College in Winnipeg, Dave is a past chair of The Writers' Union of Canada (1992-93).

About the Editor

Neil K. Besner, Dean of Humanities at the University of Winnipeg, writes mainly on Canadian literature. He has written studies of Mavis Gallant and Alice Munro, edited a special issue of *Prairie Fire* on Carol Shields, and co-edited books of short stories and poetry with Oxford University Press. His most recent book (2002) is *Rare and Commonplace Flowers*, a translation into English of a Brazilian biography of the American poet Elizabeth Bishop.